WINNING

Also by Jack Welch

Jack: Straight from the Gut
(with John A. Byrne)

Jack Welch

with Suzy Welch

WIN

NING

HarperCollins*Publishers*

HarperCollins*Publishers*
77–85 Fulham Palace Road,
Hammersmith, London W6 8JB
www.harpercollins.co.uk

Published by HarperCollins*Publishers* 2005
17

ISBN-13 978-0-00-719767-5
ISBN-10 0-00-719767-5

Printed and bound in Great Britain by
Clays Ltd, St Ives plc

To the thousands of men and women
who cared enough about business to raise their hands

The authors' profits from this book are being donated to charity.

CONTENTS

CONTENTS

YOUR COMPANY

YOUR COMPETITION

YOUR CAREER

TYING UP LOOSE ENDS

Introduction

"EVERY DAY, THERE IS A NEW QUESTION"

AFTER I FINISHED my autobiography—a fun but crazily intense grind that I wedged into the corners of my real job at the time—I swore I'd never write another book again.

But I guess I did.

My excuse, if there is one, is that I didn't actually come up with the idea for this book.

It was given to me.

It was a retirement present, if you will, from the tens of thousands of terrific people I have met since I left GE—the energized, curious, gutsy, and ambitious men and women who have loved business enough to ask me every possible question you could imagine. In order to answer them, all I had to do was figure out what I knew, sort it out, codify it, and borrow their stories—and this book was off and running.

The questions I'm referring to first started during the promotional tour for my autobiography in late 2001 and through much of 2002, when I was overwhelmed by the emotional attachment people seemed to have to GE. From coast to coast, and in many countries around the world, people told me touching stories about their experiences working for the company, or what happened when their sister, dad, aunt, or grandfather did.

But with these stories, I was also surprised to hear how much *more* people wanted to know about getting business right.

Radio call-in guests pressed me to explain GE's system of differentiation, which separates employees into three performance categories and manages them up or out accordingly. People attending book-signing events wanted to know if I really meant it when I said the head of human resources at every company should be at least as important as the CFO. (I did!) At a visit to the University of Chicago business school, an MBA from India asked me to explain more fully what a really good performance appraisal should sound like.

The questions didn't stop after the book tour. They continued—in airports, restaurants, and elevators. Once a guy swam over to me in the surf off Miami Beach to ask me what I thought about a certain franchise opportunity he was considering. But mainly they've come at the 150 or so Q & A sessions I have participated in over the past three years, in cities around the world from New York to Shanghai, from Milan to Mexico City. In these sessions, which have ranged from thirty to five thousand audience members, I sit on a stage with a moderator, usually a business journalist, and I try to answer anything the audience wants to throw at me.

And throw they have—questions about everything from coping with Chinese competition, to managing talented but difficult people, to finding the perfect job, to implementing Six Sigma, to hiring the right team, to leading in uncertain times, to surviving mergers and acquisitions, to devising a killer strategy.

What should I do, I've heard, if I deliver great results but I work for a jerk who doesn't seem to care, or if I'm the only person in my company who thinks change is necessary, or if the budget process in my company is full of sandbagging, or I'm about to launch a great new product and headquarters doesn't want to give me the autonomy and resources I need?

What can I do, people have asked, if managers in my company don't really tell it like it is, or I have to let go of an employee I really like but who just can't hack it, or I have to help lead my organization through the crisis we've been trying to deal with for a year?

There have been questions about juggling the colliding demands of kids, career, and all that other stuff you want to do, like play golf, renovate your house, or raise money in a walkathon. There have been questions about landing the promotion of your dreams—without making any enemies. There have been questions about macroeconomic trends, emerging industries, and currency fluctuations.

There have been literally thousands of questions. But most of them come down to this:

What does it take to win?

And that is what this book is about—winning. Probably no other topic could have made me want to write again!

Because I think winning is great. Not good—*great*.

Winning in business is great because when companies win, people thrive and grow. There are more jobs and more opportunities everywhere and for everyone. People feel upbeat about the future; they have the resources to send their kids to college, get better health care, buy vacation homes, and secure a comfortable retirement. And winning affords them the opportunity to

> I have been asked literally thousands of questions. But most of them come down to this: *What does it take to win?*

— 3 —

> I think winning is
> great. Not good—
> *great.* Because when
> companies win, people
> thrive and grow. There
> are more jobs and more
> opportunities.

give back to society in hugely important ways beyond just paying more taxes—they can donate time and money to charities and mentor in inner-city schools, to name just two. Winning lifts everyone it touches—it just makes the world a better place.

When companies are losing, on the other hand, everyone takes a hit. People feel scared. They have less financial security and limited time or money to do anything for anyone else. All they do is worry and upset their families, and in the meantime, if they're out of work, they pay little, if any, taxes.

Let's talk about taxes for a minute. In fact, let's talk about government in general.

Obviously, government is a vital part of society. First and foremost, it does nothing less than protect us all from the insidious and persistent challenges to national security that are with us now and for the foreseeable future. But government provides much more: the justice system, education, police and fire protection, highways and ports, welfare and hospitals. The list could go on and on.

But even with the virtues of government, it is critical to remember that all of its services come from some form of tax revenue. Government makes no money of its own. And in that way, government is the support for the engine of the economy, it is not the engine itself.

Winning companies and the people who work for them are the engine of a healthy economy, and in providing the revenues for government, they are the foundation of a free and democratic society.

That's why winning is great.

Now, it goes without saying that you have to win the right way—cleanly and by the rules. That's a given. Companies and people that don't compete fairly don't deserve to win, and thanks to well-honed internal company processes and government regulatory agencies, the bad guys are usually found and kicked out of the game.

But companies and people in business that are honest—and that's the vast, vast majority—must find the way to win.

This book offers a road map.

It is not, incidentally, a road map just for senior level managers and CEOs. If this book helps them, terrific. I hope it does. But this book is also very much for people on the front lines: business owners, middle managers, people running factories, line workers, college graduates looking at their first jobs, MBAs considering new careers, and entrepreneurs. My main goal with this book is to help the people with ambition in their eyes and passion running through their veins, wherever they are in an organization.

You will meet a lot of people in this book. Some may remind you of yourself, some may just seem very familiar:

There's the CEO who presents the company with a list of noble values—say, quality, customer service, and respect—but never really explains what it means to live them. There's the middle manager who fumes during a meeting with another division of his company, knowing that his coworkers could do so much more—if they just stopped patting themselves on the back for a minute. There is the employee who has been underperforming for years but is just so friendly and nice—and clueless—you can't bring yourself to let her go. There is the colleague you can't look in the eye because he is a "Dead Man Walking," slowly and painfully being managed out the door. There are the employees who eat lunch every day at what they have dubbed "The Table

> Have a positive attitude and spread it around, never let yourself be a victim, and for goodness' sake—have fun.

of Lost Dreams," making a show of their resentment of authority. There's the engineer who spent fifteen years building a great career, only to throw it in one day when she realized that she had juggled life and work to make everyone happy—but herself.

You'll also meet a lot of people whose stories are examples of innovation, insight, and grit.

There's David Novak, the energetic young CEO of Yum! Brands, who has turned every one of Yum!'s more than thirty-three thousand restaurant chain outlets into a laboratory of new ideas and the entire organization into a learning machine. There's Denis Nayden, the consummate change agent, who never settles for good enough and has intensity to burn. There's Jimmy Dunne, who rebuilt his company out of the ashes of the World Trade Center, using love, hope, and an attitude that anything is possible. There's Susan Peters, a working mother and the No. 2 HR executive at GE, who could write a book herself on successfully navigating the hills and valleys of work-life balance. There is Chris Navetta, the CEO of U.S. Steel Kosice, who helped transform a struggling city in Slovakia while turning a former state-owned steel mill into a flourishing, profitable enterprise. There's Kenneth Yu, the head of 3M's Chinese operations, who catapulted his businesses from modest to high growth by throwing out the phony ritual of annual budgeting and replacing it with a sky's-the-limit dialogue about opportunities. There's Mark Little, who was devastated after a demotion at GE but fought his way back to a huge promotion with courage, perseverance, and great results.

People are everything when it comes to winning, and so this book is a lot about people—in some cases, the mistakes they've made, but more often, their successes. But mostly this book is about ideas and the power of putting them into action.

Now, at this point, there might be readers out there who are skeptical. They're thinking: Winning is just too nuanced and complex a topic to cover in twenty chapters. I don't care how many people and ideas are in this book!

Yes, winning is nuanced and complex, not to mention brutally hard.

But it also happens to be achievable. You *can* win. But to do that, you need to know what makes winning happen.

This book offers no easy formulas. There are none.

Depending on the chapter, this book does, however, give you guidelines to follow, rules to consider, assumptions to adopt, and mistakes to avoid. The strategy chapter provides a three-step process; the chapter on finding the right job offers you good signs and warning signals. There are also several themes you'll hear again and again: the team with the best players wins, so find and retain the best players; don't overbrain things to the point of inaction; no matter what part of a business you're in, share learning relentlessly; have a positive attitude and spread it around; never let yourself be a victim; and for goodness' sake—have fun.

Yes, have fun.

Business is a game, and winning that game is a total blast!

THE ROAD AHEAD

Before we get started, a word on how this book is organized. It has four parts.

The first, called "Underneath It All," is conceptual. It certainly contains more management philosophy than most businesspeople have time for on any given day, and certainly more than I ever thought about in one sitting when I was working the day shift. But there is a substructure of principles to my approach to business, and so I lay them out in this first part.

In brief, the four principles are about the importance of a strong mission and concrete values; the absolute necessity of candor in every aspect of management; the power of differentiation, meaning a system based on meritocracy; and the value of each individual receiving voice and dignity.

The next section of this book, "Your Company," is about the innards of organizations. It's about mechanics—people, processes, and culture. Its chapters look at leadership, hiring, people management, letting people go, managing change, and crisis management.

After "Your Company" comes "Your Competition," the section of this book about the world outside your organization. It discusses how you create strategic advantages, devise meaningful budgets, grow organically, grow through mergers and acquisitions, and it attempts to demystify a topic that never ceases to intrigue and baffle people, the quality program Six Sigma.

The next section of this book is called "Your Career," and it's about managing the arc and the quality of your professional life. It starts with a chapter on finding the right job, not just a first job but the right job at any point in your career. It also includes a chapter on what it takes to get promoted, and another on a hard spot we all find ourselves in at one time or another—working for a bad boss. The last chapter of this section addresses the very human desire to have it all—all at the same time—which as you already know, you can't really do. You can, however, know what your boss thinks about the matter, and you should—and that's one aspect of this chapter.

The last section of this book is called "Tying Up Loose Ends," and in it, I answer nine questions that did not fall into any of the above categories. They concern managing the "China threat," diversity, the impact of new regulations like the Sarbanes-Oxley

Act, and how business should respond to societal crises like AIDS. There is also a question in there about how my successor, Jeff Immelt, is doing (in a word, great), the status of my golf game, and whether I think I'll go to heaven.

Now, that was a question that stopped me!

As for the rest of the questions in this book—they didn't exactly stop me, but they did challenge me to think hard about what I believe and why.

This book has a lot of answers, but not all—because business is always changing and the world is always changing.

As a Dutch entrepreneur said to me last year, "Every day in life, there is a new question. That is what keeps us going."

There are new questions—and new answers too. In fact, I have learned almost as much about business since I left GE as when I worked there. I learned from every single question asked of me.

And I hope my responses will help you learn too.

UNDERNEATH IT ALL

I

Mission and Values

SO MUCH HOT AIR ABOUT
SOMETHING SO REAL

B EAR WITH ME, if you will, while I talk about mission
and values.

I say that because these two terms have got to be among the
most abstract, overused, misunderstood words in business. When I
speak with audiences, I'm asked about them frequently, usually
with some level of panic over their actual meaning and relevance.
(In New York, I once got the question "Can you please define the
difference between a mission and a value, and also tell us what difference that difference makes?") Business schools add to the confusion by having their students regularly write mission statements
and debate values, a practice made even more futile for being carried out in a vacuum. Lots of companies do the same to their senior executives, usually in an attempt to create a noble-sounding
plaque to hang in the company lobby.

Too often, these exercises end with a set of generic platitudes
that do nothing but leave employees directionless or cynical. Who
doesn't know of a mission statement that reads something like,

"XYZ Company values quality and service," or, "Such-and-Such Company is customer-driven." Tell me what company doesn't value quality and service or focus on its customers! And who doesn't know of a company that has spent countless hours in emotional debate only to come up with values that, despite the good intentions that went into them, sound as if they were plucked from an all-purpose list of virtues including "integrity, quality, excellence, service, and respect." Give me a break—every decent company espouses these things! And frankly, integrity is just a ticket to the game. If you don't have it in your bones, you shouldn't be allowed on the field.

By contrast, a good mission statement and a good set of values are so real they smack you in the face with their concreteness. The mission announces exactly where you are going, and the values describe the behaviors that will get you there. Speaking of that, I prefer abandoning the term *values* altogether in favor of just *behaviors*. But for the sake of tradition, let's stick with the common terminology.

FIRST: ABOUT THAT MISSION . . .

In my experience, an effective mission statement basically answers one question: *How do we intend to win in this business?*

It does not answer: What were we good at in the good old days? Nor does it answer: How can we describe our business so that no particular unit or division or senior executive gets pissed off?

Instead, the question "How do we intend to win in this business?" is defining. It requires companies to make choices about people, investments, and other resources, and it prevents them from falling into the common mission trap of asserting they will be all things to all people at all times. The question forces companies to delineate their strengths and weaknesses in order to assess where they can *profitably* play in the competitive landscape.

Yes, profitably—that's the key. Even Ben & Jerry's, the crunchy-granola, hippy, save-the-world ice cream company based in Vermont, has "profitable growth" and "increasing value for stake-holders" as one of the elements of its three-part mission statement because its executives know that without financial success, all the social goals in the world don't have a chance.

That's not saying a mission shouldn't be bold or aspirational. Ben & Jerry's, for instance, wants to sell "all natural ice cream and euphoric concoctions" and "improve the quality of life locally, nationally and internationally." That kind of language is great in that it absolutely has the power to excite people and motivate them to stretch.

At the end of the day, effective mission statements balance the possible and the impossible. They give people a clear sense of the direction to profitability and the inspiration to feel they are part of something big and important.

Take our mission at GE as an example. From 1981 through 1995, we said we were going to be "the most competitive enter-prise in the world" by being No. 1 or No. 2 in every market—fixing, selling, or closing every underperforming business that couldn't get there. There could be no doubt about what this mission meant or entailed. It was specific and descriptive, with nothing abstract going on. And it was aspirational, too, in its global ambition.

This mission came to life in a bunch of different ways. First off, in a time when business strategy was mainly kept in an envelope in head-quarters and any information about

> **Effective mission statements balance the possible and the impossible.**

it was the product of the company gossip mill, we talked openly about which businesses were already No. 1 or No. 2, and which businesses had to get repaired quickly or be gone. Such candor shocked the system, but it did wonders for making the mission real to our people. They may have hated it when businesses were sold, but they understood why.

Moreover, we harped on the mission constantly, at every meeting large and small. Every decision or initiative was linked to the mission. We publicly rewarded people who drove the mission and let go of people who couldn't deal with it for whatever reason, usually nostalgia for their business in the "good old days."

Now, it is possible that in 1981 we could have come up with an entirely different mission for GE. Say after lots of debate and an in-depth analysis of technology, competitors, and customers, we had decided we wanted to become the most innovative designer of electrical products in the world. Or say we had decided that our most profitable route would have been to quickly and thoroughly globalize every business we had, no matter what its market position.

Either of these missions would have sent GE off on an entirely different road from the one we took. They would have required us to buy and sell different businesses than we did, or hire and let go of different people, and so forth. But technically, I have no argument with them as missions. They are concrete and specific. Without doubt, the electrical products mission would have come as a comfort to most people in GE. After all, that's what most thought we were. The global

> Setting the mission is top management's responsibility. A mission cannot be delegated to anyone except the people ultimately held accountable for it.

focus mission would have probably alarmed others. Rapid change usually does.

A final word about missions, and it concerns their creation. How do you come up with one?

To me, this is a no-brainer. You can get input from anywhere—and you should listen to smart people from every quarter. But setting the mission is top management's responsibility. A mission cannot, and must not, be delegated to anyone except the people ultimately held accountable for it.

In fact, a mission is the defining moment for a company's leadership.

It's the true test of its stuff.

. . . AND NOW ABOUT THOSE VALUES

As I said earlier, values are just behaviors—specific, nitty-gritty, and so descriptive they leave little to the imagination. People must be able to use them as marching orders because they are the *how* of the mission, the means to the end—winning.

In contrast to the creation of a mission, everyone in a company should have something to say about values. Yes, that can be a messy undertaking. That's OK. In a small enterprise, everyone can be involved in debating them in all kinds of meetings. In a larger organization, it's a lot tougher. But you can use company-wide meetings, training sessions, and the like, for as much personal discussion as possible, and the intranet for broader input.

Getting more participation really makes a difference, giving you more insights and more ideas, and at the end of the process, most importantly, much more extensive buy-in.

The actual process of creating values, incidentally, has to be iterative. The executive team may come up with a first version, but it should be just that, a first version. Such a document should go out to be poked and probed by people all over an organization, over and over again. And the executive team has to go out of their way to be sure they've created an atmosphere where people feel it is their obligation to contribute.

Now, if you're in a company where speaking up gets you whacked, this method of developing values just isn't going to work. I understand that, and as long as you stay, you're going to have to live with that generic plaque in the front hall.

But if you're at a company that does welcome debate—and many do—shame on you if you don't contribute to the process. If you want values and behaviors that you understand and can live with yourself, you have to make the case for them.

IT'S IN THE NITTY-GRITTY DETAILS

When I first became CEO, I was certainly guilty of endorsing vague, too cryptic values. For instance, in 1981, I wrote in the annual report that GE leaders "face reality" and "live excellence" and "feel ownership." These platitudes sure sounded good, but they had a long way to go toward describing real behaviors.

By 1991, we had made a lot of progress. Over the course of the previous three years, more than five thousand employees spent some portion of their time participating in the development of our values. The result was much more concrete. We printed them on laminated wallet cards. The text included imperatives such as "Act in a boundaryless fashion—always search for and apply the best ideas regardless of their source" and "Be intolerant of bureaucracy" and "See change for the growth opportunity it brings."

Of course, some of these behaviors required further explanation and interpretation. And we did that all the time, at meetings, during appraisals, and at the watercooler.

Since leaving GE, I've realized how much further still we might have been able to push the discussion about values and behaviors. In 2004, I watched Jamie Dimon and Bill Harrison work together to develop values and behaviors for the new company created by the merger of Bank One and JPMorgan Chase. The document they used to open the dialogue came from Bank One, and it listed values and their corresponding behaviors with a level of detail I had never seen before.

Take the value "We treat customers the way we would want to be treated." That's pretty tangible, but Bank One had literally identified the ten or twelve behaviors that made that value come to life. Here are some of them:

■ Never let profit center conflicts get in the way of doing what is right for the customer.

■ Give customers a good, fair deal. Great customer relationships take time. Do not try to maximize short-term profits at the expense of building those enduring relationships.

■ Always look for ways to make it easier to do business with us.

■ Communicate daily with your customers. If they are talking to you, they can't be talking to a competitor.

■ Don't forget to say thank you.

Another value Bank One had was: "We strive to be the low-cost provider through efficient and great operations." Some of the prescribed behaviors included:

- Leaner is better.

- Eliminate bureaucracy.

- Cut waste relentlessly.

- Operations should be fast and simple.

- Value each other's time.

- Invest in infrastructure.

- We should know our business best. We don't need consultants to tell us what to do.

If this level of detail feels overwhelming and even doctrinaire to you, I can sympathize. When I first saw Jamie's single-spaced, five-page values-and-behaviors document, I nearly fell over. But as I read it, I saw its power.

With all the stories I have heard in the past few years from employees in companies around the world, I'm convinced you cannot be too specific about values and their related behaviors.

AND IT'S IN THE BACKUP

Clarity around values and behaviors is not much good unless it is backed up. To make values really mean something, companies have to reward the people who exhibit them and "punish" those who don't. Believe me, it will make winning easier.

I say that because every time we asked one of our high-performing managers to leave because he didn't demonstrate the values—and we said as much publicly—the organization responded incredibly well. In annual surveys over a decade, employees would tell us that we were a company that increasingly lived its values. That made people even more committed to living them too. And as our employee satisfaction results improved, so did our financial results.

AND FINALLY, IT'S IN THE CONNECTION

A concrete mission is great. And values that describe specific behaviors are too. But for a company's mission and values to truly work together as a winning proposition, they have to be mutually reinforcing.

It seems obvious, doesn't it, that a company's values should support its mission, but it's amazingly easy for that not to be the case. A disconnect between the parts of a company's framework probably is more a sin of omission than of commission, but it often happens.

In the most common scenario, a company's mission and its values rupture due to the little crises of daily life in business: A competitor moves into town and lowers prices, and so do you, undermining your mission of competing on extreme customer service. Or a downturn hits, so you cut your advertising budget, forgetting your mission is to enhance and extend your brand.

These examples of disconnections may sound minor or tempo-

> In the most common scenario, a company's mission and its values rupture due to the little crises of daily life in business.

rary, but when left unattended, they can really hurt a company. In fact, in the worst-case scenario, they can literally destroy a business.

That's how I see what happened at Arthur Andersen and Enron.

Arthur Andersen was founded almost a century ago with the mission to become the most respected and trusted auditing firm in the world. It was a company that prided itself on having the courage to say no, even if that meant losing a client. It succeeded by hiring the most capable, highest-integrity CPAs and rewarding them for doing work that rightfully earned the confidence of corporations and regulators around the world.

Then the boom times of the 1980s arrived, and Arthur Andersen decided it wanted to start a consulting business; that's where the excitement was, not to mention the big money. The company started hiring more MBAs and paying them the constantly escalating salaries that the consulting industry demanded. In 1989, the firm actually split into two divisions, a traditional accounting division, called Arthur Andersen, and Andersen Consulting. Both fell under one corporate umbrella, called Andersen Worldwide.

Rather than valuing conscientiousness, consulting firms generally encourage creativity and reward aggressive sales behavior, taking the customer from one project to the next. In the 1990s in particular, there was a real cowboy mentality in the consulting industry, and the accounting side of Andersen felt the impact. Some of its accountants clearly got swept up in the momentum, letting go of the auditing business values that had guided them for so long.

Throughout most of the '90s, Arthur Andersen was a firm at war with itself. The consulting business was subsidizing the auditing side and didn't like it, and you can be sure the auditing side wasn't crazy about the bravado of the consulting types. In these circumstances, how could people know the answer to questions like, "What really is our mission?" "What values matter most?" and "How should we behave?" Depending on which side of the firm you pledged allegiance to, your answer would be different, and that's ultimately why the partners ended up in court with each other, trying to figure out how to divide the firm's profits.

Eventually, in 2002, the house collapsed, due in no small part to the disconnect between its mission and values.

In many ways, the same kind of dynamic was behind the Enron collapse.

In its prior life, Enron was a simple, rather mundane pipeline and energy company. Everyone was focused on getting gas from point A to point B cheaply and quickly, a mission they accomplished very well by having expertise in energy sourcing and distribution.

Then, like Arthur Andersen, the company changed missions. Someone got the idea to turn Enron into a trading company. Again, the goal was faster growth.

At Arthur Andersen, auditors wearing green eyeshades were suddenly sharing office space with MBAs in Armani suits. At Enron—again, figuratively speaking—the guys in coveralls were suddenly riding the elevator with MBAs in suspenders.

Enron's new mission meant it focused first on trading energy and then on trading anything and everything. That change was probably pretty exciting at the time, but obviously no one stopped to figure out and explicitly broadcast what values and corresponding behaviors would support such a heady goal. The trading desk was the place to be, and the pipeline and energy generation businesses got shoved to the background. Unfortunately, there were no processes to provide checks and balances for the suspenders crowd. And it was in that context—*of no context*—that Enron's collapse occurred.

Like Arthur Andersen's, this story of a mission and values disconnect ends with thousands of innocent people losing their jobs. What a tragedy.

This chapter opened with the observation that people in business talk a lot about mission and values, but too often the result is more hot air than real action. No one wants it that way, but the loftiness and the imprecision inherent in both terms always seem to make it end up like that.

But there is too much to lose by not getting your mission straight and by not making your values concrete. I'm not saying your company will collapse in flames the way Arthur Andersen and Enron did—they are extreme examples of a mission-and-values meltdown. But I am saying your company will not reach anywhere near its full potential if all that is guiding it is a list of pleasant platitudes hanging on the lobby wall.

Look, I realize that defining a good mission and developing the values that support it takes time and enormous commitment. There will be long, contentious meetings when you would rather go home. There will be e-mail debates when you wish you could just go do real work. There will be painful times when you have to say good-bye to people you really like who just do not get the mission or live its values. On days like those, you might wish your mission and values were vague and generic.

They can't be.

Take the time. Spend the energy.

Make them real.

2

Candor

THE BIGGEST DIRTY LITTLE
SECRET IN BUSINESS

I HAVE ALWAYS BEEN a huge proponent of candor. In fact,
I talked it up to GE audiences for more than twenty years.

But since retiring from GE, I have come to realize that I un-
derestimated its rarity. In fact, I would call lack of candor the
biggest dirty little secret in business.

What a huge problem it is. Lack of candor basically blocks
smart ideas, fast action, and good people contributing all the stuff
they've got. It's a killer.

When you've got candor—and you'll never completely get it,
mind you—everything just operates faster and better.

Now, when I say "lack of candor" here, I'm not talking about
malevolent dishonesty. I am talking about how too many people—too often—instinctively don't express themselves with
frankness. They don't communicate straightforwardly or put forth
ideas looking to stimulate real debate. They just don't open up. Instead they withhold comments or criticism. They keep their

> **Lack of candor blocks smart ideas, fast action, and good people contributing all the stuff they've got. It's a killer.**

mouths shut in order to make people feel better or to avoid conflict, and they sugarcoat bad news in order to maintain appearances. They keep things to themselves, hoarding information.

That's all lack of candor, and it's absolutely damaging.

And yet, lack of candor permeates almost every aspect of business.

In my travels over the past few years, I have heard stories from people at hundreds of different companies who describe the complete lack of candor they experience day to day, in every type of meeting, from budget and product reviews to strategy sessions. People talk about the bureaucracy, layers, politicking, and false politeness that lack of candor spawns. They ask how they can get their companies to be places where people put their views on the table, talk about the world realistically, and debate ideas from every angle.

Most often, I hear that lack of candor is missing from performance appraisals.

In fact, I hear about that so often that I always end up asking audiences for a show of hands to the question "How many of you have received an honest, straight-between-the-eyes feedback session in the last year, where you came out knowing exactly what you have to do to improve and where you stand in the organization?"

On a good day, I get 20 percent of the hands up. Most of the time, it is closer to 10 percent.

Interestingly, when I turn the question around and ask the audience how often they've given an honest, candid appraisal to their people, the numbers don't improve much.

Forget outside competition when your own worst enemy is the way you communicate with one another internally!

THE CANDOR EFFECT

Let's look at how candor leads to winning. There are three main ways.

First and foremost, candor gets more people in the conversation, and when you get more people in the conversation, to state the obvious, you get idea rich. By that, I mean many more ideas get surfaced, discussed, pulled apart, and improved. Instead of everyone shutting down, everyone opens up and learns. Any organization—or unit or team—that brings more people and their *minds* into the conversation has an immediate advantage.

Second, candor generates speed. When ideas are in everyone's face, they can be debated rapidly, expanded and enhanced, and acted upon. That approach—surface, debate, improve, decide—isn't just an advantage, it's a necessity in a global marketplace. You can be sure that any upstart five-person enterprise down the street or in Shanghai or in Bangalore can move faster than you to begin with. Candor is one way to keep up.

Third, candor cuts costs—lots—although you'll never be able to put a precise number on it. Just think of how it eliminates meaningless meetings and b.s. reports that confirm what everyone already knows. Think of how candor replaces fancy PowerPoint slides and mind-numbing presentations and boring off-site conclaves with real conversations, whether they're about company strategy, a new product introduction, or someone's performance.

Put all of its benefits and efficiencies together and you realize you just can't afford not to have candor.

SO WHY NOT?

Given the advantages of candor, you have to wonder, why don't we have more of it?

Well, the problem starts young.

The facts are, we are socialized from childhood to soften bad news or to make nice about awkward subjects. That is true in every culture and in every country and in every social class. It doesn't make any difference if you are in Iceland or Portugal, you don't insult your mother's cooking or call your best friend fat or tell an elderly aunt that you hated her wedding gift. You just don't.

What happened at a suburban cocktail party we attended recently is classic. Over white wine and sushi rolls, one woman standing in a cluster of five others started lamenting the horrible stress being endured by the local elementary school's music teacher. Other guests chimed in, all agreeing that fourth-graders were enough to send you to the insane asylum. Fortunately, just before the music teacher was canonized, another guest entered the conversation, saying, "Are you guys crazy? That teacher gets fifteen weeks off a year!" She pointed to the doctor standing in the circle, who had been nodding away in agreement. "Robert," she said, "you make life-and-death decisions every day. Surely you don't buy this sad story, do you?"

Talk about killing polite chitchat. The new guest sent everyone scattering, mostly toward the bar.

> **We are socialized from childhood to soften bad news or make nice about awkward subjects.**

Candor just unnerves people.

That was a lighthearted example, of course, but when you try to understand candor, you are really trying to understand human nature. For hundreds of years, psychologists and social scientists have studied why people don't say what they

> Eventually, you come to realize that people don't speak their minds because it's simply easier not to.

mean, and philosophers have been reflecting on the same subject for literally thousands of years.

A good friend of mine, Nancy Bauer, is a professor of philosophy at Tufts University. When I ask her about candor, she tells me that most philosophers have come to the same conclusions on this topic as most of us laypeople do with age and experience. Eventually, you come to realize that people don't speak their minds because it's simply easier not to. When you tell it like it is, you can so easily create a mess—anger, pain, confusion, sadness, resentment. To make matters worse, you then feel compelled to clean up that mess, which can be awful and awkward and time-consuming. So you justify your lack of candor on the grounds that it prevents sadness or pain in another person, that not saying anything or telling a little white lie is the kind, decent thing to do. But in fact, Nancy says, classic philosophers like Immanuel Kant give powerful arguments for the view that not being candid is actually about self-interest—making your *own* life easier.

Nancy tells me that Kant had another point, too. He said that people are often strongly tempted not to be candid because they don't look at the big picture. They worry that when they speak their minds and the news isn't good, they stand a strong chance of alienating other people. But what they don't see is that lack of candor is the ultimate form of alienation. "There was a huge irony in this for Kant," Nancy says. "He believed that when people avoid candor in order to curry favor with other people, they actually destroy trust, and in that way, they ultimately erode society."

I tell Nancy the same could be said about eroding business.

FROM THEN TO NOW

The make-or-break importance of candor in U.S. business is relatively new, actually. Up until the early 1980s, big companies like GE and thousands of others operated largely without it, as did most companies regardless of size. These companies were a product of the military-industrial complex that grew up after World War II. They had virtually no global competition, and, in fact, companies within industries were so similar to one another that they could often seem more collegial than competitive.

Take the steel industry. Every three years or so, union workers across several companies would demand higher pay and benefits. The steel companies would meet those demands, passing their increased costs on to the automotive industry, which would pass their increased costs on to the consumer.

It was a nice party until the Japanese arrived at the door with their average-quality, low-cost imported cars that within a few years became high-quality, low-cost cars, many of them made in nonunion U.S. factories.

But until the foreign threat spread, most American companies had very little to do with the kind of frank debate and fast action that characterizes a candid organization. They had little use for it. And so countless layers of bureaucracy and old-fashioned social codes of behavior led to a kind of enforced politeness and formality throughout most organizations. There were very few overt confrontations about strategy or values; decisions were made mostly behind closed doors. And when it came to appraisals, those too were conducted with a kind of courteous remoteness. Good performers were praised, but because companies were so financially strong, poor performers could be warehoused in a far-flung department or division until retirement.

Without candor, everyone saved face, and business lumbered along. The status quo was accepted. Fake behavior was just a day at the office. And people with initiative, gumption, and guts were labeled troublesome—or worse.

You would predict, perhaps, that given all its competitive advantages, candor would have made a grand entrance with the Japanese. But Japan didn't make it happen, nor did Ireland, Mexico, India, or China, to name a few of the big hitters in the global marketplace today. Instead, most companies have fought global competition through more conventional means: layoffs, drastic cost reductions, and in the best cases, with innovation.

Candor, while inching its way in, still remains a very small part of the arsenal.

IT CAN BE DONE

Now for the really bad news. Even though candor is vital to winning, it is hard and time-consuming to instill in any group, no matter what size.

Hard because you are fighting human nature and entrenched organizational behaviors, and time-consuming, as in years and years. At GE, it took us close to a decade to use candor as a matter of course, and it was by no means universal after twenty.

Still it can be done. There is nothing scientific about the process. To get candor, you reward it, praise it, and talk about it. You make public heroes out of people who demonstrate it. Most of all, you yourself demonstrate it in an exuberant and even exaggerated way—even when you're not the boss.

> **To get candor, you reward it, praise it, and talk about it. Most of all, you yourself demonstrate it in an exuberant and even exaggerated way.**

Imagine yourself for a second at a meeting where the subject is growth and how to get it at an old-line division. Everyone is sitting around the table, civilly talking about how hard it is to win in this particular market or industry. They discuss the tough competition. They surface the same old reasons why they can't grow and why they are actually doing well in this environment. In fact, by the time the meeting ends, they've managed to pat themselves on the back for the "success" they've enjoyed "under the circumstances."

Inside your head, you're about ready to burst, as you tell yourself, "Here we go again. I know Bob and Mary across the room feel the same way I do—the complacency around here is killing us."

Outside, all three of you are playing the game. You're nodding.

Now imagine an environment where you take responsibility for candor. You, Bob, or Mary would ask questions like:

"Isn't there a new product or service idea in this business somewhere that we just haven't thought of yet?"

"Can we jump-start this business with an acquisition?"

"This business is taking up so many resources. Why don't we get the hell out of it?"

What a different meeting! What a lot more fun, and how much better for everyone.

Another situation that happens all the time is a high-growth business with a self-satisfied crowd managing it. You know the scene at the long-range planning meeting. The managers show up with double-digit growth—say 15 percent—and pound out slide after slide showing how well they are doing. Top management nods their approval, but you're sitting there knowing there's a lot more juice in that business. To compound matters, the people presenting the slides are peers of yours, and there's that age-old code hanging in the air: if you don't challenge mine, I won't challenge yours.

Frankly, the only way I know of to get out of this bind—and introduce candor—is to poke around in a nonthreatening way:

"Jeez, you're good. What a terrific job. This is the best business we've got. Why not put more resources into it and go for more?"

"With the great team you've put in place, there must be ten acquisitions out there for you. Have you looked globally?"

Those questions, and others like them, have the power to change the meeting from a self-congratulatory parade to a stimulating working session.

TRUTH AND CONSEQUENCES

Now, you may be thinking, I can't raise those questions because I don't want to look like a jerk. I want to be a team player.

It is true that candid comments definitely freak people out at first. In fact, the more polite or bureaucratic or formal your organization, the more your candor will scare and upset people, and, yes, it could kill you.

That's a risk, and only you can decide if you're willing to take it.

Needless to say, you'll have an easier time of installing candor in your organization if you are closer to the top. But don't blame your boss or the CEO if your company lacks candor—open dialogue can start anywhere. I was speaking my mind when I had four employees at Noryl, the smallest, newest unit of a hierarchical company that had a very dim view of straight talk.

> It is true that candid comments definitely freak people out at first.

My bosses cautioned me about my candor. Now my GE career is over, and I'm telling you that it was my candor that helped make it work.

I was too young and politically clueless to notice at the time, but I was covered because our business was growing by leaps and bounds.

If we had the guts to be candid, it didn't feel that way at the time—we didn't know enough to know what candor was. It just felt natural to us to speak openly, argue and debate, and get things to happen fast. If we were anything, it was crazily competitive.

Every time I got promoted, the first cycle of reviews—be it budgets or appraisals—was often awkward and unpleasant. Most of the new team I was managing wasn't used to wide-open discussions about everything and anything. For example, we'd be talking about a direct report at a personnel review, and in conversation, we would agree that the guy was really awful. His written appraisal, however, made him look like a prince. When I challenged the phoniness, I'd hear, "Yeah, yeah, but why would we ever put that in writing?"

I'd explain why, making the case for candor.

By the next review, we'd already be seeing candor's positive impact with a better team in place, and with each successive cycle, more and more people made candor's case with me.

Still, it wasn't like I was singing with the whole chorus.

From the day I joined GE to the day I was named CEO, twenty years later, my bosses cautioned me about my candor. I was labeled abrasive and consistently warned that my candor would soon get in the way of my career.

Now my GE career is over, and I'm telling you that it was candor that helped make it work. So many more people got into the game, so many voices, so much energy. We gave it to one another straight, and each of us was better for it.

We've talked a lot in this chapter about one word. But it's really very simple—candor works because candor unclutters.

Yes, yes, everyone agrees that candor is against human nature. So is waking up at five in the morning for the 6:10 train every day. So is eating lunch at your desk so you won't miss an important meeting at one. But for the sake of your team or your organization, you do a lot of things that aren't easy. The good thing about candor is that it's an unnatural act that is more than worth it.

It is impossible to imagine a world where everyone goes around saying what they really think all the time. And you probably wouldn't want it anyway—too much information! But even if we get halfway there, lack of candor won't be the biggest dirty little secret in business anymore.

It will be its biggest change for the better.

Differentiation

CRUEL AND DARWINIAN? TRY FAIR AND EFFECTIVE

IF THERE IS ONE OF MY VALUES that really pushes buttons, it is differentiation.

Some people love the idea; they swear by it, run their companies with it, and will tell you it is at the very root of their success. Other people hate it. They call it mean, harsh, impractical, demotivating, political, unfair—or all of the above. Once, during a radio talk show about my first book, a woman in LA pulled off the highway to call in and label differentiation "cruel and Darwinian." And that was just the beginning of her commentary!

Obviously, I am a huge fan of differentiation. I have seen it transform companies from mediocre to outstanding, and it is as morally sound as a management system can be. It works.

Companies win when their managers make a clear and meaningful distinction between top- and bottom-performing businesses and people, when they cultivate the strong and cull the weak. Companies suffer when every business and person is treated equally and bets are sprinkled all around like rain on the ocean.

> A company has only so much money and managerial time. Winning leaders invest where the payback is the highest. They cut their losses everywhere else.

When all is said and done, differentiation is just resource allocation, which is what good leaders do and, in fact, is one of the chief jobs they are *paid* to do. A company has only so much money and managerial time. Winning leaders invest where the payback is the highest. They cut their losses everywhere else.

If that sounds Darwinian, let me add that I am convinced that along with being the most efficient and most effective way to run your company, differentiation also happens to be the fairest and the kindest. Ultimately, it makes winners out of everyone.

When I was at GE, people discussed differentiation vigorously, but over the years, most people came to strongly support it as our way of doing business. By the time I retired, differentiation was not really a hot topic anymore. The same can't be said for outside the company! Without a doubt, differentiation receives the most questions I get from audiences around the world. As I said, people tend to love it or hate it, but a pretty large number are just confused by it. If I could change one thing about my first book, it would be to add more pages to the discussion of differentiation, explaining the topic inside and out, and stressing that differentiation cannot—and must not—be implemented quickly. At GE, it took us about a decade to install the kind of candor and trust that makes differentiation possible.

But this chapter is not about implementation. It's about why I believe in differentiation and why you should too.

DIFFERENTIATION DEFINED

One of the main misunderstandings about differentiation is that it is only about people. That's to miss half of it. Differentiation is a way to manage people *and* businesses.

Basically, differentiation holds that a company has two parts, software and hardware.

Software is simple—it's your people.

Hardware depends. If you are a large company, your hardware is the different businesses in your portfolio. If you are smaller, your hardware is your product lines.

Let's look first at differentiation in terms of hardware. It's pretty straightforward and a lot less incendiary.

Every company has strong businesses or product lines and weak ones and some in between. Differentiation requires managers to know which is which and invest accordingly.

To do that, of course, you have to have a clear-cut definition of "strong." At GE, "strong" meant a business was No. 1 or No. 2 in its market. If it wasn't, the managers had to fix it, sell it, or as a last resort, close it. Other companies have different frameworks for investment decisions. They put their money and time only into businesses or product lines that promise double-digit sales growth, for instance. Or they invest only in businesses or product lines with a 15 percent (or better) discounted rate of return (DCRR).

Now, I generally don't like investment criteria that are financial in nature, like DCRR, because the numbers can be jiggered so easily by changing the residual value, or any other number of assumptions, in an investment proposal. But my point is the same: differentiation among your businesses or product lines requires a transparent framework that everyone in the company understands. People may not like it, but they know it and they manage with it.

In fact, differentiation among businesses and product lines is a powerful management discipline in general. At GE, the No. 1 or No. 2 framework stopped the decades-long practice of sprinkling money everywhere. Most GE managers in the old days probably knew that spreading money all around didn't make sense, but it's so easy to do. There's always that pressure—managers jockeying and politicking for their share of the pie. To avoid warfare, you give everyone a little slice and hope for the best.

Companies also sprinkle money evenly for sentimental or emotional reasons. GE hung on to a marginally profitable central air-conditioning business for twenty years because people thought it was necessary in order to have a full-line major appliance company. In reality, headquarters hated air-conditioning because its success was so dependent on the installers. These independent contractors would put our machines into homes and then drive off, and GE lost control of the brand. Worse, we had a small share of the market and just couldn't make much money on central air-conditioning. With the No. 1 or No. 2 framework, we had to sell the business, and when we did—to a company that lived and breathed air-conditioning very successfully—GE's former employees discovered the joy of being loved! Moreover, management attention was no longer diverted to an under-performing business, and shareholders had better returns. Everybody won.

Running your company without differentiation among your businesses or product lines may have been possible when the world was less competitive. But with globalization and digitization, forget it. Managers at every level have to make hard choices and live by them.

THE PEOPLE PART

Now let's talk about the more controversial topic, differentiation among people. It's a process that requires managers to assess their employees and separate them into three categories in terms of performance: top 20 percent, middle 70, and bottom 10. Then—and this is key—it requires managers to *act* on that distinction. I emphasize the word "act" because all managers naturally differentiate—in their heads. But very few make it real.

When people differentiation is real, the top 20 percent of employees are showered with bonuses, stock options, praise, love, training, and a variety of rewards to their pocketbooks and souls. There can be no mistaking the stars at a company that differentiates. They are the best and are treated that way.

The middle 70 percent are managed differently.

This group of people is enormously valuable to any company; you simply cannot function without their skills, energy, and commitment. After all, they are the majority of your employees. And that's the major challenge, and risk, in 20-70-10—keeping the middle 70 engaged and motivated.

That's why so much of managing the middle 70 is about training, positive feedback, and thoughtful goal setting. If individuals in this group have particular promise, they should be moved around among businesses and functions to increase their experience and knowledge and to test their leadership skills.

To be clear, managing the middle 70 is not about keeping people out of the bottom 10. It is not about saving poor performers. That would be a bad investment decision. Rather, differentiation is about managers looking at the middle 70, identifying people with potential to move up, and cultivating them. But *everyone* in the middle 70 needs to be motivated and made to feel as if they truly belong. You do not want to lose the vast majority of your middle 70—you want to improve them.

As for the bottom 10 percent in differentiation, there is no sugar-coating this—they have to go. That's more easily said than done; It's awful to fire people—I even hate that word. But if you have a candid organization with clear performance expectations and a performance evaluation process—a big if, obviously, but that should be everyone's goal—then people in the bottom 10 percent generally know who they are. When you tell them, they usually leave before you ask them to. No one wants to be in an organization where they aren't wanted. One of the best things about differentiation is that people in the bottom 10 percent of organizations very often go on to successful careers at companies and in pursuits where they truly belong and where they can excel.

That's how differentiation works in a nutshell. People sometimes ask where I came up with the idea. My answer is, I didn't invent differentiation! I learned it on the playground when I was a kid. When we were making a baseball team, the best players always got picked first, the fair players were put in the easy positions, usually second base or right field, and the least athletic ones had to watch from the sidelines. Everyone knew where he stood. The top kids wanted desperately to stay there, and got the reward of respect and the thrill of winning. The kids in the middle worked their tails off to get better, and sometimes they did, bringing up the quality of play for everyone. And the kids who couldn't make the cut usually found other pursuits, sports and otherwise, that they enjoyed and excelled at. Not everyone can be a great ballplayer, and not every great ballplayer

> I didn't invent differentiation! I learned it on the playground when I was a kid.

can be a great doctor, computer programmer, carpenter, musician, or poet. Each one of us is good at something, and I just believe we are happiest and the most fulfilled when we're doing that.

It's true on the playground, and it's true in business.

REASONS TO HATE DIFFERENTIATION—AND NOT

I could spend the next couple of pages explaining all the reasons to love differentiation, but instead I'm going to list the most common criticisms the concept receives. I'm leaving aside "hardware" differentiation here, because it doesn't get anything like the heat that 20-70-10 does.

So here are the criticisms of people differentiation. Some have truth in them, but more often than not, they don't! Here's what I mean:

> *Differentiation is unfair because it's always corrupted by company politics—20-70-10 is just a way of separating the people who kiss the boss's rear from those who don't.*

It is true, without question, that at some companies, differentiation is corrupted by cronyism and favoritism. The top 20 percent are the boss's head-nodders and buddies, and the bottom 10 percent are the outspoken types who ask difficult questions and challenge the status quo. The middle 70 are just ducking and getting by. That happens and it stinks, and it is a function of a leadership team lacking in brains or integrity or both.

The only good thing I can say about a merit-free system like this is that eventually it destroys itself. It collapses from its own weight or has to change. The results just won't be good enough to sustain the enterprise.

Luckily, cases of "differentiation abuse" can generally be prevented by a candid, clear-cut performance system, with defined expectations and goals and timelines, and a program of consistent appraisals. In fact, differentiation can be implemented only after such a system is in place, a process that we will discuss more specifically in the chapter on people management.

> *Differentiation is mean and bullying. It's like the playground in the worst possible way—weak kids are made into fools, outcasts, and objects of ridicule.*

I've heard this one a hundred times, and it really drives me crazy because one of the major advantages of differentiation is that it is good and fair—to everyone!

When differentiation is working, people know where they stand. You know if you have a strong shot at a big promotion or if you need to be looking for other opportunities, inside or outside the company. Maybe some information is hard to swallow at first, and yes, "bad" news often hurts, but soon enough, like all knowledge, it's power—in fact, it's liberating. When you know where you stand, you can control your own destiny, and what is more fair than that?

Interestingly, when people raise this criticism with me at speaking engagements, I often ask them a question back. I ask if they ever received grades in school. Naturally, everyone says yes. I then ask, "Did you think getting grades was mean?"

"Well, no," they usually say. Sometimes grades sting, but kids somehow always live through it. And grades have a way of making everything pretty clear. Some people graduate and go on to be astronauts or research scientists or college professors, others become marketing managers or advertising executives, and still others become nurses, chefs, or even professional surfers. Grades, in fact, guide us, telling us something about ourselves that we need to know.

So why should we stop getting grades at age twenty-one? To prevent meanness? Please!

Corollary: I'm just too nice to implement 20-70-10.

Usually, people with this complaint about differentiation assert that differentiation, as a managerial system, does not value people who add intangible things to a business, like a "feeling of family" or "humanity" or "a sense of history." And we all know of organizations that continue to employ underperformers for a long time mainly because they are really nice individuals.

I fully understand not wanting to manage out somebody nice.

But the fact is protecting underperformers always backfires. First of all, by not carrying their weight, they make the pie smaller for everyone. That can cause resentment. It's also not what you could call fair, and an unfair culture never helps a company win; it undermines trust and candor too much.

The worst thing, though, is how protecting people who don't perform hurts the people themselves. For years, they are carried along with everyone looking the other way. At appraisals, they are vaguely told they are "great" or "doing just fine." They are thanked for their contributions.

Then a downturn occurs, and layoffs are necessary. The "nice" underperformers are almost always the first to go, and always the most surprised, because no one has ever told them the truth about their results, or lack thereof. The awful thing is that this often happens when the underperformers are in their late forties or

> Protecting under-performers always backfires. The worst thing, though, is how protecting people who don't perform hurts the people themselves.

fifties; they've been carried along for most of their careers. Then suddenly, at an age when starting over can be very tough, they are out of a job with no preparation or planning and a kick in the stomach they may never get over. They feel betrayed, and they should.

As harsh as it may seem at first, differentiation prevents that tragedy because it is based on performance measures that really count. That's why I believe you are never "too nice" to implement 20-70-10, only too cowardly.

Differentiation pits people against one another and undermines teamwork.

Try telling that to Joe Torre!

The New York Yankees function perfectly well as a team (much to the dismay of Red Sox fans like myself, I might add) with a highly transparent system of differentiation in place. Stars are lavishly rewarded; underperformers are shown the clubhouse exit. And if that's not enough to make a system of differentiation perfectly clear, the players' salaries are very public! You can have no doubt that differentiation is going on when some team members make $18 million a year, and others wearing the same uniform make the Major League minimum of $300,000.

And yet everyone pulls together for the *team* to win. Alex Rodriguez loves the thrill of hitting a grand slam home run, but I'm sure it feels a lot better to him when the Yankees win. In July 2004, Derek Jeter made the catch of the year, diving into the stands and coming up with a black eye and a cut face, a photo of which graced every newspaper in New York. A lot of the pain had to be relieved when the Yankees won, coming from behind in the thirteenth inning, in one of the great baseball games of all time.

Without question, these two stars love to excel for their own sakes. But you can bet it is always more fun and exciting when the team wins.

> Differentiation rewards those members of the team who deserve it.

Their teamwork is a testament to two other things. First, great leadership. Joe Torre obviously understands the challenges of managing in a differentiation environment.

Second, the cohesiveness of the Yankees, and of so many other sports teams, shows the positive impact of an open, honest management system built on candid performance assessments and aligned rewards. In that way, differentiation doesn't undermine teamwork, it enhances it.

In business, there probably would be pandemonium if companies started publishing everyone's salary, and I'm not advocating that here. And yet, people always seem to know what their coworkers are making, don't they? That's why they get mad when everyone on a team gets rewarded the same way when only a few people have done the work. They feel cheated and wonder why management can't see the obvious—that not every team member is created equal.

Differentiation rewards those members of the team who deserve it. By the way, that annoys only the underperformers. To everyone else, it seems fair. And a fair environment promotes teamwork. Better yet, it motivates people to give their all, and that's what you want.

Differentiation is possible only in the United States. I wish I could implement it, but because of our cultural values, the people in my country simply won't accept it.

I have heard this critique of differentiation since its earliest days at GE, when one of our managers explained that 20-70-10 couldn't be implemented in Japan because in that culture politeness was valued far more than candor. Since then, I have heard the national-culture excuse from people in hundreds of companies in dozens of nations. Recently, managers in Denmark told us that their country values egalitarianism too much for differentiation to be widely accepted. We've heard that case made in France too. A manager at a meeting in Amsterdam told us last year that there was too much "Calvinism in Dutch bones" for the system to work in the Netherlands. I guess the manager believed all rewards come only in Heaven, if you're chosen to get there! And in China we heard that differentiation is a long time coming because in most state-owned enterprises—still more than 50 percent of the economy despite market reforms—many of the best jobs and rewards go to the most loyal members of the party whether they are the most talented or not.

Basically, I think the excuses we hear about differentiation's cultural obstacles are just that—excuses. At GE, we couldn't have a company where differentiation existed only in our U.S. operations. First of all, we just believed too much in differentiation's effectiveness. But we also knew that having differentiation only in the United States would have been unfair and confusing, especially for the businesses with both U.S. and global divisions, and for the people who moved around the world for us. We decided early on that we would push through differentia-

> Once we made the case for differentiation and we linked it to a candid performance appraisal system, it worked as well in Japan as it did in Ohio.

tion everywhere we did business, dealing with whatever cultural issues that confronted us.

Then an amazing thing happened. Very many cultural issues *didn't* confront us. Once we made the case for differentiation and we linked it to a candid performance appraisal system, it worked as well in Japan as it did in Ohio. In fact, people who at first thought it could never work in their country came to support it strongly for its honesty, fairness, and clarity.

As I mentioned, very often when I get the comment "We can't have differentiation in *my* country," it comes from managers who admit they themselves support the approach. Their resistance grows out of the *assumption* that their people will object based on cultural values. My advice to them is to move slowly but go for it anyway. They will be surprised that they are not alone because differentiation, once in practice for a while, makes its own case in any language.

> *Differentiation is fine for the top 20 percent and the bottom 10 because they know where they are going. But it is enormously demotivating to the middle 70 percent, who end up living in an awful kind of limbo.*

Again, an element of truth in this complaint. The middle 70 percent is the hardest category to manage in differentiation. The biggest problem comes with the individuals in the top tier of the 70 percent because they know they are not a whole lot different from the top-20 performers, and often a whole lot better than the bottom tier of their own "guard." And yes, that can be enervating, and sometimes talented middle-70 people leave because of it.

The silver lining to this difficult situation is that the existence of a middle 70 forces companies to manage themselves better. It

> While being in the middle 70 percent can be demotivating to some people, it actually revs the engines of many others.

forces leaders to scrutinize people more closely than they would ordinarily and to provide more consistent, candid feedback. It pushes companies to build training centers that really make a difference. For instance, before differentiation, our Crotonville, New York, training center was often used in the 1970s as a warehouse where businesses could afford to send their underperformers. It was like a way station on the road to early retirement.

The rigor of 20-70-10 helped us change that. We turned Crotonville into a place where the top 20 and the best of the middle 70 talked about ideas, debated our approach to business, and got to know and understand one another a lot better. And since senior management spent several hours with each class, it also gave us a rough idea as to just how rigorously differentiation was being practiced in the field.

Another piece of silver lining is that while being in the middle 70 percent can be demotivating to some people, it actually revs the engines of many others. For the people in the top 20, for instance, the very existence of a middle 70 gives them yet another reason to pull out all the stops every day. They have to *keep getting better* to keep their high standing—what a rush that can be! After all, most people want to improve and grow every day.

For a lot of people in the middle 70, getting better is energizing too. Getting into the top 20 gives them a tangible goal, and having that goal makes them work harder, think more creatively, share more ideas, and, overall, fight the good fight every day. It makes work more of a challenge and a lot more fun.

Differentiation favors people who are energetic and extroverted and undervalues people who are shy and introverted, even if they are talented.

I don't know if it's good or bad, but the world generally favors people who are energetic and extroverted. That's also something you learn young, and it's reinforced in school, at church, at camp, in clubs, and usually at home too. By the time you get to work, if you are still shy and introverted and somewhat low in energy, there are professions and jobs where those characteristics are advantageous. If you know yourself, you will find them. This criticism of differentiation, which I hear now and then, is not really about differentiation, but about society's values.

I might add that in business, energetic and extroverted people generally do better, but *results* speak for themselves, loud and clear. Differentiation hears them.

If you want the best people on your team, you need to face up to differentiation. I don't know of any people management system that does it better—with more transparency, fairness, and speed. It isn't perfect. But differentiation, like candor, clarifies business and makes it run better in every way.

4

Voice and Dignity

EVERY BRAIN IN THE GAME

RUDY GIULIANI HAS A SAYING: "Know what you believe." I think he's right, so I want to conclude this section of the book with one of my core beliefs. I mention it because it is the hinge for every principle you've just read about—mission and values, candor, and differentiation.

The belief is this: every person in the world wants voice and dignity, and every person deserves them.

By "voice," I mean people want the opportunity to speak their minds and have their ideas, opinions, and feelings heard, regardless of their nationality, gender, age, or culture.

By "dignity," I mean people inherently and instinctively want to be respected for their work and effort and individuality.

If you've just read the above and said, "Well, obviously," then fine. I am assuming that most people are having that response. And maybe the belief in voice and dignity doesn't even need to be stated, it is so widely accepted and its importance is so self-evident. But I have been surprised over the past couple of years at how often I end up coming back to this value when I talk about winning.

Last year in China, a young woman in the audience stood and, literally in tears, asked how any businessperson in her country could practice candor and differentiation when "only the voice of the boss is allowed."

"We, the people underneath, have so many ideas. But we cannot even imagine speaking them until we are the boss," she said. "That is fine if you are an entrepreneur and start your own company. Then you are the boss. But some of us are not able to do that."

I said that in the early days of GE's operations in China, I had seen the difficulties she had just described at our factories in Nansha, Shanghai, and Beijing. But as the plants developed and business practices evolved, I had seen an enormous improvement in how the Chinese leaders who worked for GE were listening to employees. I told her that I was confident that, with China's expanding market economy and the maturation of its management practices, a more inclusive approach would eventually spread.

But the repression of voice and dignity is hardly a Chinese problem. In fact, while the Chinese woman was very emotional in her questioning, people in every country I've visited share some of her frustration and concern on this matter.

> In China, a young woman asked how any businessperson in her country could practice candor and differentiation when "only the voice of the boss is allowed."

Now, when you are running a unit or a division, you rarely think that people aren't speaking up or that they're not respected. It feels like the people around you certainly are, and your days are filled with visits, calls, and notes from people with strong opinions. But it ends up that what you experience is a skewed sample. The majority of people in most organizations don't say anything because they feel they can't—and because they haven't been asked.

> I'd ask, "Why aren't you asking those questions to your own bosses?" The answer would come back, "I can't bring that up. I'd get killed."

That became clear to me in the late 1980s, just about every time I had a marathon session at our training center in Crotonville. Detailed questions about local business issues—questions that should have been answered back on home turf—were thrown at me from every direction. "Why is the refrigeration plant getting all the new equipment while we're letting laundry suffer?" and "What are we moving the GE90 engine assembly to Durham for, when we can do it right here in Evandale?"

In frustration, after several such questions, I'd invariably stop the class to ask, "Why aren't you asking those questions to your own bosses?"

The answer would come back, "I can't bring that up. I'd get killed."

"Why can you ask *me*?" I'd say.

"Because we feel anonymous here."

After a year or so of these kinds of exchanges, we realized we had to do something to create an environment back in the businesses where people at every level would speak out the way they did at Crotonville.

The Work-Out process was born. These were two- or three-day events held at GE sites around the world, patterned after New England town meetings. Groups of thirty to a hundred employees would come together with an outside facilitator to discuss better

> Some people have better ideas than others; some are smarter or more experienced or more creative. But everyone should be heard and respected.

ways of doing things and how to eliminate some of the bureaucracy and roadblocks that were hindering them. The boss would be present at the beginning of each session, laying out the rationale for the Work-Out. He or she would also commit to two things: to give an on-the-spot yes or no to 75 percent of the recommendations that came out of the session, and to resolve the remaining 25 percent within thirty days. The boss would then disappear until the end of the session, so as not to stifle open discussion, returning only at the end to make good on his or her promise.

Tens of thousands of these sessions took place over several years, until they became a way of life in the company. They are no longer big events but part of how GE goes about solving problems.

Whether it was a refrigeration plant in Louisville, Kentucky, where employees debated faster and better paint systems, or a jet engine plant in Rutland, Vermont, where employees had recommendations on how to cut cycle time in blade manufacturing, or a credit card processing facility in Cincinnati, where employees had ideas about billing efficiency, Work-Outs led to an explosion in productivity.

They brought every brain into the game.

A middle-aged appliance worker who was at one Work-Out spoke for thousands of people when he told me, "For twenty-five years, you paid for my hands when you could have had my brain as well—for nothing."

At last, because of Work-Out, we were getting both. In fact, I believe Work-Out was responsible for one of the most profound changes in GE during my time there. For the vast majority of employees, the boss-knows-all culture disappeared.

A big bureaucracy like GE needed something as systematized as Work-Out to break the ice and get people to open up. But it is not the only method to make sure that your team or company is getting every voice heard. Find an approach that feels right to you.

I'm not saying that everyone's opinions should be put into practice or every single complaint needs to be satisfied. That's what management judgment is all about. Obviously, some people have better ideas than others; some people are smarter or more experienced or more creative. But everyone should be heard and respected.

They want it and you need it.

YOUR COMPANY

5

Leadership

IT'S NOT JUST ABOUT YOU

$O^{NE \ DAY,}$ you become a leader.

On Monday, you're doing what comes naturally, enjoying your job, running a project, talking and laughing with colleagues about life and work, and gossiping about how stupid management can be. Then on Tuesday, you *are* management. You're a boss.

Suddenly, everything feels different—because it is different. Leadership requires distinct behaviors and attitudes, and for many people, they debut with the job.

Before you are a leader, success is all about growing yourself.

When you become a leader, success is all about growing others.

Without question, there are lots of ways to be a leader. You need to look only as far as the freewheeling, straight-talking Herb Kelleher, who ran Southwest Airlines for thirty years, and Microsoft's quiet innovator, Bill Gates, to know that leaders come in all varieties. In politics, take Churchill and Gandhi. In football, take Lombardi and Belichick.

Each of these leaders would give you a different list of leadership "rules."

If asked, I would give you eight. They didn't feel like rules when I was using them. They just felt like the right way to lead.

This is not the last you will hear of leadership in this book. Virtually every chapter touches on the subject, from crisis management to strategy to work-life balance.

But I'm starting with a separate chapter on leadership because it is always on people's minds. Over the past three years, during my talks with students, managers, and entrepreneurs, leadership questions invariably were asked. "What does a leader really do?" for instance, and "I was just promoted and I've never run anything before. How can I be a good leader?" Micromanagement often comes up as an area of concern, as in, "My boss feels as if he has to control everything—is that leadership or babysitting?" Similarly, charisma gets a lot of queries; people ask, "Can you be introverted, quiet, or just plain shy and still get results out of your people?" Once, in Chicago, an audience member said, "I have at least two direct reports who are smarter than I am. How can I possibly appraise them?"

These kinds of questions have pushed me to make sense of my own leadership experiences over forty years. Across the decades, circumstances varied widely. I ran teams with three people and divisions with thirty thousand. I managed businesses that were dying and ones that were bursting with growth. There were acquisitions, divestitures, organizational crises, moments of unexpected luck, good economies and bad.

And yet, some ways of leading always seemed to work. They became my "rules."

WHAT LEADERS DO

1. Leaders relentlessly upgrade their team, using every encounter as an opportunity to evaluate, coach, and build self-confidence.

2. Leaders make sure people not only see the vision, they live and breathe it.

3. Leaders get into everyone's skin, exuding positive energy and optimism.

4. Leaders establish trust with candor, transparency, and credit.

5. Leaders have the courage to make unpopular decisions and gut calls.

6. Leaders probe and push with a curiosity that borders on skepticism, making sure their questions are answered with action.

7. Leaders inspire risk taking and learning by setting the example.

8. Leaders celebrate.

THE DAILY BALANCING ACT

Before we look at each rule, a word on paradoxes. Leadership is loaded with them.

The granddaddy of them all is the short-long paradox, as in the question I often get: "How can I manage quarterly results and still do what's right for my business five years out?"

My answer is, "Welcome to the job!"

Look, anyone can manage for the short term—just keep squeezing the lemon. And anyone can manage for the long—just keep dreaming. You were made a leader because someone believed you could squeeze and dream at the same time. They saw in you a person with enough insight, experience, and rigor to balance the conflicting demands of short- and long-term results.

Performing balancing acts every day *is* leadership.

Take rule 3 and rule 6. One says you should show positive energy and optimism, showering your people with a can-do attitude. The other says you should constantly question your people and take nothing they say for granted.

Or take rule 5 and rule 7. One says you need to act like a boss, asserting authority. The other says you need to admit mistakes and embrace people who take risks, especially when they fail.

Of course, life would be easier if leadership was just a list of simple rules, but paradoxes are inherent to the trade.

That's part of the fun of leading, though—each day is a challenge. It is a brand-new chance to get better at a job that, when all is said and done, you can never be perfect at.

You can only give it everything you've got.

Here's how.

> RULE 1. Leaders relentlessly upgrade their team, using every encounter as an opportunity to evaluate, coach, and build self-confidence.

After the Boston Red Sox finally broke an eighty-six–year drought and won the World Series, you couldn't turn on the TV or open a paper without hearing speculation as to why 2004 was "the year." There were theories about everything, from center-fielder Johnny Damon's hairstyle to the lunar eclipse!

Most people agreed, however, that the reason wasn't mysterious at all. The Red Sox had the best players. The pitching staff was the league's best, the fielders were good enough, and the hitters . . . well, they were sensational. And they were all bound together by a winning spirit so palpable you could feel it in the air.

There are lucky breaks and bad calls in any season, but the team with the best players usually does win. And that is why, very simply, you need to invest the vast majority of your time and energy as a leader in three activities.

■ You have to **evaluate**—making sure the right people are in the right jobs, supporting and advancing those who are, and moving out those who are not.

■ You have to **coach**—guiding, critiquing, and helping people to improve their performance in every way.

■ And finally, you have to **build self-confidence**—pouring out encouragement, caring, and recognition.

Self-confidence energizes, and it gives your people the courage to stretch, take risks, and achieve beyond their dreams. It is the fuel of winning teams.

Too often, managers think that people development occurs once a year in performance reviews. That's not even close.

People development should be a daily event, integrated into every aspect of your regular goings-on.

Take budget reviews. They are a perfect occasion to focus on people. That's right, people. Yes, you need to talk about the business and its results, but in a budget review you can really see team dynamics in action. If everyone around the table sits silent and frozen while the team leader pontificates, you've got some serious coaching to do. If everyone's involved in the presentation and the whole team is alive, you've got a great opportunity to give immediate feedback that you like what you see. If the team has a real star or a dud in its midst, share your impressions with its leader as soon as you can.

There is no event in your day that cannot be used for people development.

Customer visits are a chance to evaluate your sales force. Plant tours are an opportunity to meet promising new line managers and see if they have the ability to run something bigger. A coffee break at a meeting is an opening to coach a team member who is about to give his first major presentation.

And remember in all these encounters, evaluating and coaching are great, but building self-

> Take every opportunity to inject self-confidence into those who have earned it. Use ample praise, the more specific the better.

confidence is, in the end, probably the most important thing you can do. Take every opportunity to inject self-confidence into those who have earned it. Use ample praise, the more specific the better.

Besides its huge impact on upgrading the team, the best thing about using every encounter for people development is how much fun it is. Instead of mind-numbing meetings about numbers and plant tours showing off new machines, every day is about growing people. In fact, think of yourself as a gardener, with a watering can in one hand and a can of fertilizer in the other. Occasionally you have to pull some weeds, but most of the time, you just nurture and tend.

Then watch everything bloom.

> **RULE 2. Leaders make sure people not only see the vision, they live and breathe it.**

It goes without saying that leaders have to set the team's vision and most do. But there's so much more to the "vision thing" than that. As a leader, you have to make the vision come alive.

How do you achieve that? First of all, no jargon. Goals cannot sound noble but vague. Targets cannot be so blurry they can't be hit. Your direction has to be so vivid that if you randomly woke one of your employees in the middle of the night and asked him, "Where are we going?" he could still answer in a half-asleep stupor, "We're going to keep improving our service to individual contractors and expand our market by aggressively reaching out to small wholesalers."

I had just that kind of experience last year when I was out

> **There were times I talked about the company's direction so many times in one day that I was completely sick of hearing it myself.**

hawking an investment fund for Clayton, Dubilier & Rice, where I consult. At one dinner session in Chicago, the room was filled with about a dozen investors, all focused on our investment criteria and projections for returns.

Steve Klimkowski, the chief investment officer of Northwestern Memorial HealthCare, was one of them. But in the midst of all the financial chatter, he was just as interested in talking about his hospital's mission to deliver "excellent patient care—from the patient's perspective." He had examples of how employees at every level—including him, the investment guy—had transformed their work to fulfill the vision. He had been coached, for example, never to give outpatients directions to a location in the hospital, but to walk them there. At his performance review, Steve had been asked to list several ways in which he personally had improved the patient's experience at Northwestern Memorial. In fact, Steve's understanding of his role in achieving the mission, and his passion for it, were so real that after talking to him for fifteen minutes, you could wake me in the middle of the night and I could tell you about it!

Clearly, Northwestern Memorial's leaders had communicated the hospital's vision with amazing clarity and consistency. And that's the point. You have to talk about vision constantly—basically, to the point of gagging. There were times I talked about the company's direction so many times in one day that I was completely sick of hearing it myself. But I realized the message was always new to someone. And so, you keep on repeating it.

And you talk to *everyone*.

One of the most common problems in organizations is that

leaders communicate the vision to their closest colleagues and its implications never filter down to people in frontline positions. Think about all the times you have bumped into a rude or harried clerk at a high-service department store, or been put on hold by a call center operator at a company that promises speed and convenience.

Somehow, they haven't heard the mission, maybe because it wasn't shouted in their direction, loud enough or often enough.

Or maybe their rewards weren't aligned.

And that's the final piece of this particular leadership rule. If you want people to live and breathe the vision, "show them the money" when they do, be it with salary, bonus, or significant recognition of some sort. To quote a friend of mine, Chuck Ames, the former chairman and CEO of Reliance Electric, "Show me a company's various compensation plans, and I'll show you how its people behave."

Vision is an essential element of the leader's job. But no vision is worth the paper it's printed on unless it is communicated constantly and reinforced with rewards. Only then will it leap off the page—and come to life.

> RULE 3. Leaders get into everyone's skin, exuding positive energy and optimism.

You know that old saying "The fish rots from the head." It's mainly used to refer to how politics and corruption filter down into an organization, but it could just as easily be used to describe the effect of a bad attitude at the top of any team, large or small. Eventually, everyone's infected.

The leader's mood is, for lack of a better word, catching. You've seen the dynamic a hundred times. An upbeat manager who goes through the day with a positive outlook somehow ends up running a team or organization filled with . . . well, upbeat people with positive outlooks. A pessimistic sourpuss somehow ends up with an unhappy tribe all his own.

Unhappy tribes have a tough time winning.

Of course, sometimes there are good reasons to be down. The economy is bad, competition is brutal—whatever. Work can be hard.

But your job as leader is to fight the gravitational pull of negativism. That doesn't mean you sugarcoat the challenges your team faces. It does mean you display an energizing, can-do attitude about overcoming them. It means you get out of your office and into everyone's skin, really caring about what they're doing and how they're faring as you take the hill *together*.

Now, you might be thinking, "That kind of emotional bonding—it just ain't me."

And it isn't for some people. I've seen a few capable managers run their businesses while keeping their people at arm's length. These managers often demonstrated the right values, like candor and rigor, and they delivered good results.

But in never really getting inside their people, something was lost. Work stayed work.

The right attitude could have made it so much more.

Make that attitude yours.

RULE 4. Leaders establish trust with candor, transparency, and credit.

For some people, becoming a leader can be a real power trip. They relish the feeling of control over both people and information.

And so they keep secrets, reveal little of their thinking about people and their performance, and hoard what they know about the business and its future.

This kind of behavior certainly establishes the leader as boss, but it drains trust right out of a team.

> Leaders never score off their own people by stealing an idea and claiming it as their own.

What is trust? I could give you a dictionary definition, but you know it when you feel it. Trust happens when leaders are transparent, candid, and keep their word. It's that simple.

Your people should always know where they stand in terms of their performance. They have to know how the business is doing. And sometimes the news is not good—such as imminent layoffs—and any normal person would rather avoid delivering it. But you have to fight the impulse to pad or diminish hard messages or you'll pay with your team's confidence and energy.

Leaders also establish trust by giving credit where credit is due. They never score off their own people by stealing an idea and claiming it as their own. They don't kiss up and kick down because they are self-confident and mature enough to know that their team's success will get them recognition, and sooner rather than later. In bad times, leaders take responsibility for what's gone wrong. In good times, they generously pass around the praise.

When you become a leader, sometimes you really feel the pull to say, "Look at what *I've* done." When your team excels, it's only normal to want some credit yourself.

After all, you run the show. You hand out the paychecks, so people listen to your every word (or pretend to) and they laugh at all your jokes (or pretend to). In some companies, being boss means getting a special parking place or traveling first class. It could go to your head. You could really start to feel pretty big.

Don't let it happen.

Remember, when you were made a leader you weren't given a crown, you were given a responsibility to bring out the best in others. For that, your people need to trust you. And they will, as long as you demonstrate candor, give credit, and stay real.

RULE 5. Leaders have the courage to make unpopular decisions and gut calls.

By nature, some people are consensus builders. Some people long to be loved by everyone.

Those behaviors can really get you in the soup if you are a leader, because no matter where you work or what you do, there are times you have to make hard decisions—let people go, cut funding to a project, or close a plant.

Obviously, tough calls spawn complaints and resistance. Your job is to listen and explain yourself clearly but move forward. Do not dwell or cajole.

You are not a leader to win a popularity contest—you are a leader to lead. Don't run for office. You're already elected.

Sometimes making a decision is hard not because it's unpopular, but because it comes from your gut and defies a "technical" rationale.

> You are not a leader to win a popularity contest—you are a leader to lead.

Much has been written about the mystery of gut, but it's really just pattern recognition, isn't it? You've seen something so many times you *just know* what's going on this time. The facts may be incomplete or the data limited, but the situation feels very, very familiar to you.

Leaders are faced with gut calls all the time. You're asked to invest in a new office building, for instance, but visiting the city, you see cranes in every direction. The deal's numbers are absolutely perfect, you're told, but you've been here before. You know that overcapacity is around the corner and the "perfect" investment is about to be worth sixty cents on the dollar. You've got no proof, but you've got a real uh-oh feeling in your stomach.

> If you're left with that uh-oh feeling in your stomach, don't hire the guy.

You have to kill the deal, even if that pisses people off.

Sometimes the hardest gut calls involve picking people. You meet a candidate who has all the right stuff. His résumé is perfect: prestigious schools and great experience. His interview is impressive: firm handshake, good eye contact, smart questions, and so on. But something nags at you. Maybe he's moved around an awful lot—he's just had too many jobs in too few years without a plausible enough explanation. Or his energy seems too frantic. Or one previous boss said nice things about him but didn't sound as though he really meant them.

And you're left with that uh-oh feeling in your stomach again. Don't hire the guy.

You've been made a leader because you've seen more and been right more times. Listen to your gut. It's telling you something.

RULE 6. Leaders probe and push with a curiosity that borders on skepticism, making sure their questions are answered with action.

When you are an individual contributor, you try to have all the answers. That's your job—to be an expert, the best at what you do, maybe even the smartest person in the room.

When you are a leader, your job is to have all the questions. You have to be incredibly comfortable looking like the dumbest person in the room. Every conversation you have about a decision, a proposal, or a piece of market information has to be filled with you saying, "What if?" and "Why not?" and "How come?"

When I was first made a manager, in 1963, I was running a start-up with a product that went to market through a large pool sales force. I knew we weren't getting enough attention from the people in the field. So every weekend I would take home carbon copies of the sales reports filed after every customer visit—piles of them. On Mondays, I would make a pest of myself with a round of phone calls, asking the salespeople or the plant manager to explain everything I didn't understand. Why, for instance, were we giving truckload pricing to one customer for small lot sales? Why was another customer getting a product with black specks?

These questions got the sales team to give our product the attention it needed and increased my understanding of how it was sold.

Questioning, however, is never enough. You have to make sure your questions unleash debate and raise issues that get action.

Remember, just because you are a leader, saying something doesn't mean it will happen.

That was the case back in the early '90s when I was pretty much obsessed with the idea of an MRI machine with a larger opening. If you have ever had an MRI, you'll know what I am talking about. You lie on your back and are slid inside a tunnel containing a spinning magnet.

At the time, the tunnel—or bore, as it was called—was very narrow, and patients were experiencing claustrophobia during the forty-minute MRI process. Word was that Hitachi was coming up with a machine with a much wider bore, but some members of our medical business dismissed the product. Hospitals, they said, would never accept the low-quality images such large-bore machines produced.

> "We'll look into it," they kept assuring me. I was a know-nothing, meddling pain in the neck, and they were just trying to mollify me.

Having experienced an MRI myself, I just wasn't convinced. The machines did make you feel claustrophobic! Every chance I got, I asked the medical team to look at the situation again. Won't hospitals compromise image quality for patient comfort, especially for simple procedures, like elbows and knees? Won't the technology eventually improve?

In response, the medical team gave me the all-too-common business head fake. "We'll look into it," they kept assuring me. Of course they didn't. I was a know-nothing, meddling pain in the neck, and they were just trying to mollify me.

A year later, Hitachi rolled out a large-bore machine and captured a significant piece of the market. We spent two years playing catch-up.

The last thing I want to sound like with this story is a hero.

Just the opposite.

I should have pushed a whole lot harder with my questioning. In fact, I should have insisted we put resources into developing our own large-bore machine. All we were left with at the end was me thinking, "I knew it," and wanting to say, "I told you so."

Both of those sentiments are worth nothing. You would assume that was obvious, but I've seen more leaders believe that second-guessing absolves them from responsibility when things go wrong. Years ago, I used to see a well-known CEO socially on a fairly regular basis. Whenever his company had been in the news for screwing up, he'd always say something like, "I knew they shouldn't have done that." For some reason that made him feel better, but what did it matter?

We've all been guilty at one point or another in our careers of boasting of perfect hindsight.

It's a terrible sin.

If you don't make sure your questions and concerns are acted upon, *it doesn't count*.

I realize most people don't love the probing process. It's annoying to believe in a product or come into a room with a beautiful presentation only to have it picked apart with questions from the boss.

But that's the job. You want bigger and better solutions. Questions, healthy debate, decisions, and action will get everyone there.

RULE 7. Leaders inspire risk taking and learning by setting the example.

Winning companies embrace risk taking and learning.

But in reality, these two concepts often get lip service—and little else. Too many managers urge their people to try new things and then whack them in the head when they fail. And too many live in not-invented-here worlds of their own making.

If you want your people to experiment and expand their minds, set the example yourself.

Consider risk taking. You can create a culture that welcomes risk taking by freely admitting your mistakes and talking about what you've learned from them.

I cannot count the number of times I've told people about my first big mistake—and it was huge—blowing up a pilot plant in Pittsfield, Massachusetts, in 1963. I was across the street in my office when the explosion occurred, set off by a spark igniting a large tank of volatile solution. The noise was enormous, and then roof shingles and shards of glass flew everywhere. Smoke blanketed the area. Thank God no one was hurt.

Despite the enormity of my mistake, my boss's boss, a former MIT professor named Charlie Reed, didn't beat me up. Instead, his sympathetic, scientific probing of the reasons for the incident taught me not only how to improve our manufacturing process, but more importantly, how to deal with people when they were down.

That wasn't the only mistake in my career; I made plenty. I bought the investment bank Kidder Peabody—a cultural fit disaster—and made many wrong hires, to name just two more.

These experiences were nothing to feel great about, but I talked about them openly in order to show that it was OK to take swings and miss, as long as you learned from them.

You don't need to be preachy or particularly somber about your errors. In fact, the more humorous and lighthearted you can be about them, the more people will get the message that mistakes aren't fatal.

As for learning—again, live it yourself. Just because you're the boss doesn't mean you're the source of all knowledge. Whenever I learned about a best practice that I liked at another company, I would come back to GE and make a scene. Maybe I often overstated the case, but I wanted people to know how enthusiastic I was about the new idea. And I was!

> Just because you're the boss doesn't mean you're the source of all knowledge.

You can—and should—learn from one another too. Remember that executive in Chicago who asked me how he could appraise people who were smarter than he was? The answer I gave him was, "Learn from them. In the best-case scenario, all your people will be smarter than you. It doesn't mean you can't lead them."

There is no edict in the world that will make people take risks or spend their time learning. In most cases, their risk-reward equation just isn't obvious enough.

If you want to change that, set the example yourself. You'll love the exciting culture you create and the results you get—and so will your team.

RULE 8. Leaders celebrate.

What is it about celebrating that makes managers so nervous? Maybe throwing a party doesn't seem professional, or it makes managers worry that they won't look serious to the powers that be, or that, if things get too happy at the office, people will stop working their tails off.

Whatever the reason, there is just not enough celebrating going on at work—anywhere. When I travel, I frequently ask audiences if they've done anything to recognize their team's achievements—large or small—over the past year. I'm not talking about those stilted, company-orchestrated parties that everyone hates, in which the whole team is marched out to a local restaurant for an evening of forced merriment when they'd rather be home. I'm talking about sending a team to Disney World with their families, or giving each team member two tickets to a great show in New York, or handing each team member a new iPod or the like.

But to my question "Do you celebrate enough?" almost no one raises a hand.

It's not as if GE was immune to this phenomenon. I harped on the importance of celebrating for twenty years. But during my last trip as CEO to our training center in Crotonville, I asked the hundred or so managers in the class, "Do you celebrate enough in your units?" Even knowing what I wanted them to say, less than half answered yes.

> Work is too much a part of life not to recognize moments of achievement. Grab as many as you can. Make a big deal out of them.

What a lost opportunity. Celebrating makes people feel like winners and creates an atmosphere of recognition and positive energy. Imagine a team winning the World Series without champagne spraying everywhere. You just can't! And yet companies win all the time and let it go without so much as a high five.

Work is too much a part of life not to recognize moments of achievement. Grab as many as you can. Make a big deal out of them. If you don't, no one will.

◼

There is no easy formula for being a leader. If only!

Leadership is challenging—all those balancing acts, all the responsibility, all that pressure.

And yet, good leadership happens—and it comes in all kinds of packages. There are quiet leaders and bombastic ones. There are analytical leaders and more impulsive ones. Some are tough as nails with their teams, others more nurturing. On the surface, you would be hard-pressed to say what qualities these leaders share.

Underneath, you would surely see that the best care passionately about their people—about their growth and success. And you would see that they themselves are comfortable in their own skins. They're real, filled with candor and integrity, optimism and humanity.

I am often asked if leaders are born or made. The answer, of course, is both. Some characteristics, like IQ and energy, seem to come with the package. On the other hand, you learn some leadership skills, like self-confidence, at your mother's knee, and at school, in academics and sports. And you learn others at work through iterative experience—trying something, getting it wrong and learning from it, or getting it right and gaining the self-confidence to do it again, only better.

For most of us, leadership happens one day when you become a boss and the rules change.

Before, your job was about yourself.

Now, it's about them.

6

Hiring

WHAT WINNERS ARE MADE OF

SOMETIMES WHEN I APPEAR before business audiences, I get a question that totally stumps me, as in: I have no clue about the right answer. A couple of years ago at a convention of insurance executives in San Diego, for instance, a woman stood up and said, "What is the one thing you should ask in an interview to help you decide whom to hire?"

I shook my head. "The *one* thing?" I said. "I can't come up with *one*. What do you think?"

"That's why I'm asking you!" she replied.

The audience roared, certainly because I was so floored, but also because they could probably relate.

Hiring good people is hard.

Hiring great people is brutally hard.

And yet nothing matters more in winning than getting the right people on the field. All the clever strategies and advanced technologies in the world are nowhere near as effective without great people to put them to work.

Because hiring right is so important—and so challenging—there is a lot of territory to cover in this chapter.

■ First, we'll take a short look at three acid tests you need to conduct before you even think about hiring someone.

■ Next we'll lay out the 4-E (and 1-P) framework for hiring that I have used for many years. It's named after the four characteristics it contains, which all begin with *E,* a nice coincidence. There's a *P* (for passion) in there too.

■ After that, we'll explore the four special characteristics you look for when hiring leaders. The previous chapter was about what you do when you are a leader—the rules of leadership, as it were. This section is about how to hire leaders in the first place.

■ Finally, I'll answer six FAQs (frequently asked questions) about hiring that I get during my travels—plus that "impossible" one from that insurance executive in San Diego. After all, I've had a couple of years to think it over!

THE ACID TESTS

Before you even think about assessing people for a job, they have to pass through three screens. Remember, these tests should come at the outset of the hiring process, not right before you're about to sign on the dotted line.

The first test is for *integrity*. Integrity is something of a fuzzy word, so let me tell you my definition. People with integrity tell the truth, and they keep their word. They take responsibility for past actions, admit mistakes, and fix them. They know the laws of their

> Over time, many of us develop an instinct for integrity. Just don't be afraid to use it.

country, industry, and company—both in letter and spirit—and abide by them. They play to win the right way, by the rules.

How can you test for integrity? If a candidate comes from inside your company, that's pretty easy. You've seen him or her in action or know someone who has. From the outside, you need to rely on reputation and reference checks. But those aren't foolproof. You also have to rely on your gut. Does the person seem real? Does she openly admit mistakes? Does he talk about his life with equal measures of candor and discretion?

Over time, many of us develop an instinct for integrity. Just don't be afraid to use it.

The second test is for *intelligence*. That doesn't mean a person must have read Shakespeare or can solve complex physics problems. It does mean the candidate has a strong dose of intellectual curiosity, with a breadth of knowledge to work with or lead other smart people in today's complex world.

Sometimes people confuse education with intelligence. I certainly did that at the start of my career. But with experience, I learned that smart people come from every kind of school. I've known many extremely bright people from places like Harvard and Yale. But some of the best executives I've worked with have attended places like Bryant University in Providence, Rhode Island, and the University of Dubuque, in Iowa.

GE was lucky to have all these people on its team.

My point is that a candidate's education is only a piece of the picture, especially when it comes to intelligence.

The third ticket to the game is *maturity.* You can, by the way, be mature at any age, and immature too. Regardless, there are certain traits that seem to indicate a person has grown up: the individual can withstand the heat, handle stress and setbacks, and, alternatively, when those wonderful moments arise, enjoy success with equal parts of joy and humility. Mature people respect the emotions of others. They feel confident but are not arrogant.

In fact, mature people usually have a sense of humor, especially about themselves!

As with integrity, there is no real test for maturity. Again, you have to rely on reference checks, reputation, and most important, gut.

THE 4-E (AND 1-P) FRAMEWORK

The 4–E framework took years for me to solidify. No doubt other people have other frameworks that work very well in building winning teams. But I've found this one was consistently effective, year after year, across businesses and borders.

The first E is positive energy. We just talked about this characteristic in the chapter on leadership. It means the ability to go go go—to thrive on action and relish change. People with positive energy are generally extroverted and optimistic. They make conversation and friends easily. They start the day with enthusiasm and usually end it that way too, rarely seeming to tire in the middle. They don't complain about working hard; they love to work.

They also love to play.

People with positive energy just love life.

The second E is the ability to energize others. Positive energy is the ability to get other people revved up. People who energize can inspire their team to take on the impossible—and enjoy the hell out of doing it. In fact, people would arm wrestle for the chance to work with them.

> People with positive energy just love life.

Now, energizing others is not just about giving Pattonesque speeches. It takes a deep knowledge of your business and strong persuasion skills to make a case that will galvanize others.

A great example of an energizer is Charlene Begley, who started with GE as a financial management trainee in 1988. After several years in various jobs, Charlene was selected to run GE's Six Sigma program in the transportation business. That's where her leadership really began to shine. Galvanized by her intensity, her team really got its Six Sigma program on the corporate radar screen.

It's hard to unpick Charlene's ability to energize because it's a brew of skills all mixed together. She is a great communicator, who can clearly define objectives. She's dead serious about work, but she doesn't take herself too seriously. In fact, she has a good sense of humor and shares credit readily. Her attitude is always upbeat: no matter how hard the job, it can get done.

Charlene's ability to energize that Six Sigma team was one of the key characteristics that got her out of the pile and set her on GE's fast track. After Six Sigma and a couple of other leadership roles, she was made head of GE's corporate audit staff and eventually became CEO of GE Fanuc Automation. Today, at thirty-eight, Charlene is CEO and president of GE's $3 billion rail business.

The third E is edge, the courage to make tough yes-or-no decisions. Look, the world is filled with gray. Anyone can look at an issue from every different angle. Some smart people can—and will—analyze those angles indefinitely. But effective

> **Effective people know when to stop assessing and make a tough call, even without total information. Little is worse than a manager who can't cut bait.**

people know when to stop assessing and make a tough call, even without total information.

Little is worse than a manager at any level who can't cut bait, the type that always says, "Bring it back in a month and we'll take a good, hard look at it again," or that awful type that says yes to you, but then someone else comes into the room and changes his mind. We called these wishy-washy types last-one-out-the-door bosses.

Some of the smartest people that I've hired over the years—many of them from consulting—had real difficulty with edge, especially when they were put into operations. In every situation, they always saw too many options, which inhibited them from taking action. That indecisiveness kept their organizations in limbo. In the end, for several of them, that was a fatal flaw.

Which leads us to the fourth E—execute—the ability to get the job done. Maybe this fourth E seems obvious, but for a few years, there were just the first three Es. Thinking these traits were more than sufficient, we evaluated hundreds of people and labeled a slew of them "high-potentials," and moved many of them into managerial roles.

In that period, I traveled to personnel review sessions in the field with GE's head of HR, Bill Conaty. At the review sessions, we would refer to a single page that had each manager's photo on it, along with his or her boss's performance review and three circles, one for each E we were using at the time. Each one of these Es would be colored in to represent how well the individual was doing. For instance, a person could have half a circle of energy, a full circle of energize, and a quarter circle of edge.

Then one Friday night after a weeklong trip to our midwestern businesses, Bill and I were flying back to headquarters, looking over page after page of high-potentials

> Some of the smartest people I hired had real difficulty with edge. For several of them, that was a fatal flaw.

with three solidly colored-in circles. Bill turned to me. "You know, Jack, we're missing something," he said. "We have all these great people, but some of their results stink."

What was missing was execution.

It turns out you can have positive energy, energize everyone around you, make hard calls, and still not get over the finish line. Being able to execute is a special and distinct skill. It means a person knows how to put decisions into action and push them forward to completion, through resistance, chaos, or unexpected obstacles. People who can execute know that winning is about results.

If a candidate has the four Es, then you look for that final P—passion. By passion, I mean a heartfelt, deep, and authentic excitement about work. People with passion care— really care in their bones—about colleagues, employees, and friends winning. They love to learn and grow, and they get a huge kick when the people around them do the same.

The funny thing about people with passion, though, is that they usually aren't excited just about work. They tend to be passionate about everything. They're sports trivia nuts or they're fanatical supporters of their alma maters or they're political junkies.

Whatever—they just have juice for life in their veins.

HIRING FOR THE TOP

The three preliminary acid tests and the 4-E (and 1-P) framework apply to any hiring decision, no matter what level in the organization. But sometimes, you need to hire a senior-level leader—someone who is going to run a major division or an entire company. In that case, there are four more highly developed characteristics that really matter.

The first characteristic is authenticity. Why? It's simple. A person cannot make hard decisions, hold unpopular positions, or stand tall for what he believes unless he knows who he is and feels comfortable with that. I am talking about self-confidence and conviction. These traits make a leader bold and decisive, which is absolutely critical in times when you must act quickly.

Just as important, authenticity makes leaders likable, for lack of a better word. Their "realness" comes across in the way they communicate and reach people on an emotional level. Their words move them: their message touches something inside.

When I was at GE, we would occasionally encounter a very successful executive who just could not be promoted to the next level. In the early days, we would struggle with our reasoning. These executives demonstrated the right values and made the numbers, but usually their people did not connect with them. What was wrong? Finally, we figured out that these executives always had a certain phoniness to them. They pretended to be something they were not—more in control, more upbeat, more savvy than they really were. They didn't sweat. They didn't cry. They squirmed in their own skin, playing a role of their own inventing.

Leaders can't have an iota of fakeness. They have to know themselves—so that they can be straight with the world, energize followers, and lead with the authority born of authenticity.

The second characteristic is the ability to see around corners. Every leader has to have a vision and the ability to predict the future, but good leaders must have a special capacity to anticipate the radically unexpected. In business, the best leaders in brutally competitive environments have a sixth sense for market changes, as well as moves by existing competitors and new entrants.

The former vice-chairman of GE, Paolo Fresco, is a gifted chess player. He carried that skill into every global business deal he made over the course of thirty years. Somehow, because of his intuition and savvy, he could put himself in the chair of the person across the table, allowing him to predict every move in a negotiation. To our amazement, Paolo always saw what was coming next. No one ever came close to getting the better of him—because he knew what his "adversary" was thinking before the adversary himself knew.

The ability to see around corners is the ability to imagine the unimaginable.

The third characteristic is a strong penchant to surround themselves with people better and smarter than they are. Every time we had a crisis at GE, I would quickly assemble a group of the smartest, gutsiest people I could find at any level from within the company and sometimes from without, and lean on them heavily for their knowledge and advice. I would make sure everyone in the room came at the problem from a different angle, and then I would have us all wallow in the information as we worked to solve the crisis.

> The best leaders in brutally competitive environments have a sixth sense for market changes. They can imagine the unimaginable.

These sessions were almost always contentious, and the opinions that came at me strong and varied. And yet, my best decisions arose from what I learned in these debates. Disagreement surfaced meaningful questions and forced us to challenge assumptions. Everyone came out of the experience more informed and better prepared to take on the next crisis.

A good leader has the courage to put together a team of people who sometimes make him look like the dumbest person in the room! I know that sounds counterintuitive. You want your leader to be the smartest person in the room—but if he acts as if he is, he won't get half the pushback he must get to make the best decisions.

The fourth characteristic is heavy-duty resilience. Every leader makes mistakes, every leader stumbles and falls. The question with a senior-level leader is, does she learn from her mistakes, regroup, and then get going again with renewed speed, conviction, and confidence?

The name for this trait is resilience, and it is so important that a leader must have it going into a job because if she doesn't, a crisis time is too late to learn it. That is why, when I placed people in new leadership situations, I always looked for candidates who had one or two very tough experiences. I particularly liked the people who had had the wind knocked clear out of them but proved they could run even harder in the next race.

The global business world today is going to knock any leader off her horse more than once. She must know how to get back in the saddle again.

HIRING FAQS

Finally, let's look at the six FAQs—frequently asked questions— I've received about hiring over the past several years. At the end of them, I will try (at last) to answer the insurance executive from San Diego about the one best question to ask in an interview. As I said earlier, I've been thinking about it for a long time now.

1. How do you actually interview somebody for a job? My immediate answer to this question is: don't ever rely entirely on one meeting!

No matter how pressed for time you are or how promising someone looks, make sure every candidate is interviewed by several people. Over time, you will find that there are some people in your organization who have a special gift for picking out stars and phonies. Rely on them. (Bill Conaty, my HR head, was a master at this. Whether it was with a handshake, a smile, or a way of talking about their family, job candidates were transparent to him.) And listen when a trusted colleague tells you that his or her gut is negatively responding to a candidate. That uh-oh feeling is usually a sign that the candidate is not what he seems.

At some point in the interview process, when it's your turn, make sure you exaggerate the challenge of the open job; describe it on its worst day—hard, contentious, political, full of uncertainty. As you crank it up, see if the candidate keeps saying, "Yes, yes, yes!" If he does, you should worry that he has few other options, if any. You may even be his sole hope of employment.

Be impressed if the candidate starts peppering you back with hard questions like, "How soon do you expect the results to be achieved?" or "Do I have enough people to make this happen?" Be even more impressed if she asks you about the company's values. The difficulty of a job will bring good candidates to

I particularly liked the people who had had the wind knocked clear out of them but proved they could run even harder in the next race.

the edge of their seats with curiosity and firm self-confidence, not overenthusiastic acquiescence.

Finally, after all the talking is done, don't check just the references the candidate gives you. Call around—but you know that. When you do, don't allow the conversation to be perfunctory. Stop yourself from doing something natural—just hearing the good news you want to hear. Force yourself to challenge anything that sounds like lawyer-speak. Use your chits. Promise you won't repeat what you hear. Doing that, you'll get what I did more times than I can count: "You've got to be kidding! We were happy to get rid of that guy!"

2. I just need to hire someone for technical expertise. Why do I need to bother with the four Es? Obviously, hiring a person who is both a technical star and demonstrates the four Es would be very nice! But if you're really just desperate for a person with a certain specialty—say, a computer programmer or a research scientist—then I'd be satisfied with energy and passion, along with a bucketful of raw intelligence, great prior experience, and, of course, integrity. You need that with any person you hire.

3. What if someone is missing one or two of the Es? Can training fill in the gaps? Any candidate you hire in a managerial role must have the first two Es, positive energy and the ability to energize. Those are personality traits, and I don't think they can be trained into someone. And frankly, I would encourage you not to hire any team member—manager or not—without a good dose of positive energy. People without it just enervate an organization.

Edge and execution, on the other hand, can be developed with experience and management training. Time after time, I've seen people learn how to make tough calls and deliver results.

The GE audit staff offers numerous examples. Every year, it brings on board about 120 people, primarily from GE's financial management training program, but about a quarter from other functions, such as engineering and manufacturing. The typical new hire in auditing has about three years of experience with the company.

Their first year, these "new kids" travel to GE businesses around the world as members of three- to six-person audit teams. After twelve weeks of grueling analysis, they return to the headquarters of the business they've just audited to present their findings to the CFO and CEO. Often, they've got plenty to tell, some of it not so pretty.

Early on, these young auditors are tentative, holding their comments while the more senior members of the team run the show. But over time, usually three to five years, I've seen these auditors develop an edge that is razor sharp. It comes from observing their more experienced teammates, lots of coaching, and plenty of practice. They also develop an incredible knack for execution. After all, they are responsible for making sure their recommendations have been implemented. If they haven't, all hell breaks loose—and that's a good teacher.

The proof that edge and execution can be learned is clear: several CEOs of GE's biggest businesses and a vice-chairman are veterans of the audit staff development process.

4. Can a person get ahead in business without the four Es or passion? Absolutely yes.

A person can reach great heights just by being very smart. Or just by the sheer ability to get things done. We can all think of examples of these individuals. Many are the inventors and entrepreneurs of the world, and usually they run their own shows.

But within an organization, I just haven't seen too many who have sustained success, especially as leaders, without the four Es and passion.

5. I've always tried to hire people who can hit the ground running. What do you think about that as a decisive factor?

When hiring, you have to make a trade-off. Do you hire someone to get a job done fast, or do you hire him based on his potential for growth? My advice is: try to pick the second option.

I didn't always feel that way.

The first time I hired managers was when I was twenty-eight years old and I needed to build a functional team. I hired a PhD who was a peer of mine to be manager of R & D. For marketing, I hired a good fellow who was smart and was there, and for manufacturing manager, my selection was an experienced hand. I'd seen him in action in another part of the same division.

Although I didn't think of it at the time, most of these people had no future beyond the jobs I had just put them in. Our business was growing rapidly, and they didn't have the skills to grow with it. In fact, by the time the business was four years old, all of them were gone and we were filling the positions again.

With my first shot at hiring managers, I didn't know any better. I just wanted to get the job done. But I eventually learned that it pays to go for the high-potentials who can grow with the business or are capable of moving up elsewhere in the organization. Hiring a highly skilled "blocker"—someone who will hit the ground running but has no future beyond the open position—is tempting because it solves an immediate need. But blockers soon become enervating. They get bored by the familiarity of the work or, as in my early case, swamped by its challenges. Their people get discouraged because they see their bosses going nowhere, which makes them wonder about their own opportunities.

A good rule of thumb, then, is not to hire someone into the last job of his or

A good rule of thumb is not to hire someone into the last job of his or her career, unless it's to be head of a function or CEO.

her career, unless it's to be head of a function or CEO.

6. How long does it take to know if you've hired right? Usually within a year—and certainly within two—it is pretty clear if someone is getting the results you'd hoped for.

> Don't beat yourself up if you get hiring wrong some of the time. Just remember, the mistake is yours to fix.

It's relatively easy to notice when a person lacks the energy and execution you anticipated. But the ability to energize and the capacity for edge sometimes take longer to show up in a new environment. People want to fit in before they start rousing the team to a cause or making the tough calls. But as I said, within two years at the most, if an employee is still falling short of your expectations, it is time to admit your mistake and start the process of moving the person out. If you have been doing your job and giving honest evaluations along the way, the employee shouldn't be surprised, and an equitable severance package will likewise soften the blow.

Hiring right is hard. I'd say as a young manager, I picked the right people about 50 percent of the time. Thirty years later, I had improved to about 80 percent.

My point is: don't beat yourself up if you get hiring wrong some of the time, especially when you're starting out.

Situations change. People change. You change.

But just remember, every hiring mistake is yours. You have to fix it, not an HR person you call in to do your dirty work. Take responsibility and make sure the ending is candid and fair.

And now for our San Diego question.

What is the one thing you should ask in an interview to help you decide whom to hire? If I had just one area to probe in an interview, it would be about why the candidate left his previous job, and the one before that.

Was it the environment? Was it the boss? Was it the team? What exactly made you leave? There is so much information in those answers. Keep digging and dig deep. Maybe the candidate just expects too much from a job or a company—he wants a boss who is entirely hands-off or teammates who always agree. Maybe he wants too much reward too fast. Or maybe she's leaving her last job because she has just what you want: too much energy to be held back, so much ability to energize she wants to manage more people, too much edge for a namby-pamby employer, and such a strong ability to execute she needs more challenge.

The key is: Listen closely. Get in the candidate's skin. Why a person has left a job or jobs tells you more about them than almost any other piece of data.

■

Your goal in hiring is to get the right players on the field.

Luckily, great people are everywhere. You just have to know how to pick them.

It's so easy to just hire people you like. After all, you'll be spending the majority of your waking hours with them. It's also easy to hire people with relevant experience. They'll get the job done.

But friendship and experience are never enough. Every person you hire has to have integrity, intelligence, and maturity. Once you've got those, look hard for people with the four Es and passion. Beyond that, at the senior level, look for authenticity, foresight, the willingness to draw on others for advice, and resilience.

Put it all together, and those are the people who win.

7

People Management

YOU'VE GOT THE RIGHT PLAYERS. NOW WHAT?

You've got the right players on the field—that's a great start. Now they need to work together, steadily improve their performance, be motivated, stay with the company, and grow as leaders.

In other words, they need to be managed.

There are libraries of books on people management, not to mention plenty of courses in business schools. There are training programs, magazines, and Web sites, many offering sound advice. And then there is experience.

That's mainly what this chapter draws on. During my years at GE, once I was out of the laboratory at Plastics, managing people was really what I did. After all, I didn't have the expertise to design jet engines, build CT scanners, or create a comedy program for NBC. Obviously, as CEO, I got involved in everything: strategy, new products, sales, M & A, and the like. But in that job, I always believed the people part was how I could help GE the most.

People management covers a wide range of activities, but it really comes down to six fundamental practices.

No person can undertake these activities alone—far from it—so let me phrase them as company-wide practices. To manage people well, companies should:

1. Elevate HR to a position of power and primacy in the organization, and make sure HR people have the special qualities to help managers build leaders and careers. In fact, the best HR types are pastors and parents in the same package.

2. Use a rigorous, nonbureaucratic evaluation system, monitored for integrity with the same intensity as Sarbanes-Oxley Act compliance.

3. Create effective mechanisms—read: money, recognition, and training—to motivate and retain.

4. Face straight into charged relationships—with unions, stars, sliders, and disrupters.

5. Fight gravity, and instead of taking the middle 70 percent for granted, treat them like the heart and soul of the organization.

6. Design the org chart to be as flat as possible, with blindingly clear reporting relationships and responsibilities.

After being on the road for several years, I realize that some people may read these practices and wonder how, if they adopt them, they'll ever get any real work done.

I always thought they *were* real work! But many Q & A sessions have left me with the impression that at lots of companies, people management is what's done when there's time left over.

In the hope that that might change, here are the practices in more detail.

> **PRACTICE 1:** Elevate HR to a position of power and primacy in the organization, and make sure HR people have the special qualities to help managers build leaders and careers. In fact, the best HR types are pastors and parents in the same package.

About three years ago I was in Mexico City, speaking at a convention of five thousand human resource executives. As usual, the event was set up as a Q & A session with two seats on the stage. In this case, the interviewer was Daniel Servitje, the thoughtful and engaging CEO of Grupo Bimbo, one of the country's largest food companies.

Daniel and I spent the first forty-five minutes talking about strategy, budgets, global competition, and other business topics before the microphone went into the audience for their questions. The first person to speak identified herself as the head of personnel for a Brazilian manufacturer. With an urgent voice, she asked me about the role of HR in a company—what did I think it should be?

My answer was immediate, and to be honest with you, even though I have been making this point publicly for years, I thought it would get a round of applause, given the makeup of the audience.

"Without doubt, the head of HR should be the second most important person in any organization," I said. "From the point of view of the CEO, the director of HR should be at least equal to the CFO."

There was a strange hush in the place. In fact, it was so quiet I thought my Boston accent had thrown off the translator.

"Isn't that what happens in your companies?" I asked. "I mean, let's get a show of hands. How many of you work at companies where the CEO treats the director of HR and the CFO with equal respect?"

Fifty hands went up—fifty out of five thousand people! No wonder no one had clapped! I had accidentally stepped on the toes of about 99 percent of the crowd.

Later, at a reception after the session, one person after another from the audience told me how HR was belittled and under-utilized in their organizations. In all, about thirty people told me stories in the same vein.

Worse, their reports turned out not to be an exception. I have asked my stature-of-HR question at about seventy-five other speaking events since Mexico City. The results are always dis-turbingly similar.

It blows my mind. Even if your company is too small to have its own HR department, *somebody* has to be doing HR.

And HR has just got to be as important as any other function in a company.

> If you managed a baseball team, would you listen more closely to the team accountant or the director of player personnel?

In fact, why wouldn't HR be as important as finance? After all, if you managed a baseball team, would you listen more closely to the team accountant or the director of player personnel? The input of the team accountant matters—he sure knows how much they can pay a player. But his input certainly doesn't count *more* than input from the director of player personnel, who knows just how good each player is. Both belong, alongside the CEO, at the table where decisions are made.

Unfortunately, at a lot of companies, HR isn't even in the same room.

The reasons, I think, are threefold. First, the impact of HR is hard to quantify. You can see how sales and R & D affect performance, and how finance tallies it up. But HR deals with "air"— people skills. Not only are people skills squishy-soft, most people assume they have them in spades. How many times have you heard someone say, "I'm a people person!"

Second, HR too often gets relegated or pushed into a benefits trap—administering insurance plans and overseeing scheduling issues like vacation and flextime. It also gets saddled with health and happiness activities—putting out the plant newspaper and organizing the summer picnic. Someone has to take care of these tasks, but if HR gets stuck doing them all the time, its stature will never be what it should.

Third, HR becomes twisted up in palace intrigue.

Back in the 1960s and early '70s, GE went through a period like that. Its HR system ran on gossip, whispers, and tattling. A small and frankly terrifying group of HR executives held secretive opinions about every manager, and they could tar you for life if they wanted. On the other hand, they could also move you up very quickly. They thought of themselves as kingmakers.

The game changed completely when Reg Jones, the CEO at the time, appointed Ted LeVino to run HR. Ted threw open the shutters and let the light shine in. HR processes soon became transparent, and more importantly, they began to make sense. By the time Ted retired in 1985, HR was on its way to doing exactly what it should: listening to people vent, brokering internal differences, and helping managers develop leaders and build careers.

Pastor-parent types see the hidden hierarchies in people's minds—the invisible org chart that exists at every company.

That's why the best HR people are a kind of hybrid: one part pastor, who hears all sins and complaints without recrimination, and one part parent, who loves and nurtures, but gives it to you fast and straight when you're off track.

I've found over the years that the best pastor-parent types have usually run something once in their careers—a factory, a product line, or another function. But I've also seen some come right up through HR. Either way, the best have stature beyond their rank and title. They *know* the business—its every detail. They understand the tensions between marketing and manufacturing, or between two executives who once went after the same job. They see the hidden hierarchies in people's minds—the invisible org chart of political connections that exists in every company. They know the players and the history.

Along with stature, pastor-parent types have got integrity oozing out of them. That integrity comes from unrelenting candor and trustworthiness. Pastor-parents listen with uncommon care, tell the truth, and hold confidences tight.

They also know how to settle a disagreement.

We'd all like to believe that good companies don't need referees. But they do. People get passed over for promotions. Interdivisional sales cause all kinds of who-gets-the-credit issues. Bonus pools are perceived to be unfairly distributed.

I was lucky enough to have a few pastor-parent types on my team at various points in my career, the last one being Bill Conaty, whom I've mentioned before in this book. Bill started out in GE's manufacturing training program and eventually became the manager of the locomotive diesel engine plant in Grove City, Pennsylvania. He then jumped ship to the HR business. He was a natural. No matter with whom he was dealing—a senior executive or an hourly worker—he was as straight as could be with good news and bad. He was a great listener and so discrete that you couldn't squeeze a secret out of him with a vise.

I came to appreciate Bill when he was head of HR for Aircraft Engines. The business had a huge crisis in '89, when it was discovered that one of its employees had bribed an Israeli air force general to get a jet engine contract. What impressed me was how Bill dealt with the people involved in the mess, some of whom were his peers and friends. He had to make incredibly painful recommendations about letting people go, and he did it with the kind of candor, compassion, and diplomacy that is the ultimate hallmark of a pastor-parent.

If your HR is on track, pastor-parents are ready to handle frictions and crises—channeling anger, forging compromises, and if need be, negotiating dignified endings.

They are there to help managers manage people well.

PRACTICE 2: Use a rigorous, nonbureaucratic evaluation system, monitored for integrity with the same intensity as Sarbanes-Oxley Act compliance.

Remember what happened when corporate scandals rocked the American economy? The government reacted quickly by passing the Sarbanes-Oxley Act, which mandates a fine or jail time or both for any CEO or CFO who wittingly signs off on bad numbers.

The Sarbanes-Oxley Act was necessary to get credibility in financial reporting and restore investor confidence.

> Very few companies have meaningful evaluation systems in place. That's not just bad—it's terrible!

I just wish that evaluation systems got the same kind of attention and rigor. After all, financial violations happen because of people.

Yet people evaluation systems are too often just exercises in paper pushing.

Earlier in this book, in the chapter on candor, I mentioned that I often ask audiences, "How many of you have received an honest, straight-between-the-eyes feedback session in the past year, where you came out knowing exactly what you have to do to improve and where you stand in the organization?"

To repeat: 20 percent of the audience raises its hand on a good day, but the average yes-response is about 10 percent.

If this unscientific research is anywhere near right, very few companies have meaningful evaluation systems in place.

That's not just bad—it's terrible!

You simply cannot manage people to better performance if you do not give candid, consistent feedback through a system that is loaded with integrity.

There is no one right way to evaluate people. Every company will devise different forms and different methodologies. But any good evaluation system should share some characteristics.

■ **It should be clear and simple, washed clean of time-consuming bureaucratic gobbledygook.** If your evaluation system involves more than two pages of paperwork per person, something is wrong. I evaluated my twenty or so direct reports with frequent handwritten notes that included two pieces of information: what I thought the person did well, and how I thought they could improve.

■ **It should measure people on relevant, agreed-upon criteria that relate directly to an individual's performance.** The criteria should be quantitative, based on how people deliver on certain goals, and qualitative, based on how they deliver on desired behaviors.

■ **It should ensure that managers evaluate their people at least once a year, and preferably twice, in formal, face-to-face sessions.** Informal appraisals should happen all the time. But when it comes to formal reviews, one of the face-to-face sessions should let people know where they stand in relation to others. If your company practices differentiation, a good evaluation system is where the rubber meets the road.

■ **Finally, a good evaluation system should include a professional development component.** Managers should not only talk to their employees about next career steps, but should elicit from them the names of the two or three people who they think could replace them should they be promoted.

Even with all these characteristics, no evaluation system is first-rate unless it is constantly monitored for integrity. Someone has to have the responsibility—and the accountability—to ask if the evaluation system is capturing the truth, just as a good audit team does with the numbers.

Does the evaluation system really measure company values, or does it just measure financial results?

Does it really get implemented with sincerity, or do people blow it off as a waste of time?

Do people really learn at the end of it what they must do to improve their performance?

Only integrity can keep evaluation systems from becoming paper-pushing. And since there is no law to make it happen, and no audit team either, it is up to every boss giving an evaluation—with the vigorous support of HR—to take this responsibility upon himself or herself.

You won't get thrown in jail if you don't, but do it anyway because it will make you and your team better.

PRACTICE 3: Create effective mechanisms—read: money, recognition, and training—to motivate and retain.

I'll never forget the time I was at a meeting about how GE should reward the winner of the Steinmetz Award, given annually to the company's best scientist. I was a group VP at the time, and so my ears really perked up when one of the vice-chairmen, a guy with a lot of stature and a lot of dough, registered his opinion.

"These people don't want money," he said, "they want recognition."

He must have forgotten where he came from!

Of course, people want to be recognized for great performance. Plaques and public fanfare have their place. But without money, they lose a lot of their impact. Even the Nobel and Pulitzer prizes come with cash awards.

If your company is managing people well, it tightly aligns good performance with rewards. The better you do, the more you get—and you get it in *both* the soul and the wallet.

There is hardly anything more frustrating than working hard, meeting or exceeding expectations, and discovering that it doesn't matter to your company. You get nothing special, or you get what everyone else does.

People need to get differentiated rewards and recognition to be motivated. And companies need to deliver both for retention.

It's that simple.

Take the case of a woman I know who graduated with a degree in theater design from an Ivy League college and eagerly went to work as a buyer at a prestigious New York City retailer. Despite the grueling hours and low pay, this woman showed immediate promise. Her selections for the sportswear department broke sales records for six straight quarters, and she managed to repair the store's relationships with two disgruntled vendors. Although it was not part of the job—and other buyers teased her for "overdoing it"—she worked the floor and the cash register to better understand her department's customers.

For two years, this buyer got very little public recognition for her success. That was bad enough, but her bonus was also standard—exactly what the company described as average during the interview process.

She had to quit to find out how much she was valued. When she handed in her resignation, her boss was shocked.

"But why are you leaving?" she asked. "You have a great future here!"

"It's so draining—no one ever tells me I'm doing a good job."

> Plaques and public fanfare have their place. But without money, rewards lose a lot of their impact.

"No one ever tells *me* I'm doing a good job," her boss shot back. "That's just the way it goes here. You've got to get a thick skin."

Retail is a notoriously tough working environment. But the practice of not rewarding performance is commonplace in plenty of industries and one of the main reasons good people leave.

A winning company does not let good people walk out the door for lack of recognition, financial or otherwise.

Another key way to motivate and retain is through training.

If you've hired the right people, they will want to grow. They will be bursting with the desire to learn and do more. A good machinist will want to know how to operate more machines and eventually how to run the shop. A good manufacturing engineer will want to travel to Japan to visit companies using advanced techniques that he has only read about. A good PR person will want to learn how to communicate more effectively on the Web.

Good people never think they have reached the top of their game. But they're dying to get there!

A company that manages people well helps make that happen. If it can afford it, it has in-house training led by its own executives, who serve not only as teachers but as role models. A company with fewer resources can facilitate training outside at any number of good programs. In either case, it makes sure that training is seen as a reward for performance, not a sop for time served.

> Good people never think they've reached the top of their game. But they're dying to get there!

Companies cannot promise their people lifetime employment. Global competition is too fierce and economic cycles too frequent for any such guarantees.

But they can promise to give

their people every chance for employability—skills that will make them more attractive if they are forced to part ways.

Like rewards and recognition, training does that. It motivates people by showing them a way to grow, that the company cares, and that they have a future.

If you are doing it right, they will want to make that future with you.

PRACTICE 4: Face straight into charged relationships—with unions, stars, sliders, and disrupters.

Like families, companies have relationships filled with history or fraught with tension.

But managing people well means paying special attention to these hard relationships, not just letting them fester or float into neglect—approaches that are entirely human but often end in a mess.

Good people management requires companies to confront their charged relationships with candor and action.

Let's start with unions. When I was at GE, it was well known that I was not a fan of unions. I thought they created conditions that made the company less competitive, and they drove an unnecessary wedge between management and employees.

I use the word "unnecessary" because in my experience, unions arise only when a plant or an office is being managed by someone who is abusive, remote, or indifferent, and whose actions have taken away the voice and dignity of employees. Without a doubt, that boss needs to be reformed or removed because unionization is an excessive response with negative long-term consequences—really for everyone.

We did have several longtime unions at GE during my time as CEO. I always felt our relationship was candid and respectful, and we never had a national strike. I can think of two reasons why.

First, we always stated our principles and stuck to them, and second, we never started our relationship at the negotiating table.

Principles first.

The most important thing to remember about unions is that they are made up of your own people. You work together, reside in the same towns, and oftentimes your kids go to school or play together. Your lives and futures are intertwined.

That is why all you have with unions is your integrity—your word. You can fight about issues, and you will. But your fighting will be more productive if you are always clear about what issues are negotiable and which are untouchable. During negotiations, waffle only on those matters you identified as negotiable and nothing else. Otherwise, your word will be meaningless and your relationship will be without trust.

Now to the negotiating table. Make every effort not to have your first date there. A war zone is no place to get acquainted.

Almost every time I traveled to the businesses with Bill Conaty, we met with local union representatives. These sessions were mainly to get to know one another better and lay out positions without any immediate agenda. Everyone would get a chance to talk, and even better, in these settings, we were all more inclined to listen. Bill and I always learned a lot, and it served Bill and the company well in every national negotiation.

Let's look at another charged relationship to manage: with stars. One thing is certain. You need stars to win, and I have always advocated identifying your stars—that top 20 percent—and stroking and rewarding them in an outsize way.

But stroking can backfire. A star's ego can be a dangerous thing.

I've seen talented young people promoted too quickly and

their ambition spin out of control. I've seen terrific financial analysts, engineers, and network executives get told one too many times that they are irreplaceable, and they start swaggering around to the point that their teams resent them. I've seen smart, capable individuals come to believe they are so indispensable that they should not be bound by anything, including the company's values.

Stars can become monsters if you let them.

That's why someone has to be on the lookout, namely the star's boss, with support from HR, if you have it. This job cannot fall through the cracks. The minute a star seems to be getting arrogant or out of control, someone has to call the person in to have a candid conversation about values and behaviors. You can never be afraid of your stars; they can't hold a company hostage.

Now, sometimes stars surprise you and up and leave. That can be a defining moment. Ideally, the star will be replaced within eight hours. That's right, eight hours. This immediate reaction sends the message to the organization that no one is indispensable. It shouts out that no single individual is bigger than the company.

One morning in the summer of 2001, just as Jeff Immelt was about to take over as CEO, Larry Johnston, who was CEO of our appliances business, came to headquarters to tell us he was taking the job as CEO of Albertsons, the large West Coast food and drug chain. Larry was a big presence in GE, with a strong track record and great reputation. Even though the announcement of his departure knocked the wind out of us, we moved quickly. By four o'clock that afternoon, we appointed Jim Campbell, the sales manager in Appliances, to the job. Albertsons

> Ideally, the star will be replaced within eight hours. This sends the message that no single individual is bigger than the company.

> A slider just shows up at work and goes through the motions.

got a great CEO, and we never missed a beat. Jim was off and running from day one.

The only way to be able to replace a star swiftly is to have a slate of people ready to do so. That's where good evaluation systems come in, in particular, career development planning. That process can surface one or two in-house candidates to replace any star who departs.

Just don't wait until the star leaves to start the replacement process. By then it's too late to make the point.

A third complicated relationship is with what I call sliders. These are employees who were once good performers but have hit a wall for some reason or another, ranging from a midlife crisis to a job-related disappointment.

A slider, while generally well liked, now just shows up at work and goes through the motions. In most cases, no one knows what to do about it. In fact, the situation is usually so awkward, people look away.

You can't. Sliders need to be reenergized, either with new jobs or training. Otherwise, they fossilize in their jobs, and they often grow bitter, slowly but surely infecting their groups with disaffection. Often, managers take a long time to let these individuals go because their previous accomplishments were more than acceptable. But a company that manages people well quickly moves to get its sliders back in the game, and if that doesn't work, tells them the game is over.

The final relationship that cannot be ignored is with disrupters. These are the individuals who cause trouble for sport—inciting opposition to management for a variety of reasons, most of them petty.

Usually these people have good performance—that's their cover—and so they are endured or appeased.

A company that manages people well takes disrupters head-on. First they give them very tough evaluations, naming their bad behavior and demanding it change. Usually it won't. Disrupters are a personality type. If that's the case, get them out of the way of people trying to do their jobs. They're poison.

> **PRACTICE 5. Fight gravity, and instead of taking the middle 70 percent for granted, treat them like the heart and soul of the organization.**

As practice 4 would suggest, managers end up spending the vast majority of their people-management energy on charged relationships—too often trying to salvage sliders or disrupters. That's natural, but it's a mistake.

Most work in an organization gets done by the people in the middle 70, those solid performers who don't quite shine but work hard and well, and perhaps could shine with enough care and attention. You just can't allow the middle 70 to toil away in a form of obscurity, like a well-behaved, mild-mannered middle child in a family of attention-grabbing prodigies and troublemakers.

Well-managed companies fight that pull. In fact, they make sure managers spend at least 50 percent of their people time on their biggest constituency, evaluating and coaching them. Further, they don't forget the middle 70 when it comes to rewards, recognition, and training.

One important note. In larger companies, the middle 70 can be a highly differentiated group. In a way, it has its own top 20, valuable middle, and bottom 10 percent. You need to recognize those performance variations—you can be sure the employees do. In fact, a common and damaging dynamic is the departure of the best performers in the middle 70. Some of these individuals are almost stars—their performance is that close. But when they get lumped with the middle 70 and are not managed attentively, they leave in frustration for a company where they will be more appreciated. That's a real loss.

Future stars are very often hard at work—quietly—in the middle 70. A good company recognizes that and makes it clear that this ranking is just a snapshot in time. It encourages this group, using every tool in its people management kit.

The point is: The middle 70 matters a lot. It is the heart and soul—the central core—of any company.

If you're going to manage people well, you simply cannot forget the majority of them.

PRACTICE 6. Design the org chart to be as flat as possible, with blindingly clear reporting relationships and responsibilities.

In 2004, Clayton, Dubilier & Rice purchased Culligan International, the water treatment and supply business with about $700 million in annual sales and about five thousand employees spread across thirteen countries. One of CD&R's partners, George Tamke, the former co-CEO of Emerson Electric, was named chairman. George was well aware that Culligan had been through ten owners in the previous fifteen years, but he couldn't believe the organizational disarray that hit him when he walked through the door. George found that many employees simply didn't know where they fit in—whom they reported to, who reported to them, and what results each person was responsible for.

George had had the luxury of studying the business for ninety days prior to CD&R's closing the deal, so he had a clear idea of how Culligan should be organized. Within thirty days, George and Culligan's relatively new CEO, Mike Kachmer, had designed and implemented a new org chart that eliminated any confusion.

It's too early to talk about the impact of this change on Culligan's bottom line, but based on my all-too-frequent GE experience clearing up confusing and otherwise ambiguous structures, it will be significant.

Culligan's situation, unfortunately, is not unique to old, established multinationals. Just recently, I spoke with Dara Khosrowshahi, the new CEO at the online travel company Expedia. Dara also walked into an org chart quagmire when he arrived on the job at the end of 2004. Expedia, less than ten years old and highly entrepreneurial, had been growing so fast, no one had taken the time to clarify reporting roles and responsibilities. As his first priority, Dara set out to fix that.

My goal here is not to describe how to come up with the perfect org chart. Each company will do that differently, based on its size and the business it's in. But some principles apply across the board. If you want to manage people effectively, help them by making sure the org chart leaves as little as possible to the imagination. It should paint a crystal-clear picture of reporting relationships and make it patently obvious who is responsible for what results.

Just as important, it should be flat.

Look, every layer in an organization puts spin on a new initiative or organizational event. It's like that children's whispering game, tele-

> Hierarchies tend to make little generals out of perfectly normal people who find themselves in organizations that respond only to rank.

Make your company flatter. Managers should have ten direct reports at the minimum and 30 to 50 percent more if they are experienced.

phone. Every time a piece of information travels through another person, it changes. Layers do that too, adding interpretation and buzz as information travels up and down the ladder. The trick, then, is to have fewer rungs.

Layers have other vices. They add cost and complexity to everything. They slow things down because they increase the number of approvals and meetings required for anything to move forward. They have an odious way of burying new businesses, or small units in big companies, in honeycombs of bureaucracy. They tend to make little generals out of perfectly normal people who find themselves in hierarchies that respond only to rank.

The awfulness of layers is nothing new to anyone. And yet companies gravitate toward them. For some, layers feel like the only way to respond to growth. More sales—quick, add more district managers in the field. More employees—quick, add more staff at headquarters.

For others, the reasoning is even worse. Layers are a way to give people the feeling of growth when there is none. Layers allow you to give employees promotions instead of raises. That's better than doing nothing, right? Wrong!

The inexorable pull toward layers is why I suggest you make your company 50 percent flatter than you'd normally feel comfortable with. Managers should have ten direct reports at the minimum and 30 to 50 percent more if they are experienced.

When you've got great players, you'll get the most out of them if their reporting relationships and responsibilities are blindingly clear. Your org chart is not the only way to accomplish that, but it's a necessary first step.

■

After you've hired great people, your job becomes managing them into a winning team.

Make HR matter, with a cadre of pastor-parent types at the helm. Ensure people really know how they're doing, with evaluation systems that are honest and real. Motivate and retain wisely with money, recognition, and training. Face into charged relationships without flinching. Pay ample attention to your largest constituency, the middle 70 percent. And finally, get that org chart flattened and straightened out.

These six practices take time, that's true. But companies are not buildings, machines, or technologies. They are people.

Besides managing them, what work matters more?

Parting Ways

LETTING GO IS HARD TO DO

Now for the hard part.

For the previous three chapters of this book, I've talked about the exciting, energizing stuff of work—leading, finding great players, and managing people into a winning team.

But we all know that work isn't a perpetual paradise.

Work is more like the Garden of Eden. Sometimes people have to be let go.

That event—be it a firing for nonperformance or a layoff for economic reasons—is awful, both for the person doing the casting out and, obviously, for the person being asked to leave. Most good managers find the actual deed incredibly difficult—feeling guilt and anxiety before, during, and after. As for the person being let go, it can be the worst day of his or her career. For some, work has been their identity, central routine, or second family, and being forced to leave is a kind of public death. For others, work may mean less emotionally, but it is a financial necessity, and the prospect of unemployment is frightening.

This chapter is about how to manage a parting of ways with as little pain and damage as possible.

Importantly, not all partings are created equal.

- First, there are **firings for integrity violations—stealing, lying, cheating, or any other form of ethical or legal breach.**

- Then, there are **layoffs due to economic downturns.**

- Finally, there are **firings for nonperformance.**

The last of these is the main focus of this chapter because those are the ones that usually turn into bitter messes.

It doesn't have to be that way.

The antidote is actually very straightforward: managers need to accept that letting people go is not something to be avoided, delegated to HR, or done quickly with eyes closed. Instead, it is a process that they must fully own, guided by two principles: no surprise and minimal humiliation.

But before we look in more depth at how to achieve those goals, let's talk about the first two forms of separation.

INTEGRITY VIOLATIONS

. . . are no-brainers. In such cases, you don't need to hesitate for a moment before firing someone or fret about it either. Just do it, and make sure the organization knows why, so that the consequences of breaking the rules are not lost on anyone.

LAYOFFS DUE TO THE ECONOMY

. . . are more complicated.

Think of all the times you've turned on the evening news to see angry employees protesting outside the gates of a plant or the front door of an office building. Layoffs have just been announced, and people are in shock. They feel as though a bomb has dropped on them out of nowhere.

You can bet the top team doesn't feel that way. They probably knew layoffs were in the offing for months.

The fact that everyone else didn't is really unconscionable. Every employee, not just the senior people, should know how a company is doing.

Of course, financial information is not always that easy to get your hands on. If you are running a ten-person division of a conglomerate, for instance, you may have access to data about your business but know little about how other businesses are performing. On the other hand, if you are running a ten-person machine shop, there is no reason in the world why employees shouldn't know about every vital sign of the business—the volume of orders, the size and trend line of profit margins, emerging low-cost competitors, and so forth.

For most managers, the availability of financial data lies somewhere between these extremes. Your job is to get as much as you can and get it to your people as clearly and frequently as possible. That way, if layoffs must occur, at least people will have some level of preparation.

The same principle holds for layoffs due to market changes. During

> Every employee, not just the senior people, should know how a company is doing.

the Internet boom, for example, lots of companies scrambled frantically to hire technical gurus by the truckload. As the reality of e-commerce settled in, it quickly became obvious that this hiring had been excessive and some of the techies would have to go. Most managers in this situation had help making their case, thanks to intensive media coverage of the industry's collapse. But open communication should be the order of the day no matter what.

Last year at a Q & A session in Orlando, Florida, I was introduced to the audience by the owner and CEO of a New England–based consulting and training firm. Before the session, I asked her about her business. She told me it had taken a real hit after the Internet bubble burst. She'd had to lay off half of her thirty employees.

"How did it go?" I asked.

"Incredibly well," she answered, to my surprise. "My husband and I practiced open-book management. Our employees knew everything about the state of our business. When the time came for the layoffs, people were sad but they understood."

Today, the business is flourishing, and many of the CEO's former employees have returned without bitterness.

Needless to say, this is an ideal situation—the firm was small and it too benefited from coverage of the Internet industry collapse. But even if your company is large and economic conditions are more vague, it always helps to have your cards on the table for employees to see in the event of a downturn.

FIRINGS FOR NONPERFORMANCE

Now for the most complex and delicate kind of firing, when an individual has to be let go because of poor performance.

Earlier I used "straightforward" to describe the no-surprise, minimal-humiliation approach to these situations. I didn't mean to make it sound easy—it is not.

Unfortunately, you learn how to fire on the job, under the most stressful of circumstances. Nothing really prepares you. Managers don't sit around talking about how to do it, comparing notes. I'm not aware of any business schools that actually teach the process, and while company training programs might talk a lot about evaluations,

> The most complex and delicate kind of firing is when an individual has to be let go because of poor performance.

none that I know of offer a lot of help on how to actually let people go.

Which leaves you to your instincts. Maybe some people are born to fire well. I know I wasn't. I did it for years and never got used to it. I was particularly bad at it in my early years as a manager. One of my most painful memories from Pittsfield, where I ran Plastics, is of the day that a boy got on the school bus and punched my son John in the face. I had fired the boy's dad the day before, and obviously, I had done it wrong. It didn't make any difference that I thought I had handled the matter well. The boy's family didn't perceive it that way.

THE THREE BIG MISTAKES OF FIRING

Sometimes people screw up so royally they deserve to be fired without much ado.

I once had a manager in Plastics who had to be let go after ninety days because, while he had a résumé loaded with prestigious degrees and was as charming as could be in chitchat, he was completely ineffective at every single task. A friend of mine was fired from her job as a clothing store clerk in the first week because she forgot to ask half the customers to sign their credit

> He blew up in anger, shouting, "You've got to be crazy. We don't fire people at this company!"

card slips. She says that if her boss hadn't fired her, she would have fired herself.

Usually, however, firings for nonperformance aren't so black-and-white. There's lots more gray about who did what and what went wrong to lead up to the finale.

Because of that, there are three main ways that managers get firing wrong—moving too fast, not using enough candor, and taking too long.

For an example of the first dynamic, take the case of a friend of mine who ran a sixty-person unit within a three-hundred-employee company. The company had been growing and things were generally going well. It was privately held and had a family-like culture, meaning mediocre performance was generally tolerated in the name of congeniality. It was not uncommon for employees to carpool on weekdays and socialize on weekends. As with many small companies, performance reviews were generally informal events with lots of generic pleasantries.

When my friend was promoted to head the unit, she soon realized that one of her chief lieutenants, the man in charge of distribution, whom I'll call Richard, was not up to the demands of the growing business. To exacerbate matters, Richard was a true disrupter, as described in the last chapter. He never missed an opportunity to challenge the authority of the new boss or her boss; usually, his negative comments came in the form of sarcastic humor with peers in the hallways.

Richard's performance wasn't terrible, but it was pretty close. He regularly missed deadlines and seemed unable to handle increasingly complex logistics. My friend spoke to Richard several times about his shortcomings, to no avail. Finally, after a particularly tough period of Richard's corridor sniping, an important customer called to complain that his shipment was a week late. My friend had had it—Richard had to go.

The official dismissal meeting could not have gone worse. To say Richard was surprised is an understatement. He blew up in anger, shouting, "You've got to be crazy. We don't fire people at this company!" and "You're going to pay for this." He then stormed out, ran back to his office in another part of the building, and called an impromptu meeting with his own eight-person staff. Even though he cleaned out his desk and was gone within hours, a hate-management movement had been launched. Some of the unit's employees—in particular, Richard's circle of friends—felt that he had been fired without enough warning, and they complained they no longer trusted the boss or the organization. In the fraught weeks that followed, productivity dropped by an order of magnitude as people spent inordinate amounts of time gathering behind closed doors to talk about Richard's departure, how it was handled, and who might be next.

It took my friend about three months to restore equilibrium and get her unit moving again.

The second firing mistake is a variation of Richard's case, and it involves lack of candor and a misunderstanding about fairness.

Say you've got an employee named Gail. She can't reach her sales quotas, and her coworkers really can't count on her for one reason or another. She's damaging the unit's performance and morale. But Gail's friendly to everyone, she tries hard, and she's been with the company for years. Every time you attempt to tell her how badly she's doing, she's so cheerful and oblivious that the conversation gets muddled, and you end up hiding your negative feelings behind a forced smile and a mixed message about "working smarter."

Then the situation reaches a crisis stage. Gail really screws up, and in a burst of impulsive anger, you fire her. She's shocked and starts to remind you of all the positive feedback you've given her over the years. You respond by coming up with a severance package that feels pretty rich to you, given how much she's underperformed. She hates the package—it's insulting, she says—and she gets angry. You get angry back because you can't believe she's angry. You feel she should be grateful you carried her for so long! The next thing you know, Gail's gone from shocked to angry to bitter as she walks out the door.

This may not be the last you hear of her. Think about the last time you lost a promising hire or a potential customer. They might have been talking to Gail, who went out to become an "ambassador" for your company.

Every employee who leaves goes on to represent your company. For the next five, ten, or twenty years, they can bad-mouth or praise. In the most extreme cases, people fired take their anger public, and a few become so-called whistleblowers. I say "so-called" because I've seen too many companies "exposed"—wrongly—by people seeking nothing more than revenge for a firing conducted by a manager who should have and could have done it better.

> **Every person who leaves goes on to represent your company. They can bad-mouth or praise.**

And now for the third mistake. It occurs when a firing happens too slowly and you get a kind of Dead Man Walking effect. Everyone knows a person is about to be fired, including the person himself, but the boss waits a long time to pull the trigger. The result is enormous awkwardness in the office that can lead to a form of paralysis.

I've seen the Dead Man Walking effect more times than I care to remember. I can recall a staff meeting at headquarters when I was a division VP. About ten people were there, including one of my peers—"Steve"—who had been having consistently bad results. Before the meeting even started, everyone already sensed that Steve was a goner. But once the meeting began, the discomfort got worse. The group's boss picked apart Steve's quarterly results and wouldn't allow Steve to open his mouth for a rebuttal. Steve could do nothing right. At the coffee break, everyone milled around, avoiding Steve as much as possible. None of us could look him in the eye.

> Unfortunately, it took about a year before Steve was let go. At every staff meeting, we watched in agony as the self-confidence seeped out of him.

Unfortunately, it took about a year before Steve was let go. At every staff meeting, we watched in agony as the self-confidence seeped out of him. You just knew the people in Steve's businesses had to be crippled, as they were undoubtedly seeing the same thing and were only waiting to find out who his replacement would be.

The question, of course, is why do bosses allow the Dead Man Walking effect to occur? One reason is that firing is so tough that no one likes to do it, and so the event often gets delayed. But with the Dead Man situation, something more subtle is often going on. Bosses let an employee twist in the wind because they want the victim's peers to see—and, figuratively speaking, sign off on—the necessity of the firing decision. In a way it's cruel, but most bosses would rather be known as careful than quick-triggered.

Richard, Gail, and Steve are examples of how firing goes wrong. How can you get it right?

FIRST, NO SURPRISES

You can take the surprise out of economic downturn layoffs with lots of financial information. But how do you take the surprise out of gray-area nonperformance firings?

We've actually already dealt with that question in the chapters preceding this one—in those discussing candor, differentiation, and good people management practices. In particular, the answer lies in using a rigorous evaluation system, with its regular formal and informal reviews. Very simply, a good performance evaluation process informs and prepares people in the fairest, most open way I know.

If people know where they stand, in fact, a firing actually never happens. Instead, when things are not working out, eventually there is a mutual understanding that it's time to part ways.

In this kind of environment, where the employee is doing OK but not quite what you want, it can take a couple of years for the endgame to be clear to everyone. Over that time period, there will be many candid conversations about performance and career goals. The possibility of parting ways will have been raised and discussed openly.

In the ideal situation, the last conversation will go like this:

BOSS: Well, I think you know what this meeting is about.

EMPLOYEE: Yes, I guess I do. So, what are your thoughts on timing and what's the deal?

Moreover, as a result of this process, sometimes you get lucky, and the employee will come to you first:

EMPLOYEE: I've got a great job offer, and I think I'm going to go for it. What do you think?

BOSS: What a great career move for you. I think you should take it.

These kinds of partings are rarely acrimonious, and surprise is the last thing anyone feels.

Cases like Richard, Gail, and Steve can never be eliminated entirely, but with candid and consistent evaluation processes in place, they can become less and less common every year.

SECOND, MINIMIZE HUMILIATION

To take the stinging embarrassment out of a firing, you first have to understand the emotional timeline of the experience.

For the boss, the timeline begins long before the actual event. In preparing for it, you feel nervous, frustrated, and anguished. Unless you are a complete jerk, you dread the whole thing, especially the conversation itself. For weeks, you lose sleep, rehearsing how it will go. You talk to your spouse or best friend about the situation to help get your nerve up.

Meanwhile, your employee is scared, but from my experience, usually optimistic until the end. Denial is the operative emotion. Most people walk into termination meetings hoping against hope this isn't the day, a feeling usually mixed with gut-wrenching fear.

So, the day finally comes, and you sit down.

You deliver the bad news, and suddenly you feel relieved; the anxiety flows out of you. It's over, you think. I did it kindly, I said nice things. The package is fair. Phew. At last I can get on to other work, including hiring someone great to fill the soon-to-be-vacant spot. You go home feeling that a terrible weight is finally

> Yes, the employee has done a poor job. But until he departs, your job is to make sure he doesn't feel as if he is in a leper colony.

off your shoulders. Dinner that night tastes better than it has in a while.

Your employee is in another emotional time zone, to put it mildly.

Even if he has been well prepared by candid evaluations, he is crushed—his self-esteem is in the tank. If you've done everything right, he won't be surprised, but he could still be feeling terribly sad and hurt.

The next day at work is when you must start to act against your instincts. Yes, the employee has done a poor job, and yes, he has taken up a disproportionate amount of your time and energy already. But until he departs, your job is to make sure he doesn't feel as if he is in a leper colony.

Build up his self-confidence. Coach him. Let him know there is a good job for him out there, where his skills are a better match. You may even help him find that job. Your goal for the fired employee is a soft landing wherever he goes.

A firing may take an hour, but someone's departure can take six months. You'll save a lot of pain—and preserve a lot of pride—if you don't rush it.

■

The unfortunate reality is, firings are a part of business. But that doesn't mean they have to end up as the bitter messes they often do. If you handle them right, they'll never be enjoyable, but they can be tolerable for all involved.

The legacy of a firing lasts a long time—for you, your company, and, most of all, the person who has been fired.

Obviously, if your company is collapsing, you can't handle lay-offs with kid gloves. And if someone has an integrity violation, you need to kick that person out the door, and fast.

But for everyone else, leaving for reasons more in the gray area, remember that every time there is a parting of ways, you own the process.

When it's time to let someone go, do it right. No surprises. No humiliation.

Change

MOUNTAINS DO MOVE

I'M SURE YOU'VE NOTICED the hand-wringing and hyperventilating about change out there. For more than a decade, there has been a whole industry devoted to the topic, all of it selling pretty much the same line: change or die.

Well . . . it's true.

Change is an absolutely critical part of business. You do need to change, preferably before you have to.

What you've heard about resistance to change is also true. People hate it when their bosses announce a "transformation initiative." They run back to their cubicles and frantically start e-mailing one another with reasons it's going to ruin everything.

Frankly, most people hate it when they find out their favorite coffee shop is closing. The *Times* of London changed to a tabloid format, and the editor told me he received a letter asking him how it felt to be the person responsible for ending Western civilization.

People love familiarity and patterns. They cling to them. The phenomenon is so entrenched it can only be chalked up to human nature.

But attributing a behavior to human nature doesn't mean you have to be controlled by it. Yes, managing change can sometimes feel like moving a mountain. But managing change can also be incredibly exciting and rewarding, particularly when you start seeing results.

During my years at GE, we were in a pretty constant state of change. Most companies today are. You have to be if you want to stay in the game, let alone win.

That said, I realize that change is not a layup. Over the past couple of years, I have been struck by the number of people at Q & A sessions who have asked me, "My organization needs to change. How can I get them to do it when everyone wants things to stay the same?" The question is usually delivered with a level of despair.

My first answer always is a question back. "Are you really the *only* person who sees a need for change?" I ask. "If you are, and you don't have some authority, make your case, and if you don't get anywhere, learn to live with the situation or get out."

But if the situation is not that extreme—that is, you have the power to get things done and a few supporters as well—then you can make something happen.

It comes down to embracing four practices:

1. Attach every change initiative to a clear purpose or goal. Change for change's sake is stupid and enervating.

2. Hire and promote only true believers and get-on-with-it types.

3. Ferret out and get rid of resisters, even if their performance is satisfactory.

4. Look at car wrecks.

If a company's leaders implement these practices with passion and reward everyone else who buys in, eventually all the noise around change will stop sounding like noise. Change will become business as usual—the norm—and when it does, mountains do move.

I've seen it happen, and it's not as earth-shattering as it's made out to be.

Now for the practices in more detail.

1. Attach every change initiative to a clear purpose or goal. Change for change's sake is stupid and enervating.

It is a disaster when companies take all the hype about change literally and grab every new management fad that comes down the pike. It's change overload! Some big companies adopt ten different change initiatives at once and run in eight different directions. Nothing meaningful ever happens in these flavor-of-the-month kinds of situations except that, for most employees, work feels very frantic and disorganized.

Actually, change should be a relatively orderly process.

But for that to occur, people have to understand—in their heads and in their hearts—why change is necessary and where the change is taking them.

This is easier, of course, when the problems are obvious—as in, the house is burning down. Earnings are collapsing, a competitor has dropped prices 20 percent, or a new product appears that totally threatens your market position. Change is made even easier when the media is writing stories about your imminent demise—perhaps the one time you welcome bad press! Many of the most notable large company turnarounds in the past decade had this going for them: GM, IBM, and Xerox, to name three.

When the whole world knows about your problem, the wind is at your back.

But sometimes the need for change isn't scrawled across the skies.

Competitive threats only seem to be emerging. They may not even be real . . . or they may be your company's death knell. You don't know—and still, you have to respond.

In those cases, lots of data and relentless communication about the business rationale for change are the best ammunition you've got.

Take the case of GE's appliances business in the late 1970s. In those days, Appliances and Lighting were the mainstays of the company—the previous two chairmen and several vice-chairmen had come from their ranks. As far as everyone in the business was concerned, GE was the leader in major appliances and it would be that way forever.

In 1978, when I was appointed head of the Consumer Products Group, I found myself staring at an appliances business whose market share had been slipping for a few years and whose margins were sliding even faster. To an outsider like me, the situation looked frighteningly similar to the television receiver and automotive businesses, where the Japanese were making tremendous inroads with higher-quality, lower-cost products while fat American companies sat by doing little.

I made my case to Appliances' business managers at their headquarters, in Louisville, Kentucky. The place was loaded with "good old boys," not to mention tons of overhead and layers of bureaucracy. I showed them chart after chart illustrating Appliances's eroding position. And yet, early buy-in was minimal, to put it mildly. At the outset, I basically forced the cost-reduction program.

Almost immediately, I got back the two refrains common to every cost-reduction program ever launched:

"We've already cut the fat. You're asking us to cut the bone."

And: "The competitors are crazy. They're giving away product. Just watch—they can't keep it up."

Fortunately, the head of the business—a "good old boy" named Dick Donegan, whom I had been prepared to write off—saw the logic of the case, came to my aid, and started to champion change at Appliances. His leadership was vital to fixing things. He had been with Appliances his entire career, so he knew the players well. He built a team of supporters around him and cleaned out detractors—literally hundreds of them—over a two-year period.

In the end, the appliances business went through drastic changes because it had to. That fact wasn't blindingly obvious in 1978, when the change was launched, nor was it overwhelmingly clear for a few years after. In fact, the Japanese never really sold large appliances in the U.S. Only recently have the Chinese and Koreans made inroads.

The domestic competition was tough enough to make change necessary. Just look at the price of a refrigerator today. That's why the appliances business continues to cut

> If the company has been through enough change programs, employees consider you like gas pains. You'll go away if they just wait long enough.

costs and still hasn't hit bone. It is now a business characterized by continual productivity improvements, modest innovation, and a team that understands that change is a way of life.

One lesson from the Appliances story is that you don't always have, at the outset of a change initiative, every bit of information you'd like to make your case. Regardless, you need to get out there and start talking about what you do know and what you fear.

Communication about change does get a lot more challenging as a company gets larger. It's one thing if you are the owner of a two-hundred-person machine tool company to walk into work one day, call a meeting, and say, "OK, everyone, I just got back from a sales trip, and guess what, we've got brutal competition from a really innovative new company in Hungary. Things are going to have to change around here." It's another thing entirely to make the case for change to a company with a hundred thousand people in multiple business units in multiple countries.

In big companies, calls for change are often greeted with a nice head fake. People nod at your presentations and pleasantly agree that given all the data, it sure looks like change is necessary. Then they go back to doing everything they always did. If the company has been through enough change programs, employees consider you like gas pains. You'll go away if they just wait long enough.

This pervasive skepticism is all the more reason that anyone leading a change process must stay far away from empty slogans and instead stick to a solid, persuasive business case.

Over time, logic will win out.

2. Hire and promote only true believers and get-on-with-it types.

Everyone in business claims they like change; to say otherwise nowadays would be career suicide. In fact, it's quite common to see someone describe himself as a "change agent" right on his résumé.

That's ridiculous.

By my estimate, real change agents comprise less than 10 percent of all businesspeople. These are the true believers who champion change, know how to make it happen, and love every second of the process.

> Real change agents comprise less than 10 percent of all businesspeople. They have courage— a certain fearlessness about the unknown.

A significant majority—about 70 to 80 percent more—may not lead the charge, but once they are convinced change is necessary, they say, "OK already, get on with it."

The rest are resisters.

To make change happen, companies must actively hire and promote only true believers and get-on-with-its. But with everyone claiming to like change, how can you tell who is for real?

Luckily, change agents usually make themselves known. They're typically brash, high-energy, and more than a little bit paranoid about the future. Very often, they invent change initiatives on their own or ask to lead them. Invariably, they are curious and forward-looking. They ask a lot of questions that start with the phrase "Why don't we . . . ?"

These people have courage—a certain fearlessness about the unknown. Something in them makes it OK to operate without a safety net. If they fail, they know they can pick themselves up, dust themselves off, and move on. They're thick-skinned about risk, which allows them to make bold decisions without a lot of data.

This description makes me think immediately about Denis

Nayden, a managing partner with Oak Hill Capital Management, whom I've known for more than twenty years. Denis joined GE Capital in 1977, right out of the University of Connecticut, and by 1989 was second in charge, helping Gary Wendt expand the business from a few hundred million dollars in net income to more than $5 billion in 2000. The best way to describe Denis is intense, but extremely smart and fanatical about growth also work well. He never saw a deal he couldn't make better; he never saw a routine or a process that couldn't be unpicked, shaken up, and improved. In fact, Denis always saw the status quo as something to be upended. And in doing so, he brought hundreds of GE Capital's deals to unparalleled heights of performance. He always gave people a view beyond what they were—to what they could be.

Now, Denis—like most change agents—is not always easy to work for. He constantly asks questions, pushes people hard, and just never settles. In the process, some people can feel threatened or scared. But Denis is not a whatever-works, smooth-things-over kind of person. Successful change agents rarely are.

The point here is that to make change, you need true believers at the top, and get-on-with-it types everywhere else. Take the case of Bob Nardelli at The Home Depot.

The Home Depot, like GE's appliances business, was a company where the idea of change seemed ludicrous to most people in the organization. When Bob arrived in December 2000, the company looked perfect from the outside, and everyone inside was thrilled with the level of earnings and growth. The founders of the company had done a remarkable job of building the company from nothing, along the way sharing stock options with thousands of employees, who loved the ride as the profits soared through the 1990s.

But two things were happening that no one wanted to face. The business had gotten big with few internal processes in place—careful inventory tracking, stocking policies, and buying guidelines, to name three—and was having trouble maintaining its competitiveness. Lowe's, its principal competitor, was chipping away at Home Depot's lead with better service and more modern stores.

Bob was running the company for about a month when he started boldly talking about these problems, using tons of data. But few people at any level were buying his story of Home Depot as a fixer-upper. Many employees from the good old days openly pined for the times when the founders ran the company and everyone was getting richer by the hour. Who could blame them for the nostalgia?

But things had to change, and Bob knew that he couldn't do that with the team he had inherited. He quickly brought in his own people—true believers—and promoted several longtime employees whom he had identified as get-on-with-its. Together, they put the missing processes into Home Depot and got growth back into the company. Bob had no wind at his back, but he did have the right people by his side.

3. Ferret out and remove the resisters, even if their performance is satisfactory.

When it comes to making change, this is the hardest practice to implement. In the last chapter, I talked about how hard it is to let anyone go, but it is particularly difficult to fire people who are not actually screwing up and may in fact be doing quite well.

But in any organization, as the Appliances and Home Depot stories show, there is a core of people who absolutely will not accept change, no matter how good your case. Either their personalities just can't take it, or they are so entrenched—emotionally, intellectually, or politically—in the way things are, they cannot see a way to make them better.

These people usually have to go.

Maybe that sounds harsh, but you are doing no one a favor by keeping resisters in your organization. They foster an underground resistance and lower the morale of the people who support change. They waste their own time at a company where they don't share the vision, and they should be encouraged to find one where they do.

Take this extraordinary example. It's about Bill Harrison, the CEO of JPMorgan Chase, who asked a well-respected, high-level executive to leave during his change process at the bank. His move was even more stunning in that Bill did it when his own political capital was low—in the middle of the Enron collapse, when many people wondered if Bill would personally take the fall for the bank's loans to Enron and to other high-profile troubled companies.

During this period, Bill was instituting an executive training initiative focused on transforming the newly merged JPMorgan and Chase into a more market-focused bank, a big change for an institution whose businesses, like many of those on Wall Street, prided themselves on their individuality. The biggest resister was the CEO of one of JPMorgan Chase's major businesses, a true star in his own right. He preferred the lone-wolf culture of an investment bank and launched a quiet revolt over Bill's direction.

So Bill asked him to leave. It took tremendous courage given the circumstances. But Bill knew, and he was right, that the transformation of

> Managers often hold on to resisters because of a specific skill set or because they've been around for a long time. Don't!

JPMorgan Chase could not move forward with such a resister—and his following—in the way. Candor and fairness made the departure go well. And Bill's program went on to succeed too. In a survey of all bank executives taken two years after his leadership program started, those who participated in the initiative had a favorable impression of the bank's direction twenty points higher than those who had not participated.

From a management perspective, few cases of removing resisters are as difficult as the one Bill Harrison faced. But even when a situation is not nearly as political or fraught, I have seen managers hold on to resisters because of a specific skill set or because they've been around for a long time.

Don't!

Resisters only get more diehard and their followings more entrenched as time goes on. They are change killers; cut them off early.

4. Look at car wrecks.

Most companies capitalize on obvious opportunities. When a competitor fails, they move in on their customers. When a new technology emerges, they invest in it and create product line extensions.

But to be a real change organization, you also have to have the guts to look at bolder, scarier, more unpredictable events, and assess and make the most of the opportunities they present. This capability takes a certain determination and sometimes a strong stomach, but the rewards can be huge.

Take the 1997 Asian financial crisis. Currency traders certainly capitalized on this awful event; they live on exploiting change. But

It goes without saying that no businessperson wants disasters to occur, but they will.

they're not the only ones who should do this. GE had real success buying undervalued Thai auto loans in this period. Others prospered by buying real estate at fire sale prices.

The Japanese banking woes of the '90s gave numerous companies a chance to pick up assets at attractive prices and participate in a market that had previously been closed to them. Companies like the buyout firm Ripplewood Holdings, AIG, Citigroup, and GE, to name a few, made huge gambles in a horrible-looking environment that had just about every pundit predicting the permanent demise of Japan. Those bets are turning out to be big winners as Japan recovers.

Bankruptcies are another calamity that provide all kinds of opportunities. They're tragic to the employees. Jobs are lost, and pensions disappear into thin air. But jobs and futures can also be created from the cinders. When Enron fell apart—a tragic business story if there ever was one—Warren Buffett was able to take a position in its former pipeline business at a bargain-basement price. And GE picked up its wind power business at what it considered a very good price. The Vivendi collapse was a disaster for CEO Jean-Marie Messier, many employees, and company shareholders. But its financial needs provided the opportunity for Edgar Bronfman to reenter the music business at an attractive price and for GE to purchase terrific media assets.

It goes without saying that no businessperson wants disasters to occur, but they will. There will be spikes in oil prices, buildings will be destroyed in earthquakes, companies will go bankrupt, and countries will come close. In today's world, there is the persistent threat of a terrorist attack. Yet even if terrorism is eventually contained—unfortunately, something that is not imminent—there will always be elections and revolutions that change the course of history.

Most companies take advantage of obvious opportunities. But some also have the ability to make the most of regrettable circumstances—those "car wrecks"—and they should. Since 9/11, for instance, an entirely new kind of security industry has emerged. Of course, you wish with everything in you that such an industry didn't have to exist. But these companies will benefit for having realized that change means seizing *every* opportunity, even the ones wrought by adversity.

With all the noise out there about change, it's easy to get over-whelmed and confused.

But there are really just four practices that matter: Communicate a sound rationale for every change. Have the right people at your side. Get rid of the resisters. And seize every single opportunity, even those from someone else's misfortune. That's it.

Don't get all caught up in your knickers over change.

You just don't need to.

10

Crisis Management

FROM OH-GOD-NO TO
YES-WE'RE-FINE

I T'S NO WONDER that crisis management is often referred to as firefighting. Like a four-alarm blaze, an event of the oh-God-no variety can really consume an organization. Managers huddle in meeting after meeting, trying to figure out what the heck is going on, while everyone else gathers in little clumps all over the office to whisper. They wring their hands over whose head is going to roll. They obsess about their jobs, pointing fingers up, down, and sideways. Often, panic rages so high that real work grinds to a halt.

Sound familiar?

Look, crises happen. As long as companies are made up of human beings, there will be mistakes, controversies, and blowups. There will be accidents, theft, and fraud. The cold truth is that some degree of unwanted and unacceptable behavior is inevitable. If people always followed the rules, there would be no police forces, courthouses, or jails.

For leaders, crises often stand out as the most painful and trying

Managers can waste a lot of time at the outset of a crisis denying that something went wrong. Skip that step.

experiences of their business lives. Crises can create anxiety-ridden days, sleepless nights, and a churning in the pit of your stomach like no other challenge you face at work.

And on top of it all, crises demand from leaders a daunting balancing act. On one hand, you've got to throw everything you've got into understanding and solving the crisis. You have to unleash a torrent of time and energy, mainly your own, at dousing the flames. At the same time, you have to put that activity into a compartment and carry on as if nothing is actually wrong. That's what leaders usually neglect—to their regret. Because when you focus only on the crisis, it can overtake the whole organization, sucking it into a vortex of blame, dread, and paralysis.

This balancing act is obviously brutal to pull off in the midst of an event that feels like a living hell. At the outset, you never have all the information you want or need, and solutions often emerge much more slowly than you'd like. And the ending to a crisis rarely seems completely fair or right. Good people sometimes get hurt, and all you can really be happy about is that the mess is finally over.

Each crisis is different. Some are entirely internal affairs with swift solutions. Others are huge media events, with all sorts of legal ramifications. The uniqueness of each crisis makes it hard to come up with rules for getting through them.

There are, however, five things you can assume about how your crisis will unfold. These assumptions played out in virtually every crisis I managed, from Aircraft Engines' bribery case involving an Israeli air force general, to the company's battle with the government over time card accuracy, to the Kidder Peabody scandal, where an employee misrepresented earnings by millions of dollars. These assumptions aren't a formula for managing a crisis, but hopefully they'll provide directional guidance as you get from oh-God-no back to yes-we're-fine again:

First, assume the problem is worse than it appears. Managers can waste a lot of time at the outset of a crisis denying that something went wrong. Don't let that happen to you. Skip the denial step, and get into the mind-set that the problem will get bigger, messier, and more awful than you can possibly imagine.

Second, assume there are no secrets in the world and that everyone will eventually find out everything. One of the most common tendencies inside the crisis vortex is containment, in which managers frantically try to clamp down on information flow. It's far better to get out ahead of the problem, exposing its scope before someone else does it for you.

Third, assume you and your organization's handling of the crisis will be portrayed in the worst possible light. It is not the job of the media to make you or your organization look good during a crisis, and they won't. And never mind the media. Your own organization can be a tough audience during times of trouble. In both cases, the implication is the same: define your own position early and often.

Fourth, assume there will be changes in processes and people. Almost no crisis ends without blood on the floor. Real crises don't just fade away. They require solutions that overhaul current processes or introduce new ones and, just as often, upend lives and careers.

Fifth, assume your organization will survive, ultimately stronger for what happened. We learned something from every single crisis that made us a smarter and more effective organization. Taking the long view might make living in the hellish moment somewhat more bearable.

SEEKING IMMUNITY

Last year in Amsterdam, we met a Dutch journalist who had recently recovered from an illness that had robbed her of her memory for two years. She recounted to us the worst aspect of amnesia for her, which she described as her lack of immunity in life. Every time she made a mistake, like touching a hot stove or not bringing an umbrella out in a rainstorm, it was as if it were for the first time. She never learned anything from experience.

At the time we met, the journalist was covering the crisis unfolding at the Dutch food retailer Ahold, which had been accused of serious accounting fraud. In our conversation, she wondered what would become of the company if its troubles passed. Having touched the stove once, would it do so again, or would its financial accounting be more tightly controlled than ever before?

I volunteered that Ahold might make other mistakes in the future, but it was highly unlikely to make a similar accounting error for a long, long time.

Companies typically go to extremes after a crisis. They throw up fortresses of rules and procedures to fight the enemy that got in once. Or to use the Dutch journalist's metaphor, they build a kind of immunity to the sickness that felled them—the way a child cannot get chicken pox twice.

So, there is a sliver of silver lining to crisis management in that you rarely have to live through the same disaster twice.

That said, you can be proactive in preventing some crises.

There are three main ways, and most companies have the first two pretty much nailed.

The first is tight controls—disciplined financial and accounting systems with tough internal and external auditing processes.

An organization's line managers should be required to review and act on every audit's findings.

The second way to try to prevent crises is with good internal processes, such as rigorous hiring procedures, candid performance reviews, and comprehensive training programs that make the company's policies

> There is a silver lining to crisis management in that you rarely have to live through the same disaster twice.

nothing short of crystal clear. When it comes to acceptable behaviors, rules, and regulations, you simply cannot train too much.

The third way is less common and certainly less of a layup—a culture of integrity, meaning a culture of honesty, transparency, fairness, and strict adherence to rules and regulations. In such cultures, there can be no head fakes or winks. People who break the rules do not leave the company for "personal reasons" or to "spend more time with their families." They are hanged—publicly—and the reasons are made painfully clear to everyone.

Perhaps the lawyers will warn you against saying too much. But if you've got the facts right, you should be comfortable laying out who broke the rules and how. There are enormous organizational benefits from making examples of people who have violated your policies.

Maybe public vilifications and punishments sound harsh. But they are the best way to increase the chances that when someone in your organization lights a match—that is, commits an integrity transgression—at least a couple of onlookers will immediately shout, "Fire!"

Prevention is by no means a perfect science, but it's your first line of defense against a crisis. Don't rely on hard experience to build your immunity—unless you have to.

THE ANATOMY OF A CRISIS

Before we talk about each assumption, let's take a short look at how crises tend to unfold—and roll—to their conclusions.

Most of the time, crises blindside you. They begin with someone stopping you in the cafeteria and asking a perplexing "Did you hear?" kind of question, or with an e-mail or letter about a possible "irregularity," or with a phone call you would never expect in a million years.

The last of those is what happened in 1985, when the general counsel of GE phoned to say there was an investigation of time card irregularities going on in our Valley Forge, Pennsylvania, factory that made missile cones for the government.

I had never worked in a business where employees apportioned their time by project, let alone filled out a job time card myself. All I knew was that the people in our aerospace business had nothing to gain from jiggering this process, since the engineers involved were all paid on salary only. My initial reaction was a totally unruffled "Uh-hunh, keep me posted."

He did, and before I knew it, the time card situation had erupted into a firestorm that took a lot of people's time and focus during my first couple of years as CEO.

Now, sometimes crises explode with a single event, like the *Exxon Valdez* breaking up off the coast of Alaska, dumping millions of gallons of crude oil, or when Johnson & Johnson suddenly discovered that someone was tampering with bottles of Tylenol.

But most crises don't detonate like bombs—they emerge in fits and starts. I don't know the details of the Merck situation with Vioxx, but I would bet that it actually started a few years ago with a couple of seemingly random incidents of heart problems in people taking the drug. Those reports might have led to a vague suspicion by some scientists that Vioxx was involved, and eventually a larger study was undertaken. From there, the situation probably grew into the full-blown recall that took place in the fall of 2004.

Most often, that's how crises go—they seep out and roll toward their solutions. Like snowballs down a mountain, they bounce and zigzag and pick up weight and speed. You can never be entirely sure where their paths will end.

You can be sure, however, that they will end. The trip to the bottom of the mountain will probably be unpleasant, but eventually it's over and normal life resumes.

That is, until another crisis emerges.

PLAN OF ACTION

And now for the five assumptions to keep in mind when a crisis happens.

Assumption 1: The problem is worse than it appears. No matter how hard you might wish and pray, very few crises start small and stay that way. The vast majority are bigger in scope than you could ever imagine with that first phone call—and they will last longer and get more ugly. More people than you thought will be involved, more lawyers than you've ever seen will poke their noses in, and more terrible things will be said and published than your worst nightmare.

So adjust your mind-set early on. Go into every crisis assuming the absolute worst has occurred somewhere in your organization and, just as important, that you completely own the problem. In other words, go so far as to assume your company did it and you have to fix it.

My tepid response to the time card crisis is case in point here about the importance of having the right mind-set, which I did not. With my lack of experience in crisis management, I assumed

> I'm not saying that the correct mind-set means you should fold at the get-go. Sometimes you are absolutely clean and you need to fight.

the problem just couldn't be that bad, given that no one stood to gain personally from misallocating their hours. Maybe a few people had been sloppy with their time cards and winged it, I thought—but so what?

The "so what" was all in the timing. Caspar Weinberger had just been named secretary of defense, and he was spearheading President Reagan's campaign against government "fraud, waste, and abuse." The newspapers were filled with stories about companies charging the government $400 for hammers and $1,000 for toilet seats. We were up next.

The facts, as we came to learn, were that 99.5 percent of the thousands of time cards filed in the Pennsylvania plant had been filled out correctly. It didn't matter—0.5 percent of them were not and that was a violation. Instead of facing that, we got all caught up in our own logic. It went like this: most of the time cards were correct and the errors were accidental . . . overall we had actually undercharged the government . . . this is all just a political witch hunt.

With a seasoned mind-set, I would have said, "We were wrong. Let's do what it takes to correct the situation and put it behind us."

I'm not saying that the correct mind-set means you should always fold at the get-go. Sometimes you are absolutely clean and you need to fight. In 1992, a former employee turned whistle-blower from our diamond business claimed that we had colluded with De Beers to set prices in the industrial diamond market.

Knowing the people charged with collusion, I felt certain that this was just a case of a disgruntled guy who should have been let go with more sensitivity. Nevertheless, we dug into the investigation as if we were guilty, looking for every shred of evidence that could be used against us. We turned up nothing. That allowed us to take on the government with everything we had, and we won big when a federal judge threw out the government's case in 1994.

The same "we own it" mind-set got us successfully through another crisis. In the late '80s, the people running our appliances business in Louisville, Kentucky, began to hear rumblings from the field that an unusual number of refrigerator compressors were requiring repair a year or two out of the factory. The highest volume of breakdowns was coming from the warm-weather states. After a few months, the problem spread north, and I was brought into the loop.

We immediately assembled a SWAT team of experts from every part of the company—metallurgists and statisticians from corporate R & D, design engineers from Aircraft Engines who had experience with rotating parts, and marketing people who had studied the consumer impact of other national product recalls.

The team met weekly for a month and spoke on the phone every day to review new data and sort through options. Within three months, it was clear that the only course of action was a national recall. We had to take a $500 million write-off, and we received some unpleasant coverage about our technical capabilities in the *Wall Street Journal*. But grasping the scope of the problem early and taking ownership of its solution ultimately resulted in a lot of goodwill from consumers.

The point is, at the first glimmer of a crisis, don't flinch. Get into a worst-case scenario mind-set and start digging.

Assume you have a major problem on your hands that's yours to fix.

Assumption 2: There are no secrets in the world, and everyone will eventually find out everything. In the chapter on people management, discussing the corrosive effect of layers, I mentioned the children's game of telephone. In it, the first person in a circle whispers a secret to the second, who passes to a third, and round it goes until the last person announces what message has reached him. Not surprisingly, the final version has no resemblance to the original.

Telephone gets played during crises too.

Information you try to shut down will eventually get out, and as it travels, it will certainly morph, twist, and darken.

The only way to prevent that is to expose the problem yourself. If you don't, you can be sure someone will do it for you, and you will look the worse for it.

Now, I know what you're thinking; "Legal won't let us." And you're right. During a crisis, your lawyers will tell you to say less, not more. They will warn you not to implicate Joe or Joyce because their involvement is not yet clear.

That advice is not all wrong. But don't take it as gospel. Push lawyers to let you say as much as you can. Just make sure that what you do say is the total truth, with no shades of gray.

Cases of full disclosure in business abound, but Johnson & Johnson probably set the gold standard with its handling of the Tylenol crisis in the 1980s. It held press conferences every day, and sometimes more than once, to describe the situation and its scope. It opened its packaging factories up for scrutiny, and kept the public posted on a frequent basis on its investigation of the problem and its recall efforts.

But perhaps some of the best examples of full disclosure come from the newspaper industry. In

> During a crisis, your lawyers will tell you to say less, not more. That advice is not all wrong. But don't take it as gospel.

1980, the *Washington Post* ran a detailed series describing how one of its reporters, Janet Cooke, managed to fool her editors, the public, and the Pulitzer Prize jury into believing a horrific tale of an eight-year-old heroin addict.

Or take the *New York Times* and its coverage of Jayson Blair, its reporter who fabricated numerous articles. The paper put its best investigative reporters on the case, and their articles left no part of the story untouched. The paper's own practices and leaders were challenged so thoroughly and personally that at times the coverage felt like an unedited family movie.

And yet, in the end, it was the *Times'* transparency during the crisis that saved its credibility. The more it said about Jayson Blair's falsifications, the more people trusted it—not less. The more it revealed the internal dynamics that let Blair's lying slip by, the more people knew the paper was invested in finding a solution to the underlying problems that caused the breach.

The same is true during any crisis. The more openly you speak about the problem, its causes, and its solutions, the more trust you earn from everyone watching, inside the organization and out.

And during a crisis, trust is what you need at every turn.

Assumption 3: You and your organization's handling of the crisis will be portrayed in the worst possible light. In some industries, insiders keep score by market share. In others, they keep score by revenue growth, or number of new franchises opened in a year, or customer satisfaction figures.

In journalism, they keep score by toppled empires and naked emperors. The profession's calling, as it were, is to question authority in its every form.

I speak, of course, from experience! During my very public divorce in 2002, a controversy erupted around the perks that made up my retention contract, and the media had a field day. But that was hardly the first time I'd gotten my clock cleaned by the press.

Not long after I was made CEO, during a period of wide-scale layoffs, I got labeled Neutron Jack, after the bomb that leaves buildings standing but kills people. A year later, I was named one of the toughest bosses in America, and believe me, the implication was not positive. During the Kidder Peabody crisis in 1994, I appeared on the cover of *Fortune* magazine under the headline "Jack's Nightmare on Wall Street." The article included a thesis about the cultural breakdown at Kidder Peabody brought on by earnings pressure from GE.

Public skewerings are awful—you're indignant and enraged. But no matter how innocent you think you are, or how superbly you think your organization is handling its troubles, it doesn't matter. Reporters are not in the business of telling your side of the story. They are in the business of telling the story as they see it.

That's the way the business works, and during normal times, you're usually happy for the good read that journalists provide. And in my case, over the course of my career, I got more than my fair share of positive media coverage.

But during a crisis, all bets are off. You and your organization will be portrayed in a light so negative you won't recognize yourselves.

Don't hunker down.

You may want to, but you can't. Along with disclosing the full extent of your problem as we discussed in the previous assumption, you've got to stand up and define your position before someone else does. If you don't, your lack of visibility will be taken as an admission of guilt, the same way it looks to lay people

> Your lack of visibility will be taken as an admission of guilt, the same way it looks to laypeople when someone does not take the stand in his own defense.

(albeit not lawyers!) when someone does not take the stand in his own defense.

Now, not all organizational crises have a public face. A middle manager leaves and takes his team with him. The reorganization of a business or unit causes enormous upset and turmoil. A big customer defects with complaints about your service. A fired employee makes angry charges of discrimination by senior management.

> With big crises, don't ever forget you have a business to run.

Even if the media has no interest in these events, your people will.

The same principles still apply.

Openly discuss the situation. Define your position. Explain why the problem happened and how you are handling it.

And just as with big, public crises, don't ever forget you have a business to run. Make sure you are running it.

Assumption 4: There will be changes in processes and people. Almost no crisis ends without blood on the floor. Most crises officially end with a settlement of some kind—financial, legal, or otherwise.

Then comes the cleanup, and cleanups mean change.

Processes usually get overhauled first.

With the time card situation, for instance, we instituted Policy 20.11, which formalized all dealings with the government. The policy was excruciatingly detailed, requiring us to cross every t and dot every i. I am no fan of bureaucracy, but the time card situation demanded just such a process fix.

Sometimes, however, process fixes are not enough. We had had a policy about improper payments on our books for more than thirty years—Policy 20.4 to be exact—that was supposed to prevent bribery. But it didn't help us back in 1990, when a regional sales manager for Aircraft Engines conspired with a general in the Israeli Air Force to divert money from major contracts for GE to supply engines for Israeli F-16 warplanes.

This was no small-potatoes operation. The two men had set up a joint Swiss bank account and a fake contractor in New Jersey to cover their tracks. The media coverage around the world lasted nineteen months, through congressional hearings and a criminal trial against the GE employee, Herbert Steindler. At the end, he went to jail, and we paid the government a $69 million fine.

In this case, the problem was not process, but people not enforcing an existing policy. No one in the business actually knew what Steindler was up to, and none of them gained a penny from the scheme, but some ignored warning signs that something was amiss. Eleven people had to resign, six were demoted, and four were reprimanded.

Crises require change. Sometimes a process fix is enough. Usually not. That's because the people affected by the crisis, or sometimes those just watching it, demand that *someone* be held responsible.

It sounds awful, but a crisis rarely ends without blood on the floor. That's not easy or pleasant. But sadly, it is often necessary so the company can move forward again.

Assumption 5: The organization will survive, ultimately stronger for what happened. There is not a crisis you cannot learn from, even though you hate every one of them.

From the time card crisis, we learned that when you deal with the government, there can be no looseness with regulations, even if it means installing lots of detailed bureaucratic procedures. That's the price you pay for doing business with public agencies.

From the compressors situation, we learned to bite the bullet early on product recalls. Doing that cuts your losses and pays off in consumer goodwill.

From Kidder Peabody, we learned to never buy a company with a culture that didn't match ours.

From the bribery case, we learned that policies age and even die unless managers work constantly to keep them alive.

After a crisis is over, there is always the tendency to want to put it away in a drawer.

Don't. Use a crisis for all it's worth. Teach its lessons every chance you get.

In doing so, you'll spread the immunity.

There will always be crises.

And when they erupt, it's awful! It really does feel like your house is on fire and you can't get out.

As hard as it sounds, try to remember in the heat of it all that eventually the flames will die down. And they will die down because of what you do. You will face the enormity of the problem and own its solution, while at the same time running the business as if there is a tomorrow.

Then one day, you will realize tomorrow has arrived. The smoke will have cleared, and the damaged parts of the structure will have been replaced or repaired.

You will never be happy for what happened, but stepping back, you'll see something that might surprise you—the whole place looks better than ever.

YOUR COMPETITION

11

Strategy

IT'S ALL IN THE SAUCE

$\mathbf{M}$ORE THAN A FEW TIMES over the past three years, I have been on a speaking program or at a business conference with one big strategy guru or another. And more than a few times, I have listened to their presentations in disbelief.

It's not that I don't understand their theories about competitive advantage, core competencies, virtual commerce, supply chain economics, disruptive innovation, and so on, it's just that the way these experts tend to talk about strategy—as if it is some kind of high-brain scientific methodology—feels really off to me.

I know that strategy is a living, breathing, totally dynamic *game.* It's fun—and fast. And it's alive.

Forget the arduous, intellectualized number crunching and data grinding that gurus say you have to go through to get strategy right. Forget the scenario planning, yearlong studies, and hundred–plus-page reports. They're time-consuming and expensive, and you just don't need them.

In real life, strategy is actually very straightforward. You pick a general direction and implement like hell.

When it comes to strategy, ponder less and do more.

Yes, theories can be interesting, charts and graphs can be beautiful, and big, fat stacks of PowerPoint slides can make you feel like you've done your job. But you just should not make strategy too complex. The more you think about it, and the more you grind down into the data and details, the more you tie yourself in knots about what to do.

That's not strategy, that's suffering.

Now, I don't want to write off strategy gurus. Some of their concepts have merit.

But I do want to disagree with the scientific approach to strategy that they propagate. It is taught in many business schools, peddled by countless consulting firms, and practiced in far too many corporate headquarters.

It's just so unproductive! If you want to win, when it comes to strategy, ponder less and do more.

I'm certainly not alone in this view. In speaking with many thousands of businesspeople around the world, I can count the number of strategy questions on one hand. Virtually every other topic—from managing a temperamental employee to the dollar's effect on trade—gets more interest by orders of magnitude.

Obviously, everyone *cares* about strategy. You have to. But most managers I know see strategy as I do—an approximate course of action that you frequently revisit and redefine, according to shifting market conditions. It is an iterative process and not nearly as theoretical or life-and-death as some would have you believe.

Given this view, you may be wondering what I'm going to say in this chapter.

The answer is, nothing that's going to get me tenure!

Instead, I'm going to describe how to do strategy in three steps. Over my career, this approach worked incredibly well across varied businesses and industries, in upturns and downturns, and in competitive situations from Mexico to Japan. Who knows—maybe its simplicity was part of its success.

The steps are:

First, come up with a big aha for your business—a smart, realistic, relatively fast way to gain sustainable competitive advantage. I don't know any better way to come up with this big aha than by answering a set of questions I have long called the Five Slides, because each set fits roughly onto one page. This assessment process should take a group of informed people somewhere between a couple of days and a month.

Second, put the right people in the right jobs to drive the big aha forward. This may sound generic; it's not. To drive your big aha forward, you need to match certain kinds of people with commodity businesses and a different type entirely with high-value-added businesses. I don't like to pigeonhole, but the fact is, you get a lot more bang for your buck when strategy and skills fit.

Third, relentlessly seek out the best practices to achieve your big aha, whether inside or out, adapt them, and continually improve them. Strategy is unleashed when you have a learning organization where people thirst to do everything better every day. They draw on best practices from anywhere, and push them to ever-higher levels of effectiveness. You can have the best big aha in the world, but without this learning culture in place, any sustainable competitive advantage will not last.

Strategy, then, is simply finding the big aha and setting a broad direction, putting the right people behind it, and then executing with an unyielding emphasis on continual improvement.

I couldn't make it more complicated than that if I tried.

SO WHAT IS STRATEGY?

Before we look at each of the three steps in some detail, a few thoughts about strategy in general.

At the time I retired from GE, the company employed more than three hundred thousand people in about fifteen major businesses, from gas turbines to credit cards. It was a complex, wide-ranging company, but I always said I wanted it to operate with the speed, informality, and open communication of a corner store.

Corner stores often have strategy right too. With their limited resources, they have to rely on a laserlike focus on doing one thing very well.

In our Boston neighborhood, for instance, within a block of each other on Charles Street, two little shops have constantly ringing cash registers and a nonstop flow of satisfied customers. One is Upper Crust Pizza. Its space is cramped, completely unadorned, and noisy, with self-service paper plates and a limited selection of soft drinks. Customers can eat either standing up or sitting at one large, benchlike table. The staff isn't exactly rude, but they're noncommittal. It is not unusual for your order—given at the cash register—to be greeted with a bland "Whatever."

But the pizza is to die for; you could faint just describing the flavor of the sauce, and the crust puts you over the edge. Investment bankers, artists, and cops start lining up at eleven in the morning to see the "Slice of the Day" posted on the door, and around lunch and dinner, the line can run twenty deep. A fleet of delivery people work nonstop until closing.

At Upper Crust, strategy is all about product.

Then there's Gary Drug, about half the size of a New York subway car. A large, newly renovated, twenty-four–hour CVS pharmacy is a short walk away. No matter. Gary Drug, with its single, narrow aisle and shelves packed to the ceiling, is always busy. Its selection ranges from cold remedies to alarm clocks, with tweezers and pencil sharpeners mixed in. There is a personable pharmacist tucked in back, and a wide selection of European fashion magazines in a corner up front. Everything the store sells matches the mix of the neighborhood's quirky residents. Salespeople greet customers by name when they walk in and happily give advice on everything from vitamins to foot massagers. The store offers instant home delivery and a house charge account that bills you once a month.

At Gary Drug, strategy is all about service.

Look, what is strategy but resource allocation? When you strip away all the noise, that's what it comes down to. Strategy means making clear-cut choices about how to compete. You cannot be everything to everybody, no matter what the size of your business or how deep its pockets.

Corner stores have learned that survival depends on finding a strategic position where no one can beat them. Big companies have the same challenge.

When I became CEO in 1981, we launched a highly publicized initiative: "Be No. 1 or No. 2 in every market, and fix, sell, or close to get there." This was not our *strategy*, although I've heard it described that way. It was a galvanizing mantra to describe how we were going to do business going forward. There would be no more hanging on to uncompetitive businesses for old times' sake. More than anything else, the No. 1 or No. 2 initiative was a

> Strategy means making clear-cut choices about how to compete. You cannot be everything to everybody, no matter what the size of your business or how deep its pockets.

communication tool to clean up our portfolio, and it really worked.

Our strategy was much more directional. GE was going to move away from businesses that were being commoditized toward businesses that manufactured high-value technology products or sold services instead of things. As part of that move, we were going to massively upgrade our human resources—our people—with a relentless focus on training and development.

We chose that strategy after getting hammered by the Japanese in the 1970s. They had rapidly commoditized businesses where we had had reasonable margins, like TV sets and room air conditioners. We ended up playing defense in a losing game. Our quality, cost, and service—the weapons of a commodity business—weren't good enough in the face of their innovation and declining prices. Every day at work was a kind of protracted agony. Despite our productivity improvements and increasing innovation, margins were eroding, as competitors like Toshiba, Hitachi, and Matsushita were relentless.

Meanwhile, overseeing GE Capital in the late '70s, I was shocked (and delighted) to see how easy it was to make money in financial services, particularly with GE's balance sheet. There were no union factories, no foreign competition, and plenty of interesting, creative ways to offer customers differentiated products and services. I remember the excitement in that period, seeing our people develop new private-label credit card programs and find niche after niche in middle-market industrial financing. Fat margins weren't exactly low-hanging fruit, but close.

By the time I was made CEO, I knew that GE had to get as far away as it could from any business that smelled like a commodity and get as close as possible to the other end of the spectrum. That's why we divested businesses like TV sets, small appliances, air conditioners, and a huge coal company, Utah International. It is also why we invested so heavily in GE Capital; bought RCA, which included NBC; and poured resources into developing high-technology products in our power, medical, aircraft engine, and locomotive businesses.

> **If they're headed in the right direction and are broad enough, strategies don't really need to change all that often.**

Now, in such changing times, how and why did GE stick with one strategy over twenty years? The answer is that strategies, if they're headed in the right direction and are broad enough, don't really need to change all that often, especially if they are supplemented with fresh initiatives. To that end, over the years, we launched four programs to bolster our strategy—globalization, service add-ons, Six Sigma, and e-business.

More than anything, though, our strategy lasted because it was based on two powerful underlying principles: commoditization is evil and people are everything.

Virtually every resource allocation decision we made was based on those beliefs.

Yes, some companies can win in commodity situations—Dell and Wal-Mart are great examples of companies that have pulled the levers of cost, quality, and service to succeed in extremely competitive games. But that is really tough. You just can't make any mistakes.

My advice, then, is when you think strategy, think about decommoditizing. Try desperately to make products and services distinctive and customers stick to you like glue. Think about innovation, technology, internal processes, service add-ons—whatever works to be unique. Doing that right means you can even make a few mistakes and still succeed.

That's enough theory!

MAKING STRATEGY REAL

The first step of making strategy real is figuring out the big aha to gain sustainable competitive advantage—in other words, a significant, meaningful insight about how to win. To do that, you need to debate, grapple with, wallow in, and finally answer five sets of questions.

Going into this exercise, I'll assume that you have a strategy to begin with, either written somewhere or in your head.

That said, having a strategy doesn't mean it's working.

The five slides we're going to look at here are a way to test your strategy, to see if it's getting you where you want to go, and figure out how to fix it if it's not, even to the point of changing it entirely.

I strongly believe this questioning process should not be a wide-scale, bottom-up event. While others may disagree, I know that strategy is the job of the CEO or the unit leader, along with his or her direct reports. If the culture is healthy, they can see the organization in all its various, interdependent parts. They know its people, as well as its sources of ideas and innovation, and can best determine where the most exciting opportunities lie. Moreover, they are the ones who will ultimately commit the resources the strategy requires. They get the plaudits if the strategy succeeds and hold the bag if it fails.

If you have a good team—candid, insightful, passionate about the business, and willing to disagree—completing this exercise should be fun and energizing. With intensity, it should take somewhere between a couple of days and a month. After that, it's time to act.

SLIDE ONE

What the Playing Field Looks Like Now

■ Who are the competitors in this business, large and small, new and old?

■ Who has what share, globally and in each market? Where do we fit in?

■ What are the characteristics of this business? Is it commodity or high value or somewhere in between? Is it long cycle or short? Where is it on the growth curve? What are the drivers of profitability?

■ What are the strengths and weaknesses of each competitor? How good are their products? How much does each one spend on R & D? How big is each sales force? How performance-driven is each culture?

■ Who are this business's main customers, and how do they buy?

Over the years, I have been amazed at how much debate this simple grounding exercise can spawn. In fact, it's not unusual for people who share the same office space to have widely different views of the same competitive environment.

Many people have a terrible time admitting their business is a true commodity. No matter how hard we tried, it was next to impossible to get people in our motors business, for instance, to accept this reality. And I have sat through countless meetings where this set of questions has surfaced that discomfort and generated enormous heat about the level of resources to commit to R & D and marketing in an attempt to make the product more unique.

Another of the many important issues this slide surfaces is market size. Too often, people like to call themselves the market leader, so they end up limiting the scope of their playing field to make that happen. In our case, the No. 1 or No. 2 mantra inadvertently had that exact effect. After more than a decade, we realized that businesses were increasingly tightening their overall market definition so that their shares were enormous.

We fixed that by saying that businesses had to define their market in such a way that their share of any market they were in could not be more than 10 percent. With that restriction, people were forced into a whole new mind-set, and opportunities for growth were suddenly everywhere.

On the road in Q & A sessions, this is how I talk about the market definition dynamic: Since I am usually sitting in a chair, I ask audience members to imagine that they are a chair manufacturer. They can define their market as the kind of chair I am usually in—with curved metal arms, blue fabric, and wheels. Or they can define it as all chairs. Best yet, they can define their market as all furniture. Imagine the share differences and the implications for strategy!

This kind of discussion is why this slide really deserves to be wallowed in. A rich, wide-ranging conversation puts everyone on the same page—just where they have to be to ultimately find the big aha.

SLIDE TWO

What the Competition Has Been Up To

■ What has each competitor done in the past year to change the playing field?

■ Has anyone introduced game-changing new products, new technologies, or a new distribution channel?

■ Are there any new entrants, and what have they been up to in the past year?

This set of questions brings the players on the field to life. Competitor A has been stealing your key salespeople. Competitor B has introduced two new products. Competitors C and D have merged and are having all kinds of integration difficulties.

Some of this information may have surfaced during the wallowing of the first question set, but now it's time to dig deeper into each competitor's behavior.

Be granular—know what each competitor eats for breakfast.

■

SLIDE THREE

What You've Been Up To

■ What have you done in the past year to change the competitive playing field?

■ Have you bought a company, introduced a new product, stolen a competitor's key salesperson, or licensed a new technology from a start-up?

■ Have you lost any competitive advantages that you once had—a great salesperson, a special product, a proprietary technology?

The best thing about this slide is that it hits you between the eyes if you're being outflanked. Very simply, the comparison of slides two and three tells you if you are leading the market or chasing it.

Sometimes these two slides show you that your competitors are doing a whole heck of a lot more than you are. You'd better find out why.

Other times, the comparison of these two slides paints a vivid picture of your business's competitive dynamics.

Case in point is what happened in our medical business in 1976. The British company EMI had invented the CT scanner in the early '70s, forcing the traditional X-ray manufacturers—Siemens, Philips, Picker, and us—into an intense equipment war. Soon enough, all of us were coming out with million-dollar machines six months apart, each claiming to be thirty seconds faster in scan time than the last entry. No one was particularly happy with this situation. The CT competitors were in a slugfest, and our customers—the hospitals—were frustrated that they had to make big capital outlays for technology that could be outdated within a year.

Seeing that dynamic, Walt Robb, the head of our medical business, and his team, came up with a breakthrough idea. GE would allocate its resources to design scanners that could be continually upgraded with hardware or software that would cost less than $100,000 a year. We would sell our machines by saying, "Buy a CT scanner from our Continuum Series, and our upgrades will keep you from becoming obsolete for a fraction of the price of new equipment."

The Continuum concept changed the playing field. It made us No. 1 and has kept us there for twenty-five years.

The main point here is that slides two and three work as a pair. They take anything static out of strategy and get you ready for the questions that come next.

■

SLIDE FOUR

What's Around the Corner?

■ What scares you most in the year ahead—what one or two things could a competitor do to nail you?

■ What new products or technologies could your competitors launch that might change the game?

■ What M & A deals would knock you off your feet?

This set of questions is, with doubt, the one that most people miss.

They just don't give it the paranoia it deserves.

Most people answering this set of questions underestimate the power and capabilities of their competitors. Too often, the assumption going in is that competitors will always look the way they do in slide one—they'll never change.

Take the case of Aircraft Engines in the 1990s, when our engineers believed that they had designed the perfect engine for the Boeing 777—the GE90. We spent more than $1 billion to get more than 90,000 pounds of thrust out of a brand-new design, based on the assumption that Pratt & Whitney could not afford to launch a new engine and would be unable to extend their existing engines to that level.

We were wrong.

Pratt & Whitney, with only $200 million in development, did get 90,000 pounds of thrust out of their existing engines. Because their costs were less, we had to sell the GE90 at lower prices than we planned. We had underestimated the competition because we thought we had all the technical answers.

This story had a lucky ending. Several years later, Boeing developed a long-range version of the 777. It required 115,000 pounds of thrust, which the GE90 could meet since it was a new design and could be expanded. We ended up being chosen by Boeing as their sole source, but because of our early miscalculation, we suffered through a few painful, less profitable years.

Getting the right strategy means you have to assume your competitors are damn good, or at the very least as good as you are, and that they are moving just as fast or faster.

When it comes to peering into the future, you just can't be paranoid enough.

SLIDE FIVE

What's Your Winning Move?

■ What can you do to change the playing field—is it an acquisition, a new product, globalization?

■ What can you do to make customers stick to you more than ever before and more than to anyone else?

This is the moment to leap from analysis to action. You decide to launch the new product, make the acquisition, double the sales force, or invest in major new capacity. In reality, this is when Walt Robb and his team made the decision to allocate major resources to the Continuum Series, the strategic move that would keep GE's medical customers "sticky" for decades.

By the time you've finished this set of questions, the effectiveness of your strategy should be pretty clear. Your big aha is winning, or it needs to change. Even if you didn't have a strategy before, this process should help you get one.

But either way, you've only just begun.

■

THE RIGHT PEOPLE

Here's a familiar scene. Managers meet for months on end in intensive sessions about the company's competitive situation and direction. Committees and subcommittees are formed. Surveys are conducted. Sometimes consultants are brought in. And then, at last and with tons of fanfare, the company's leaders announce a new strategy.

Which just sits there.

Any strategy, no matter how smart, is dead on arrival unless a company brings it to life with people—the *right* people.

Forget speeches. They're just hot air. The organization knows who's important. Only if those important people are assigned to lead a new strategy will it take off.

Consider what happened in Power Systems when our push toward product services first got announced. Immediately, all the engineers wanted to know what the heck was going on. After all, they had joined GE because they wanted to build the biggest, highest-powered, most environmentally sensitive turbines. Suddenly, they were being told that the people who serviced their "masterpieces" were going to be the stars of the show.

Didn't service people, they thought, carry oilcans?

Although the engineers heard the speeches, they didn't take them seriously, which was easy enough, since services were buried in the existing organization.

What did we do? We eventually took Ric Artigas, a PhD and the engineering leader in Locomotives, and put him in charge of a new and separate P & L devoted to Power Systems' services business. It was a real signal—Ric was a well-respected player. With his new stature, he had no trouble recruiting the best engineers in Power Systems, who were needed to design sophisticated software packages for turbine upgrades.

The services strategy was under way. In 2005, Ric's operating profit of close to $2.5 billion will be about equal to revenues when he took over in 1997.

Getting strategy right also means matching people with jobs—a match that often depends on where a business is on the commodity continuum.

It goes without saying that you cannot pigeonhole. Good people are too multifaceted. That said, I would still make the case that due to their skills and personalities, some people work more effectively in commodities and others are better in highly differentiated products or services.

Let's look at the motors business as an example. It's about as commoditized as you'll ever find. Several good companies make the product, and all have good service, quality, and cost.

The right people for this business are hard driving, meticulous, and detail oriented. They are not dreamers, they're hand-to-hand combat fighters.

Lloyd Trotter is the perfect example. Lloyd joined GE in 1970 as a field service engineer in its high-intensity quartz lighting department, and for thirty years after that, his career was factories, factories, and more factories. He was a foreman, a production manager, and plant supervisor in Lighting, Appliances, and virtually every electrical distribution and control (ED&C) business we had. By the time Lloyd was made CEO of ED&C in 1992, he could tell you from the parking lot whether or not a factory was humming. Two steps closer and he could tell you what it could do better.

Of course, Lloyd liked thinking about strategy, but he liked implementing it more. He was in his element with people who sweated the nitty-gritty details like he did, talking about ways to squeeze efficiencies out of every process. He was a master of discipline. And that's what made him exactly the right kind of leader to drive our commodities businesses.

At the other end of the spectrum, it's generally a different kind of person who thrives. Not better or worse, just different.

> Strategy also means matching people with jobs—a match that often depends on where a business is on the commodity continuum.

Take jet engines. Each engine is a unique, high-tech engineering miracle that requires about a billion dollars of investment to develop. The product life cycle is measured in years. And the customers are tough—the airlines themselves, perennially strapped for money, and the powerful airframers, Boeing and Airbus.

For many years, the jet engine business had its own distinct culture of romance. The people who gravitated toward it weren't your usual business types—they were in love with the very idea of flying and the wonder of airplanes.

Brian Rowe was perfect for such an environment.

Brian started his career as an apprentice with DeHavilland Engines in England before joining GE as a factory-floor engineer in 1957. After stints in virtually every possible jet engine design project, he was named head of GE's aircraft engine business in 1979.

Brian was a huge, gregarious guy—outspoken, opinionated, and visionary. He loved airplanes so much he would have worn goggles and a scarf to work if he could have.

Unlike Lloyd, Brian pretty much hated the nuts and bolts of management, and discussions of operating margins and cash flow bored him. But he sure did have the guts and the vision to place the big bets, laying a billion dollars on a single investment that would take years to pay off. Likewise, Brian's personality made him a great salesman with customers, who shared his enthusiasm for every new technological advance.

Lloyd and Brian were both a case of perfect fit—right for their jobs, right for the business situation, right for the strategy. You won't always get that lucky, and strategy can get implemented without an ideal match.

But you're much better off with one.

BEST PRACTICES AND BEYOND

I've heard it said that best practices aren't a sustainable competitive advantage because they are so easy to copy. That's nonsense.

It is true that, once a best practice is out there, everybody can imitate it, but companies that win do two things: they imitate *and* improve.

Admittedly, imitating is hard enough. I remember a software company executive at one Q & A session lamenting, "My people don't copy very well. They just don't want to—they like the way they do it." This reluctance to imitate is a common phenomenon. Maybe it's just human nature.

But to make your strategy succeed, you need to fix that mind-set—and go a lot further.

In fact, the third step of strategy is all about finding best practices, adapting them, and *continually improving them*. When you do that right, it's nothing short of innovation. New product and service ideas, new processes, and opportunities for growth start to pop out everywhere and actually become the norm.

Along with getting the right people in place, best practices are all part of implementing the hell out of your big aha, and to my mind, it's the most fun.

It's fun because companies that make best practices a priority are thriving, thirsting, learning organizations. They believe that everyone should always be searching for a better way. These kinds of companies are filled with energy and curiosity and a spirit of can-do.

Don't tell me that's not a competitive advantage!

Back in the old days—after World War II and before global competition—most industrial companies, GE included, were stuck in a not-invented-here (NIH) mind-set. The focus was on their own inventors, with plaques and bonuses reserved for the people who came up with and implemented original ideas.

Once the '80s arrived, we had no choice but to radically broaden the NIH mind-set, and we did so by celebrating people who not only invented things, but found great ideas *anywhere* and shared them with *everyone* in the company. We came to call this behavior "boundarylessness." This awkward word basically described an obsession with finding a better way—or a better idea—whether its source was a colleague, another GE business, or another company across the street or on the other side of the globe.

The impact of boundaryless thinking on our strategy implementation was enormous. Here's just one example:

GE was always trying to improve its working capital usage; we were always using too much, and increasing our inventory turns would help. But try as we might with all sorts of programs and tweaks, we just couldn't seem to get our annual turns above four.

In September 1994, Manny Kampouris was scheduled to speak at a dinner for the top thirty leaders in our company. At the time, Manny was the chairman and CEO of American Standard, the global plumbing and air-conditioning supply company and one of the largest customers of our motors business.

You couldn't help but notice that Manny wore a lapel pin emblazoned with the number "15" at its center. And soon enough, we all knew why.

For most of his talk that night, Manny regaled us with stories of how they had drastically improved inventory turns at American

Standard, a company that produced a broad and varied mix of porcelain toilet bowls and sinks in factories in just about every corner of the world. Manny and American Standard were obsessed with inventory turns. The reason was simple: the company had recently gone through a leveraged buyout, and cash flow was king.

Our team was awestruck. You could hear people thinking, if American Standard can improve inventory turns with its product mix and complicated manufacturing processes, why can't we? Before Manny could finish his talk, our business leaders were peppering him with question after question.

But that was just the beginning.

What followed was an avalanche of GE people visiting American Standard facilities, meeting with foremen and factory managers—all of them wearing lapel pins like Manny's. There was the occasional black sheep with a "10," but many more plant managers who wore pins boasting of twenty or twenty-five turns. We crawled all over their plants and picked their brains.

They were happy to help. One thing I have learned from boundarylessness over the years is that companies and their people—if they're not direct competitors, of course—love to share success stories. All you have to do is ask.

The GE people who visited American Standard put what they had learned into practice in their own businesses. Over the next several years, these businesses adapted many of American Standard's processes to GE, and continually innovated and shared with each other. It worked. By 2000, GE's inventory turns had more than doubled, freeing up billions of dollars of cash.

> Companies and their people love to share success stories. All you have to do is ask.

Over the years, GE borrowed great ideas with visits to Wal-Mart and Toyota and dozens of other companies. We also borrowed ideas from one another. At our quarterly meeting of business leaders, we asked attendees to present their best practice that others could use. If a leader tried to present a practice that wasn't applicable to the other businesses, we would give him the hook.

It was in that way that the junior military officer recruiting program, which started in Transportation and spread to every corner of the company, and Internet-selling techniques that helped Plastics reach its customers, made their way to Medical Systems and beyond. The list of these best practice transfers goes on and on.

And it's hardly exclusive to GE. Yum! Brands Inc. is a case in point. Yum! is a 1997 spinoff from PepsiCo composed of five consumer restaurant brands—KFC, Taco Bell, Pizza Hut, Long John Silver's, and A&W All American Food—with more than thirty-three thousand total outlets. Yum!'s CEO, David Novak, is an enormous believer in best practice transfer and considers each outlet an individual laboratory of ideas. David told me recently that he considered the major advantage to "bulking up"—in other words, adding chains and outlets—is to share learning. Otherwise, he said, size is just a drag.

Here's what he means. A couple of years ago, Taco Bell was rated fifteenth in service for drive-in restaurants, with customer service time of 240 seconds, or four minutes, per order. The chain introduced a new process, and within two years, managed to bring that number down to 148 seconds, making it No. 2 in the drive-through industry. Immediately, the Taco Bell practice was transferred to KFC, and last year, its customer service time moved from tenth to eighth—211 seconds to 180 seconds, a full half-minute improvement.

I could tell you many other stories about how Yum!'s "laboratories" have spawned new processes, and how they have spread to improve all of its businesses. However, to make a long story short, I'll just give you the results. Even with the tough economy, in the seven years since its spinoff, Yum!'s market capitalization has jumped from $4.2 billion to $13.5 billion. Mainly because of ideas being shared and stretched!

A focus on best practices may not sound like strategy, but try implementing strategy without it.

Best practices are not only integral to making strategy happen, they are a sustainable competitive advantage if you continually improve them, with *if* being the key word here.

That's not just a mind-set. It's a religion.

■

The other evening we were eating at Torch, a wonderful little restaurant one door down from Upper Crust Pizza, and from our seats in the window, we could see its delivery people on bikes, in cars, and on foot zipping back and forth in nonstop motion.

We started to play with the economics of the place, using rough numbers, but even with the most conservative estimates, we could only conclude that Upper Crust is very profitable.

You've got to believe that the people running Upper Crust have never held a strategy review session, let alone worked through five slides to reach a big aha.

Their big aha is all in the sauce.

Look, I don't want to oversimplify strategy. But you just shouldn't agonize over it. Find the right aha and set the direction, put the right people in place, and work like crazy to execute better than everyone else, finding best practices and improving them every day.

You may not run a corner store, but when you're making strategy, act like you do.

12

Budgeting

REINVENTING THE RITUAL

NOT TO BEAT AROUND THE BUSH, but the budget-ing process at most companies has to be the most ineffective practice in management.

It sucks the energy, time, fun, and big dreams out of an organization. It hides opportunity and stunts growth. It brings out the most unproductive behaviors in an organization, from sandbagging to settling for mediocrity.

In fact, when companies win, in most cases it is despite their budgets, not because of them.

And yet, as with strategy formulation, companies sink countless hours into writing budgets. What a waste!

I'm not saying financial planning is bad. Without question, you have to have a way to keep track of the numbers—just not the way it's usually done.

In this chapter, I'm going to talk about a totally different approach to budgeting. It aligns employees with shareholders, puts growth, energy, and fun into financial planning, and inspires

> The right budgeting process can change how a company functions—and reinventing the ritual makes winning so much easier, you can't afford not to try.

people to stretch. In fact, this approach is so unlike the typical budget process that when we started using it at GE, we stopped using the word *budget* altogether.

But more on that later.

The good news is that the process I recommend is not very hard to do. It is certainly no harder than the slogging, mind-numbing budgeting process that is the status quo.

But this new process can be practiced only if a company has trust and candor flowing through its veins. As I've mentioned throughout this book, that's rare. Perhaps budgets that actually inspire creativity and growth will make the case for that to change.

Most companies use budgeting as the backbone of their management systems. And so the right budgeting process can actually change how a company functions—and reinventing the annual ritual makes winning so much easier, you just can't afford not to try.

BUDGETS, THE WRONG WAY

Before describing how to devise budgets the right way, let's look at the two killing dynamics that are the norm. I call them the Negotiated Settlement and the Phony Smile approaches to budgeting.

These dynamics, incidentally, aren't only the purview of big corporate bureaucracies. No matter what size company you work in, one of these two approaches, maybe both, will probably sound very familiar to you. In my Q & A sessions around the world, I've heard about them in virtually every country and in companies with as few as a couple hundred employees, even in organizations that call themselves entrepreneurial. Bad budgeting is just that insidious; it creeps in everywhere and establishes itself as an institutionalized process. It's amazing how many times I have heard audience members decry entrenched budgeting systems, only for them to wearily conclude, "But that's just the way it's done."

It doesn't have to be. But first you have to undo those killing dynamics I just mentioned.

SPLIT THE DIFFERENCE

Of these dynamics, the **Negotiated Settlement** is the more common.

This process begins when the ink is barely dry on the strategic plan. That's when the businesses in the field start the long slog of constructing the next year's highly detailed financial plans from the bottom up. These will be presented in several months' time at the Big Budget Meeting with headquarters. The numbers cover everything—from costs to pricing assumptions.

In all their assumptions, the people in the field are operating with one simple goal, albeit unstated: to minimize their risk and maximize their bonus. In other words, their underlying, galvanizing mission is to come up with targets that they absolutely, positively think they can hit.

Why? Because in most companies, people are rewarded for hitting budget. Missing your budget gets you a stick in the eye or worse. So of course people want to keep their budget numbers as low as possible.

> The people in the field are operating with one simple goal, albeit unstated: to minimize their risk and maximize their bonus.

No wonder their budgets are filled with layer after layer of conservatism.

Meanwhile, back at headquarters, senior managers are also preparing for the Big Budget Meeting. Their agenda, however, is the exact opposite of the field. They're rewarded for increased earnings, and so what they want from the budget review at every business is significant growth in sales and profits.

Now fast-forward to the Big Budget Meeting itself.

The two sides meet in a windowless room with a whole day set aside for what everyone knows will be an unpleasant wrestling match.

The field makes its presentation with a fat deck of PowerPoint slides, and the story is invariably dire. Despite reports of a pretty good economy, there are reasons to believe this particular business environment is going to be very difficult. "The competition has just brought a new plant online, and with its excess supply, there will be enormous pricing pressure," they might say. Later in the meeting, you get: "Raw material costs and inflation pressures are severe. In order to meet these challenges, we need new cost-reduction programs that require $10 million in additional resources."

The final pronouncement from the business managers usually goes something like this: "To be optimistic—*very* optimistic—earnings will likely grow only 6 percent."

Headquarters, needless to say, has its own view of the situation, and it is decidedly not dire. The economy is strong. GDP is estimated to rise steadily all year. Orders are up everywhere else in the company. The main competition has a big asbestos lawsuit against it that will distract management. The business can get the cost reductions with $5 million in new programs, and earnings should grow 12 percent.

You know what goes on during this marathon—the grumbling and groaning, the probing and data quoting, the back and forth and back and forth again. On occasion, it can get contentious, especially if a senior person has worked within the business earlier in his career. He'll throw out anecdotes about how they used to do it in the old days and accuse the field of lowballing. "I know where you're hiding it. I used to park reserves in there too," he might insist. "Now give it up."

The grappling concludes—finally and inevitably—when the sides split the difference. The field gets $7.5 million in resources and a budget with a commitment for 9 percent earnings growth.

Before the field packs up to leave, everyone somberly shakes hands. The mood is resigned. For all involved, the unspoken vibe in the room is: we didn't get what we wanted or what was right.

That pall lasts right up until the moment the field team pulls out of the driveway. Then the high-fiving begins.

"Those stiffs wanted us to deliver 12 percent, and we only have to hand them 9!" the people in the field exclaim. "Thank God we dodged that bullet!"

The headquarters team is also feeling pretty good about themselves. "Those sandbaggers only wanted to give us 6 percent," they crow. "Did you see where they were hiding earnings? We let them off with 9 percent. They'll deliver that, and probably more, but with their 9 and what we've got from the other businesses, we'll have enough."

Soon thereafter, the Negotiated Settlement gets officially approved, and the field and headquarters make their peace over its targets. They tell each other, "Well, we can live with the numbers this year. We guess they're OK."

When the end of the year rolls around, the awful ritual completes itself. Most often, the field hits or beats their targets and gets their bonuses, and of course headquarters congratulates them. Job well done!

Everyone is happy, but they shouldn't be. In this minimaliza-tion exercise, there has been little or no discussion about what could have been.

EVERYONE MAKE NICE

The second budgeting dynamic that saps value is the **Phony Smile.**

Again, people in the field spend a couple of weeks coming up with a detailed budget plan. Compared to the Negotiated Settle-ment approach to budgeting, the sadder part of this dynamic is that often, Phony Smile plans are filled with good ideas and excit-ing opportunities. The people in the field have bold dreams about what they can do—make an acquisition, for example, or develop new products—given the right amount of investment. They're eager to expand their business's horizons, but they need help from the mother ship.

To make their case, the managers in the field prepare the usual stacks of slides. Since retiring from GE, I've seen such presenta-tions with as many as 150 pages! Every competitive angle is covered, and usually overly so. Typically, these presentations are ev-idence of painstaking labor, wrought with angst over minutiae and born of long nights of building spreadsheets that contain precision to the last dollar. It's likely that nobody actually enjoys putting together these slide packs, but when they're done, along with exhaustion, the team understandably feels an enormous sense of pride and ownership.

On the anointed day, the team, led by a leader we'll call Sara, travels to headquarters. And there, again in a darkened room, they present their case, slide by slide, to the senior group.

When the show is over, the lights come up, and for a few minutes, the managers and the field people engage in rather pleasant chitchat. It goes like this:

"I see you expect Acme Corp. to build another plant. That's very interesting. They almost went bankrupt in '88," one senior manager musters the energy to say.

"Well, they were bought two years ago, and they've come back strong," Sara quickly answers.

"Very interesting. Very interesting," comes the vague reply from a headquarters heavy.

"And I see that you're expecting the cost of natural gas to hold steady for the first six months," another headquarters person might offer up as evidence he was listening.

"Absolutely!" Sara responds. "We don't see any change in that pricing."

"Hmm . . . interesting. . . . Yes, interesting. . . ."

Finally, after a few more perfunctory exchanges, it's over. The top team smiles brightly and says, "Nice job! Thanks for coming in! Have a safe trip home!" And pretty convinced that they did OK, the field people smile back brightly and go away.

Then there's the meeting after the meeting.

That's when the members of the top team sit around talking about how much they are *really* going to get from this business. The reality is, headquarters already knows how they are allocating the company's investment dollars, and they know exactly what revenue and earnings numbers they expect in return from each business. Those decisions, they believe, belong at headquarters, where managers can see the whole picture, pick priorities, and divvy up the goods appropriately.

A few days later, Sara gets a call from a lower-level staff person at headquarters telling her that her business will get about 50 percent of what was asked for at the Phony Smile meeting, and the earnings budget number will be 20 percent higher than the one they submitted.

What a kick in the stomach! Instantly, Sara is enraged for a slew of reasons at once: Headquarters just didn't listen! All that work for nothing! No one explains anything around here! And worst of all, now there won't be enough money for all the things we should be doing.

The next day, Sara goes back to her people for *their* meeting after the meeting. Together, they all rail against the injustice and mystery of the corporate edict.

And then, without meaning to, Sara makes matters worse. To appease her team, she takes the money from corporate, now much less than they had asked for, and she evenly parcels it out, a bit to manufacturing, a bit to marketing, a bit to sales, and so on. Of course, Sara would be smarter to place her bets on one or two programs, but that rarely happens in these situations. People stuck in the Phony Smile budget game get bitter. Too often, they lose their sense of commitment to the company and forget how excited they were about their original proposals. They just take the money from corporate and spread it like crumbs.

My argument here is not with a senior team allocating resources. That's their job because they have a strong, informed understanding of what each business can realistically deliver. The trouble arises when headquarters is secretive about the process, when they don't explain the rationale behind their decisions.

But like the Negotiated Settlement dynamic, the Phony Smile usually concludes with everyone shrugging off the whole enervating event—it's just business, right? And the next year, they start it all over again.

■

A BETTER WAY

Now, you may be wondering, "If companies manage to hit their numbers and pay bonuses with either the Negotiated Settlement or Phony Smile approaches to budgeting—as flawed as they are— why mess with them? At least they deliver."

The problem is: they often deliver only a fraction of what they could, and they take all the fun out of setting financial goals. Yes, this annual event can be fun—and it should be.

Imagine a system of budgeting where both the field and head-quarters have a shared goal: to use the budgeting process to ferret out every possible opportunity for growth, identify real obstacles in the environment, and come up with a plan for stretching dreams to the sky. Imagine a system of budgeting that is not internally focused and based on hitting fabricated targets, but one that throws open the shutters and looks outside.

The budgeting system that I'm talking about is linked to the strategic planning process described in the last chapter, in that it is focused on two questions:

■ How can we beat last year's performance?

■ What is our competition doing, and how can we beat them?

If you focus on these two questions, the budgeting process becomes a wide-ranging, anything-goes dialogue between the field and headquarters about opportunities and obstacles in the real world. Through these discussions, both sides of the table jointly come up with a growth scenario that is not negotiated or imposed and cannot really be called a budget at all. It is an *operating plan* for the next year, filled with aspiration, primarily directional, and containing numbers that are mutually understood to be targets, or put another way, numbers that could be called "best efforts."

Unlike a conventional budget, with its numbers cast in concrete, an operating plan can change as conditions change. A division or business can have two or three operating plans over the course of a year, adjusted as needed through realistic dialogue about business challenges. Such flexibility frees an organization from the shackles of a budget document that has become irrelevant—or even downright dead—because of changing market circumstances.

At this point, you might be thinking, "Yeah, yeah, this approach sounds great, but what about my bonus?"

That's a good question. It's the key question, in fact. And the answer is that this operating plan process can occur under only one condition:

> *Compensation for individuals and businesses is not linked to performance against budget. It is linked primarily to performance against the prior year and against the competition, and takes real strategic opportunities and obstacles into account.*

For many companies, this condition would involve a radical change. People have been trained for years and years to hit their budget numbers no matter what, and managers have rigidly rewarded those who did and punished those who didn't, no matter what.

That was the company I grew up in for twenty years, and largely the company that I inherited when I became CEO. Over the years, I was at the receiving end of plenty of Phony Smile meetings, and participated in dozens if not hundreds of Negotiated Settlement meetings on both sides of the table.

But as GE's culture became more infused with candor, transforming its budgeting process became more realistic. Eventually, we were able to move our businesses away from budgets with rock-hard targets and toward operating plans filled with stretch goals.

At this point, you might be thinking, "Yeah, yeah, this approach sounds great, but what about my bonus?"

That transformation took time—several years, at least. Along the way, I promoted the change as often as I could.

In 1995, for instance, Appliances was having a brutal go of it. Competitors were churning out high-quality products at very low prices, and our team was struggling like crazy to catch up. They were innovating with several new product introductions of their own and improving manufacturing processes, getting more productive by the day. Still, at the end of the year, their earnings were 10 percent below internal expectations and about flat with the previous year.

At the same time, Plastics was having a great year. Their market took off, and shortages of material quickly developed, making it a seller's market when it came to pricing. Their earnings jumped 25 percent, about ten points higher than the operating plan called for.

Back in the old budgeting days, Plastics would have gotten the big bonuses and Appliances would have gotten a lump of coal. But with the new approach, both businesses got increased payouts that were about equal in amount.

At our annual management meeting that year with five hundred of the company's top people, I went out of my way to make this story widely known. In fact, I made a point of telling it in my keynote speech to the group.

Yes, I said, Appliances' earnings were below plan and showed no rise over the previous year. But the business's performance—in a brutal environment—was really impressive compared to its closest competitors, Whirlpool and Maytag, who had done worse than we had.

As for Plastics, yes, their earnings had beaten the plan, but it had been a layup. We cared more that one of their competitors had earnings growth of 30 percent and another had a 35 percent rise. We could have done better and we didn't. In fact, we hadn't been aggressive enough on price—a mistake, pure and simple.

You might expect that people in Plastics resented the bonuses paid out to Appliances, or that they wanted and expected more from headquarters for their results. But by that time, the reinvented approach to budgeting had permeated the organization. People understood how it worked, and how it made all of us better by looking outside the company to judge our performance. After all, what good is beating targets you set in a windowless room? The real world has its own numbers, and they're all that matters.

GETTING IT GOING

As I said, it took years for this approach to financial planning to take hold at GE, but I know a case where it was up and running within two—and in China to boot, where modern management techniques in general are just taking hold.

It happened at 3M, the industrial conglomerate, which has been doing business in China for some twenty years.

To an outside observer, 3M's track record in China has always been solid. In fact, when Jim McNerney became CEO in January 2001, the company's Chinese businesses were posting 15 percent annual growth, about three times the company's average. For years at budget time, the Chinese team had been congratulated for this level of performance and sent on its way.

But after his years of experience with the impact of stretch goals and operating plans at GE—where his last job was CEO of Aircraft Engines—Jim decided to transform budgeting at 3M, including its foreign operations.

> What good is beating targets you set in a windowless room?

His first step, however, was *not* to install the stretch approach. "You can't go to stretch directly," he told me recently. "You have to get a culture of accountability first." In other words, people have to mean what they say, deliver their operational and strategic commitments, and take responsibility if that doesn't happen.

In the past, 3M had something of the Negotiated Settlement approach to budgeting, but with an added twist of benign neglect. The company called budgets "improvement plans," which, as Jim notes, "had little commitment attached to them." Headquarters and each business unit would come up with agreed-upon numbers during the budgeting ritual, and then amicably part ways until the same event the next year. In the meantime, goals would routinely be missed, and people at headquarters might have gotten angry, but nothing happened.

Over the past four years, as Jim and his team have changed the 3M culture, the "improvement plan" approach to budgeting has all but ended. There is new candor and trust—and accountability— throughout the organization. Enough, in fact, that Jim felt it was possible to introduce the stretch approach.

One of its earliest believers was Kenneth Yu, managing director of 3M China and a 3M employee for more than thirty years, first in Hong Kong, then in Taiwan, and now in Shanghai. In his early fifties and a veteran of good results under the old budgeting system, Kenneth was an unlikely candidate to embrace such a major change. But he had, as Jim describes it, "a total reawakening" as to how business could be done.

"Once Kenneth realized that the stretch approach had a safety net, he really bought into the idea that stretching, even without getting there, could be a whole lot better than the old game," Jim recalls.

Rather than come to Jim with the usual conservative growth plan and then beating it, Kenneth presented an operating plan to catapult the China operation to 40 percent annual growth. It involved bold, wide-open thinking about possibilities. For 2002, Kenneth proposed increasing 3M's R & D investment in China in order to introduce many local product adaptations, and promoted new plant investment to support rapid growth.

In three years, 3M's business in Greater China has grown from $520 million to $1.3 billion, with ambitious plans for the future.

This does not mean, of course, that stretch has totally taken hold at 3M. Jim says people are still getting used to the change, but they have definitely come to see that the company now celebrates and rewards people who think big. Today, "budgeting" at 3M is not about delivering good-enough plans and beating them. It's about having the courage and zeal to reach for what can be done.

Doesn't that sound like more fun than budgeting? And it works better too.

A WORD OF CAUTION

Before we finish up this chapter, I just want to make sure that I am not making this change sound too easy. Experience has shown me that while most people take to reinvented budgeting with enthusiasm, there are always a few diehards who do not and with their actions try to undermine it. Usually, these people are too steeped in tradition to let go of the old link between targets and bonuses.

Sometimes they are just jerks. But whatever the reason, I would be a Pollyanna if I did not acknowledge that these types of managers haunt every company that switches over to the stretch approach. At GE, we never found or converted them all, but we never stopped trying.

> While most people take to reinvented budgeting with enthusiasm, there are always a few diehards who try to undermine it.

Here's the modus operandi of these types: At the outset of the financial planning cycle, they appear to heartily buy into the new program and ask their people for big stretch goals. Then, without openly admitting it, they take the team's stretch goal and use it as a commitment number—an old-fashioned budget target. When the end of the year rolls around, these managers take terrible advantage of their people. They identify the stretch number as the target, and they nail the team for not hitting it.

This behavior stinks, and it sets the whole process back by demonstrating to the people in the trenches that they can't trust it. Next time when they're asked to dream, you can be sure their dreams will be very small.

Part of the transformation process to a nonbudgeting company is to find the managers who pull this bait and switch. Call them on it, and take whatever action you need to make sure it doesn't happen again.

When I talk to business audiences about the right way to budget, regardless of industry or country. I often get the same question: "The budgeting process in my company is too entrenched to change the way you describe. What can I do?"

My answer is not to give up. It's too important.

It may be awkward at first, but change begins when you start talking, and one conversation leads to another and then another. Everyone knows about the Negotiated Settlement and Phony Smile dynamics, they've lived them, and they know that they take the energy and reality out of budgeting. So when you bring them up, people may not know how to deal with it—but they can't just walk away.

The subject will resonate.

The fact is, there is a way to approach budgeting that blows it up and puts something much better in its place. It's a system that can take a Chinese industrial business with modest annual growth and transform it into an enterprise growing 40-plus percent a year. It can inspire people to keep innovating and becoming more productive every day, even when global competition seems insurmountable. It can take people who once sat *across* the table from one another during debates about nothing less than the company's direction and future and put them on the *same* side.

Very simply, the right "budget" process can change the way companies compete.

People usually groan when you mention budgeting—it's a necessary evil.

It doesn't have to be. It shouldn't be. But the change to a better way has to start somewhere—how about with you?

13

Organic Growth

SO YOU WANT TO
START SOMETHING NEW

O NE OF THE MOST EXHILARATING things about being in business is starting something new from inside something old—launching a product line or service, for example, or moving into a new global market. Not only is it a blast, it is one of the most rewarding paths to growth.

Another route to growth, of course, is through mergers and acquisitions, which we'll look at in the next chapter. Here we're going to talk about companies getting bigger organically.

Now, starting something new from within an established company is easier said than done for one good reason.

It requires managers to act against many of their perfectly reasonable instincts.

Few typical corporate managers, for instance, have the burning desire to send their best people to start up a manufacturing facility halfway around the world or to pour R & D dollars into a risky new technology. Nor do many have the urge to give new ventures, at home or abroad, a lot of leeway.

But to give any new venture a fighting chance to succeed, you *do* have to set it free (somewhat). And you *do* need to spend more money on it and cheer louder and longer for it than may feel comfortable.

Managing a $50,000 new product line in its first year is harder than managing a $500 million business in its twentieth year. And going global is just as challenging. New businesses and new global ventures alike have few customers or routines. Neither has a handy road map to profitability. That's why they need special treatment.

Too often they don't get it.

Over the years, I saw countless new businesses launched within GE and many expand globally. Recently, I have been involved with several companies in their quests to grow, and in Q & A sessions, I've heard people describe their difficulties in starting new ventures.

It seems there are three common mistakes companies make in launching something.

First, they don't flood start-up ventures with adequate resources, especially on the people front.

> Companies have a habit of sending expendable bodies to run new ventures. It's nuts. For a new business to succeed, it has to have the best people in charge, not the most available.

Second, they make too little fanfare about the promise and importance of the new venture. In fact, instead of cheering about the potential of the new venture, they tend to hide it under a bushel.

Third, they limit the new venture's autonomy.

All of these mistakes are completely understandable. Starting a new venture, be it a new voice-over-IP device or a call center in India, means making a bet. Most people instinctively hedge their bets, even as they place them. The irony is that such hedging can doom a new venture to failure. When launching something new, you have to go for it—"playing not to lose" can never be an option.

Here are three guidelines for making organic growth a winning proposition. Not surprisingly, they are antidotes to the mistakes just listed above.

> **GUIDELINE ONE:** Spend plenty up front, and put the best, hungriest, and most passionate people in leadership roles.

Companies tend to size their investments in new ventures according to the size of the venture's revenues or profits starting out. That's shortsighted, to be polite about it. Investments in R & D and marketing should be sized as if the venture is going to be a big winner. And people selection should be made with the same mind-set.

Speaking of people, companies have a habit of sending expendable bodies to run new ventures: The old manufacturing guy whose children have grown and is looking for added adventure in the two years before retirement is sent to a foreign location to start up a new plant. An OK but unexciting manager who has been quietly running another business is given a new product to launch.

It's nuts. For a new business to succeed, it has to have the best people in charge, not the most available.

In fact, leaders of new ventures have to have some of the "garage entrepreneur" in them. They need to have all four Es and plenty of P.

One thing is for sure: new businesses with limited resources and good-enough people stay small.

I can think of two cases when we almost killed new ventures within GE by underspending on resources and people.

PET is a cancer-detecting imaging technology that was selling about $10 million in equipment in 1990 from within the huge medical systems business.

And in 1992, we had a $50 million business making small jet engines. It was practically invisible compared to the multibillion-dollar business we had in big commercial engines.

Neither PET nor Small Jet Engines got much in terms of time, attention, or investment from their divisions or headquarters, and they languished. Luckily for Small Jet Engines, it had a VP named Dennis Williams, who believed in the business and somehow managed to keep it alive. But PET came into our gun sights only when we tried to sell it—and no one would buy.

Market conditions eventually brought us to our senses, and only then did we begin to invest heavily in both businesses. Today, they are doing well. PET is a $400 million business. Small Jet Engines has gotten an enormous boost from the growth in commuter airlines. Its sales are about $1.4 billion, and it is the fastest-growing part of GE's commercial engine business.

We got resource allocation a lot closer to right with China.

Back in the early '90s, Asia for GE was mainly about Japan, where we had revenues of about $2 billion. But we knew that Asia was a lot more than Japan and that we had to get into China.

So we took one of our best leaders and put him in charge. It was Jim McNerney, whom I mentioned in the previous chapter on budgeting.

At the time, Jim was the CEO of GE's $4 billion industrial systems business in Plainville, Connecticut. He was, in every way, a big hitter. He had twenty-five thousand people reporting to him in one of our mainstay businesses, a comfortable office, and a well-trained, hand-picked staff. Most people in the company believed that Jim had a very promising future with GE and that his next step would be vice-chairman, at the very least.

Instead, we put him in an office in Hong Kong with an assistant and a few employees.

The impact was immediate. Jim was like the Pied Piper. As soon as headquarters raised the bar and sent someone to China who was widely acknowledged to be a star, all of our businesses started sending their best people too.

Jim and his team launched GE businesses in China into the $4 billion operation they are today. He has since gone on to do a great job as CEO of 3M.

> **GUIDELINE TWO**: Make an exaggerated commotion about the potential and importance of the new venture.

When we sent Jim McNerney to Asia, we didn't just send out a press release and let the news go at that. Instead, we made a hoopla about the event. I ranted and raved about Jim's appointment at every senior management meeting, and when I was in the field visiting businesses, I made sure everyone got the message that GE was going aggressively into China and we had to send our best. Jim was the perfect role model for the point I was trying to convey.

In the same way, when NBC launched the cable channels MSNBC and CNBC, I gave them an inordinate amount of attention in every public setting I could find. At NBC business reviews, for instance, I would focus much more intently on these cable presentations than on NBC's West Coast team promoting their new network comedy shows. I didn't ask questions about the stars appearing in NBC's next promising big hit. Instead, to demonstrate my support, I would ask the executives of MSNBC and CNBC—neither one then posting any revenues to speak of—about subscriber growth and content.

Start-ups need cheerleading—constant and loud.

Cheerleading, however, isn't just about senior managers making noise. It's also about giving new ventures sponsorship. This may mean breaking old bureaucratic norms, but with a new venture, organizational visibility is critical. For instance, new ventures should report at least two levels higher than sales would justify. If possible, they should report directly to the CEO. At the very least, they should always have a special place on the CEO's priority list.

Admittedly, there is one big problem with making a huge scene about a new venture.

How dumb you look if it fails.

You can end up looking very dumb. That is part of the gamble, and I'm not going to minimize it. It was widely reported how strongly I supported the XFL, the new extreme football league that NBC launched in 2000. As a business opportunity, I couldn't think of a thing wrong with it, and I said so, over and over again! When the XFL failed after a painful twelve-week season, losing $60 million for the company, the press had real fun with it, making me and Dick Ebersol, the XFL's other vocal sponsor, the butt of plenty of jokes. Fortunately, the hammering ended relatively quickly.

So what's the bottom line here?

> New ventures should report at least two levels higher than sales would justify. If possible, they should report directly to the CEO.

Even with the risk, go ahead and make a scene for new ventures—an exaggerated scene. You'll doom them if you don't. If the venture fails anyway, recognize your part. Don't point fingers. You believed, but it didn't work out.

If the venture wins, relish the team's success. It will feel great.

GUIDELINE THREE: Err on the side of freedom; get off the new venture's back.

This is a guideline that is not really a guideline, because when it comes to how much autonomy to give a new venture, there is no formula, only an iterative process. The main thing to remember is: throughout that process, give a new venture more freedom than you might like, not less.

Finding the right balance between supporting, monitoring, and smothering a new venture is not unlike when you send your kid off to college. Now that he's on his own, you want nothing more than for him to take full responsibility for his life. You also don't want him to flunk out or carouse too heavily. And so you begin a game of give-and-take. At first, you visit and call a lot. You frequently inquire about tests, new friends, and weekend activities.

When everything seems to be running smoothly, you let out the rope.

When the first C minus comes home, you pull it in.

When the next report card is all As and Bs, you let it out.

When you get a call from the campus police because of an unfortunate drinking episode, you really crank it in.

That's how it goes with new ventures, except that you can't replace your kid. You can—and should—replace a new venture's leaders if too much cranking is required.

Ultimately, you want this iterative process to lead to a new venture having more and more autonomy.

Now, we all know that in large companies, brand-new ventures have neither the results nor the political capital to get their own shops. In small companies, it's too easy to fold a new business into the core.

But autonomy gives people ownership and pride. In ideal situations, new ventures with strong leaders should have all their own tools, like their own R & D, sales, and marketing teams. They should be allowed to place their own audacious bets on people and strategies.

My commitment to autonomy for new ventures has its roots in my earliest days as the venture manager for Noryl, the new plastic that had about as much promise as mud when we started experimenting with it in 1964. But as soon as the team got Noryl's chemical composition to work and eliminated its technical flaws, I fought for my own operation.

The higher-ups thought I should use the pool sales force and let Noryl be sold in the basket along with GE's other plastics. But I believed that no salesperson in the world would push Noryl, which was landing $500 orders in those days, when he had Lexan to sell in $50,000 batches to Boeing or IBM. As far as I was concerned, you could sell Lexan sitting in an armchair—Noryl needed maniacs running around! I made this case with enough fervor and persistence—in other words, obnoxiousness—that after a couple of years my bosses relented.

When Noryl finally got on its own, it took off—all of us felt and acted like entrepreneurs, albeit with a big bank in our back pocket. Over the next two years, Noryl grew by leaps and bounds. In 1969, when I was promoted to run the entire Plastics division, I kept Noryl as a separate business because—even with its successful launch and rapid growth—I thought it would still benefit from autonomy. In fact, Noryl (now a billion-dollar business) wasn't folded into the Plastics marketing and sales operation for fifteen years.

IF YOU'RE RUNNING THE VENTURE . . .

The guidelines I've just listed are directed in many ways at the executives sponsoring a new venture. But they have important implications for the venture's actual leaders—the people running the new show.

Consider the first guideline, about spending on resources and people. More often than not, you will find you are not getting enough money from the mother ship, nor are you getting the best people. What do you do?

Fight like hell. Get yourself in front of senior management and make your case. And work the personnel front on your own. Ferret out good candidates both inside and outside the company, and make your pitch directly to them. Just go get the best people, even if you have to throw a few elbows.

Now about hoopla. You need to realize it's a two-edged sword. You want it in order to get commitment from those above you. But when you get that commitment, it is sure to tick off your peers. In particular, established businesses with fat profits absolutely hate it when little upstarts with no profits get a disproportionate amount of company resources and attention. They are certain they need more resources and would spend them more wisely than your risky little venture.

> You will find you are not getting enough money from the mother ship, nor are you getting the best people. Fight like hell—even throw a few elbows.

> **You are always going to want more autonomy than you get. Your best shot is to earn it.**

Their attitude may annoy you, but the last thing you need is to have anyone in the company rooting for you to fail. Recognize that resentment toward new ventures is natural. Keep your mouth shut if it bothers you. Humility will serve you well with your peers; someday soon, you'll need their support.

Finally, about autonomy. The fact of the matter is, you are always going to want more of it than you get.

The best way to get autonomy is to earn it. If you play by the rules, you'll get your freedom soon enough. The spotlight of the company is on you. Don't blow it by overreacting if you feel the early constraints put upon you are stifling. They are just part of the process of your "parents" letting go.

THE PERFECT STORM

You rarely see all three guidelines at work at once, but when you do, watch out. You get a "perfect storm" like the Fox News Channel.

Fox News was launched in 1996 by Rupert Murdoch, an entrepreneur's entrepreneur, in spite of being the owner and CEO of News Corporation, a multibillion-dollar conglomerate. Rupert wanted to get into cable news and was willing to spend whatever it took.

To succeed as a cable channel, you need two things. First, you need to get subscribers from distribution providers like Comcast and Time Warner. Second, you need to get attractive content so that enough subscribers will actually watch you—the key to ad dollars.

Rupert's first step was to hire someone to run the new venture. He found a match made in heaven with Roger Ailes. After running several successful political campaigns, Roger had worked at NBC for three years, putting the cable channel CNBC on the map. He had just launched another cable channel for GE called America's Talking. But he lost it when GE used the assets of America's Talking as its contribution to creating MSNBC, a fifty-fifty joint venture with Microsoft, which put up the cash.

Roger left NBC in frustration, but Rupert was on his trail immediately. He believed that Roger was the perfect new venture manager—bursting with ideas, energy, and passion—plus the burning desire to beat the company that had taken his "baby" away.

With the right leader in place, Rupert set to work getting subscribers. He paid well above market rates to get the subscriber access the channel needed. Meanwhile, Roger was hiring the best talent—Brit Hume from ABC, Neil Cavuto and a flock of others from CNBC, and the highly rated commentator Bill O'Reilly.

As it was all happening, Rupert continuously trumpeted the new venture inside the company, making it unambiguous that he was behind Fox News through thick and thin. In the outside world, both Rupert and Roger made it so that you couldn't open a paper or turn on a TV without hearing, in some form, about the relentless advance of Fox.

Fox News is an example of everything going right at a new venture: a high bar for people, outsize spending on resources, and lots of noise about it all. Its results tell the story. Fox quickly beat MSNBC and eventually surpassed the longtime cable news leader, CNN.

Legendary entrepreneurs like Henry Ford, Dave Packard, and Bill Gates are undeniably examples of the excitement and glory of starting something new from scratch and watching it grow to astonishing proportions.

But in each of your companies, opportunities of every size and variety await.

Grab them. Pick passionate, driven people to lead them, resource them with everything you've got, and give them oxygen to breathe.

Growth is great, and in business, it doesn't always have to start in a garage. There is nothing like the fun and the sheer thrill of starting something new—especially from inside something old.

14

Mergers and Acquisitions

DEAL HEAT AND
OTHER DEADLY SINS

Y OU'VE SEEN THE BIG PARTY when two companies
announce their merger. There's the early morning press conference on CNBC, the chatter and the buzz, the vigorous pump-
ing of hands, the TV lights glaring, the glossy banner proclaiming
the new company's name. It's all there but the confetti.

And then there are the stars of the show—the merging CEOs
grinning widely, slapping each other on the back, and talking
about a brave new world of synergies, cost savings, and increased
shareholder value. At particularly jovial merger announcements,
the CEOs wrap each other in a big bear hug, like Steve Case and
Jerry Levin on that fateful day of the AOL–Time Warner deal.

With the excitement, there's exhaustion too, and sometimes
you don't have to look very hard to see it in the faces of the CEOs
at center stage. They have been working around the clock for
weeks, if not months, fighting over every last nickel, not to mention who will run what.

But usually, all you see at merger announcements is elation and relief. The battle is over, and now it's time to reap the deal's rewards.

In reality, as the veteran of any merger will tell you, the battle has just begun, and the deal's rewards won't come without a lot of blood, sweat, and tears.

If the first day of the merger is a big party, on day two, the cleanup begins. For people on the acquiring side of the deal, mountains of work stand in front of them, and while they may be pumped with optimism, there is always an undercurrent of nervousness in the room. Every deal promises cost savings, and even if you've been part of the deal team, working night and day grinding out numbers to justify doing it, a little piece of you has to wonder if the savings you've articulated will come to mean the loss of your job, or that of your boss, or your best friend down the hall, or the employee you've been mentoring for a year.

For the acquired, the nervousness in the room isn't an undercurrent, it's a tidal wave. Everyone is terrified of layoffs. But even if you think your job is safe, life has just gotten very complex. A merger can feel like a death. Everything you've worked for, every relationship you've forged—they're suddenly null and void. Your sense is that nothing will ever be the same again.

> A merger can feel like a death. Everything you've worked for, every relationship you've forged—they're suddenly null and void.

On top of it all, day two media coverage is filled with business journalists and Wall Street analysts questioning the rationale for the deal and reminding everyone that many mergers fail.

Mergers do fail. In particular, it is a hard road for mergers forged primarily to capture industry convergence benefits or revenue synergies.

It's easier to succeed when a merger is based on cost reductions from the combination, with any upside from revenue synergies considered a pure bonus. But either way, merger success is never a layup.

And yet companies persist in merging—and they should.

In the last chapter, we looked at why organic growth is great. Every company must have the patience to consistently focus on and invest in the innovation that drives it.

But mergers and acquisitions give you a faster way to profitable growth. They quickly add geographical and technological scope, and bring on board new products and customers. Just as important, mergers instantly allow a company to improve its players—suddenly there are twice as many people "trying out" for the team.

All in all, successful mergers create a dynamic where $1 + 1 = 3$, catapulting a company's competitiveness literally overnight.

You just have to do it right.

This chapter is about that process, and it is intended for everyone involved, from the people making the deal to those who are affected by it several layers away. Over my career at GE, I was involved in well over a thousand acquisitions and mergers, and over the past three years, I have consulted with managers during several more.

Obviously, not every deal I've participated in has been a success. But most were, and over time, my batting average improved as I learned from the mistakes made in situations that did not work.

In the end, I've learned that merging successfully is about more than picking the right company to fit your strategy, laying out what plants you close and what product lines you combine, or how pretty your calculations of DCRR or IRR look.

Merging right is ultimately about avoiding seven pitfalls, by which I mean mistakes or errors in judgment. There may be other pitfalls out there, but in my experience, these seven are the most common. Sometimes they can kill a merger, but more often, they significantly slow it down or reduce its value or both.

Here they are in brief. Six are related to the acquiring company, and just one to the acquired.

■ The first pitfall is believing that a merger of equals can actually occur. Despite the noble intentions of those attempting them, the vast majority of MOEs self-destruct because of their very premise.

■ The second pitfall is focusing so intently on strategic fit that you fail to assess cultural fit, which is just as important to a merger's success, if not more so.

■ The third pitfall is entering into a "reverse hostage situation," in which the acquirer ends up making so many concessions during negotiations that the acquired ends up calling all the shots afterward.

■ The fourth pitfall is integrating too timidly. With good leadership, a merger should be complete within ninety days.

■ The fifth pitfall is the conqueror syndrome, in which the acquiring company marches in and installs its own managers everywhere, undermining one of the reasons for any merger—getting an influx of new talent to pick from.

■ The sixth pitfall is paying too much. Not 5 or 10 percent too much, but so much that the premium can never be recouped in the integration.

■ The seventh pitfall afflicts the acquired company's people from top to bottom—resistance. In a merger, new owners will always select people with buy-in over resisters with brains. If you want to survive, get over your angst and learn to love the deal as much as they do.

BEWARE DEAL HEAT

Before looking at the pitfalls in detail, it's worth pointing out one thing. Many of them happen for the same reason: deal heat.

I'm sure I don't need to illustrate this phenomenon in gruesome detail; you see it every time a company is hungry to buy and the pickings in the marketplace are relatively limited. In such situations, once an acquisition candidate is identified, the top people at the acquirer and their salivating investment bankers join together in a frenzy of panic, overreaching, and paranoia, which intensifies with every additional would-be acquirer on the scene.

Deal heat is completely human, and even the most experienced peo-

> Deal heat is completely human, and even the most experienced people fall under its sway.

ple fall under its sway. But its negative impacts during the M & A process should at least be minimized if you keep these seven common pitfalls in mind.

> The first pitfall is believing that a merger of equals can actually occur. Despite the noble intentions of those attempting them, the vast majority of MOEs self-destruct because of their very premise.

Every time I hear about a so-called merger of equals taking place, I cringe thinking about all the waste, confusion, and frustration coming down the pike for the two companies, which usually strike these deals with the best of intentions.

Yes, a merger of equals makes sense *conceptually.* Some companies are equal in size and strength, and yes, they should merge as such. Moreover, during heated negotiations—and almost all negotiations are that way at one point—the MOE concept cools the flames. Both sides can claim to be winners.

But something happens to the MOE concept in practice—people balk.

They balk, in fact, *because* of the very concept of equality. On both sides, people think, if we're so equal, why shouldn't we do it *our* way? *Your* way is certainly no better.

The result, ultimately, is that no one's way gets done.

I know this negative point of view about MOEs is not shared by everyone. My friend Bill Harrison, the CEO of JPMorgan Chase during its merger with Bank One, would tell you that in the financial industry, where the assets are the brains of proud, self-confident bankers, mergers of equals are a necessity "or else everyone would walk."

He may very well be right about this exception; the merger he is overseeing with Jamie Dimon—who will become CEO of the merged enterprise in 2006—is going very well. And Bill's merger experience supports his argument as well, starting with his Chemical Bank MOE with Manufacturers Hanover, followed by the MOE with Chase Manhattan and J. P. Morgan & Co.

Despite this success, I'm convinced that in the industrial world, meaning just about anyplace but banking and consulting, mergers of equals are doomed.

DaimlerChrysler is the most glaring example I can think of. Remember all the crowing back in 1998 about how the two companies were truly equivalent in all their facets; they just needed each other to globalize? No, no, the companies proclaimed, this wasn't an acquisition by a high-end, diversified German manufacturer of a low-end American car company—no way! It was two titans of industry entering a marriage made in heaven.

Some of this posturing was surely done in order to help the merger receive regulatory approvals. But some of it also had to do with ego. The directors on Chrysler's board certainly weren't going to admit they'd been bought by a foreign company, and their counterparts in Germany were probably no more thrilled with the prospect of being taken over by a bunch of Americans.

And so the companies tried to execute their MOE. What a mess! For two torturous years, the new company had Airbus A318s shuttling hordes of people between Detroit and Stuttgart a couple of times a week in an attempt to settle on mutually satisfactory operating processes, everything from the new company's culture to its financial systems, manufacturing sites, and leadership team. In the meantime, the "merged" organization bumped along in chaos while managers awaited direction and shareholders awaited the realization of all those promised global opportunities, synergies, and cost savings.

The ending of the story, of course, came in 2002, when newspapers reported what many people had long suspected—that the so-called merger of equals was, in fact, a pure and simple takeover. With the reality of the situation finally out there, Daimler could start running the show as it had intended all along. It installed one management system, one culture, and one strategy, and the company's performance pulled out of its post-"merger of equals" dive.

The point of this story is not to pile on DaimlerChrysler— that's been done enough in the past few years. It is to illustrate the virtual impossibility of two companies with two leaders blending seamlessly into one organization with double of everything and everyone.

Forget it. People at equal companies are probably less well equipped than anyone to merge. They may claim, during deal heat, to be entering into a perfect and equivalent union, but when the integration rolls around, who is taking charge must be established quickly. Someone has to lead and someone has to follow, or both companies will end up standing still.

> The second pitfall is focusing so intently on strategic fit that you fail to assess cultural fit, which is just as important to a merger's success, if not more so.

Once again, deal heat is behind a mistake that pervades many mergers, a thoughtful predeal analysis of cultural fit.

Now, most companies have a relatively straightforward time evaluating *strategic* fit. Most managers (and their consultants or bankers) have the tools and experience to assess whether two companies fill meaningful gaps for each other in terms of geography, products, customers, or technologies (or all of these), and by combining, create a company that, even with some inevitable overlap, is stronger and more competitive.

But *cultural* fit is trickier. Even with a cool head, the compatibility of two sets of value systems is a hard call. That's because lots of companies claim they have the same DNA—they believe in customer service, analytical decision making, learning, and transparency. They value quality and integrity, etcetera, etcetera. Their cultures are high performance, results driven, family friendly, and the like.

In reality, of course, companies have unique and often very different ways of doing business. But in deal heat, people end up assessing that every company is compatible. Cultural fit is declared, and the merger marches ahead.

That was clearly the case when GE bought Kidder Peabody, a disaster I mention in the chapter on crisis management and wrote about extensively in my last book. But just to briefly summarize here: a company with GE's core values of boundarylessness, teamwork, and candor could not merge with an investment bank with three values of its own: my bonus, my bonus, and my bonus.

For me, the lack of cultural fit was never more apparent than the day that the full magnitude of our problem—for lack of a better euphemism—was really hitting the fan. It was a Sunday afternoon in April 1994, and a team of GE and Kidder Peabody executives had been working around the clock since Friday evening to figure out why we had a $300 million shortfall in reported earnings. It was already pretty clear that a Kidder trader named Joe Jett had posted phantom trades, but what we needed to understand was why and how this behavior had slipped through the bank's controls, and just as importantly, its culture.

I joined the team that day to get their report, and over the next several hours we came to understand the situation and comprehend its consequences for the company. What blew my mind was that three times during the afternoon and evening, twice in the hallway and once in the men's room, the same thing happened. A Kidder Peabody manager on the team approached me, and with a worried look on his face, asked me in one way or another: "What's this going to do to our bonuses this year?"

Ten years later, it still sends me over the top.

In the end, with the sale of Kidder Peabody to Paine Webber and ultimately to UBS, the deal ended up being OK for our shareholders. But the truth is, we should have never put the organization through the trauma that merger wrought. When it was all over, I swore I would never buy another company unless its values were a close match with GE's or it could easily be brought into the GE fold.

I passed over some deals on the West Coast in the '90s because of my concerns about cultural fit. But I just couldn't go down that values-mismatch road again. The booming technology companies in California had their cultures—filled with chest thumping, bravado, and sky-high compensation.

By contrast, our software operations in places like Cincinnati and Milwaukee were made up of hard working, down-to-earth engineers, most of whom were graduates of state universities in the Midwest. These engineers were every bit as good as the West Coast talent, and they were paid well but not outrageously.

Frankly, I didn't want to pollute the healthy culture we had.

Every deal affects the acquiring company's culture in some way, and you have to think about that going in. The acquired company's culture can blend nicely with yours. That's the best case. Sometimes, a few of the acquired company's bad behaviors creep in and pollute what you've built. That's bad enough, but in the worst case, the acquired company's culture can fight yours all the way and delay the deal's value indefinitely.

That's why if you want your merger to work, don't just look at strategic fit. Cultural fit counts just as much.

> **The third pitfall is entering a "reverse hostage situation," in which the acquirer ends up making so many concessions during negotiations that the acquired company ends up calling all the shots afterward.**

Sometimes you want to own a company so badly, you end up letting it own you!

This dynamic is a real by-product of deal heat, and it's so common, it's frightening. Every time I talk about mergers with an experienced deal maker, it comes up.

I let it happen for the first (but unfortunately not the last) time in 1977, a few years before I became CEO. By that time, I was a veteran of dozens of mergers, so I should have known better, but I was so hot to acquire a California-based semiconductor company named Intersil that I couldn't bring myself to say no to any of their demands. The CEO was convinced that his company was operating smoothly, and he made it perfectly clear that while he liked GE's money, he didn't need its advice.

Before I knew what was happening in the negotiations, I was kissing this guy's rear end in every possible way. He wanted a special (oversize) compensation scheme for himself and his people, because that's the way it was in his industry. I said OK. He said we couldn't have GE people at his planning meetings. I said OK. He said we weren't allowed to ask his finance people to change their reporting system to match ours. I said OK.

I couldn't pay them $300 million fast enough.

What was I thinking?

Well, obviously, I wasn't. That's deal heat for you.

For several years, we muddled along, "merged" with Intersil. Frequently, when we made a suggestion about how the CEO might improve his operating systems—in HR, for instance—he would brush us off with, "You don't understand this industry. Just leave us alone and you'll get your earnings at the end of the quarter."

It was unpleasant, to put it mildly, and far from productive. I found that I could call their headquarters for information, but unless I asked my question in *exactly* the right way, I would get nothing but a head fake. GE managers stopped visiting because they were given such a cold reception. Technically, we owned the company, but for all intents and purposes, it was running the show.

Finally, we sold Intersil at about break-even. The only thing we got from the deal was an important lesson: don't ever buy a company that makes you its hostage.

The facts are, I was hamstrung with Intersil. We didn't have sufficient knowledge of semiconductors or a senior manager with enough stature and experience in the industry to replace the CEO, let alone his management team.

> Technically, we owned the company, but for all intents and purposes, it was running the show.

When we bought RCA ten years later, a similar situation rolled around, but we were prepared for it. During negotiations we were told that the head of NBC, Grant Tinker, was thinking of leaving. We certainly didn't have direct experience in managing TV networks, but I knew I had the bench strength in Bob Wright, the CEO of GE Capital at the time, to put a capable all-around leader in Grant's place quickly, should he depart. I tried hard to keep Grant but couldn't, and when he left, Bob stepped right in and eighteen years later is still running NBC.

A couple of years later, a potential hostage situation developed in one of NBC's divisions, News. Its leaders openly—you might say brazenly—questioned GE's ability to manage a journalistic enterprise and started throwing up the information firewalls that are so typical of this hostage dynamic. The division's manager, Larry Grossman, led the resistance and wasn't willing to put together a reasonable budget—that is, a budget where we made money. We asked him to leave and brought in Michael Gartner, who had significant journalistic and business experience. Michael took a lot of heat for starting the process of ridding NBC News of its entitlement mentality, and he did a good job, but unfortunately, he had to leave because of a crisis that occurred on his watch. (The NBC News show *Dateline* rigged a General Motors car to explode for a report on automobile safety; we publicly apologized for the incident.) We next turned to a CBS executive producer filled with journalistic credentials, Andy Lack. And it was Andy who really made NBC News into the high-integrity, highly profitable business it is today.

A final word on the reverse hostage dynamic. In the last moments of deal heat, companies often strike an earn-out package for the acquired company's founder or CEO, hoping they will get retention and great performance of an important player in return.

All they usually get is strife.

The reason is that earn-out packages most often motivate their recipients to keep things the same. They will want you to let them run the business the way they always did—that's how they know how to make the numbers. At every opportunity, they will block personnel changes, accounting systems consolidation, and compensation plans—you name it.

But an integration will never fully happen if there's someone blocking every change, especially if that person used to be the boss.

What can you do? Well, if you absolutely want to keep the former CEO or founder around for reasons of performance or continuity, cut your losses and forget an earn-out package. Offer a flat-rate retention deal instead—a certain sum for staying a certain period of time. That gives you the free hand you need and want to create a new company.

Earn-outs are just one aspect of the reverse hostage pitfall. Yes, sometimes you have to make concessions to get a company you really want.

Just don't make so many that, when the deal is sealed, your new acquisition can hold you up—with your own gun.

> **The fourth pitfall is integrating too timidly. With good leadership, a merger should be complete within ninety days.**

Return for a second to those partylike press conferences that accompany most merger announcements. Even in pure buyout situations, the CEOs promise a new partnership ahead. The two companies will cooperate, reach consensus, and then smoothly integrate.

Unfortunately, if partnership building isn't done right it can create paralysis. The two sides talk and talk and talk about culture, strategy, operations, titles, letterheads, and the rest—while the integration waits.

For a change, deal heat is not the culprit behind this pitfall. Instead, it is something more admirable—a kind of politeness and consideration for the other side's feelings. No one wants to be an obnoxious winner, pushing through changes without any appearance of discussion or debate. In fact, many acquirers want

> It is uncertainty that causes organizations to descend into fear and inertia. The objective should be full integration within ninety days of the deal's close.

to preserve whatever positive vibes existed at the end of negotiations, and they think moving slowly and carefully will help.

I'm not saying that acquirers shouldn't engage in debate about how the two companies will combine their ways of doing business—they absolutely should. In fact, the best acquirers are great listeners. They ask a lot of questions and take in all the information and opinions swirling around, and usually there are plenty.

But then they have to act. They have to make decisions about organizational structure, people, culture, and direction, and communicate those decisions relentlessly.

It is uncertainty that causes organizations to descend into fear and inertia. The only antidote is a clear, forward-moving integration process, transparent to everyone. It can be led by the CEO or an official integration manager—a top-level, widely respected executive of the acquirer—vested with the power of the CEO. The process should have a rigorous timetable with goals and people held accountable for them.

The objective made clear to everyone should be full integration within ninety days of the deal's close.

Every day after that is a waste.

A classic case of moving too cautiously—and paying the price for it—is New Holland's acquisition of Case Corporation in November 1999.

New Holland, a Dutch company with headquarters in London and a division of the giant Italian manufacturer Fiat, was the No. 3 player in the agriculture and construction equipment industry. Strategically, its managers were right in thinking that buying the Wisconsin-based Case, a solid No. 2, would allow it to finally take on the longtime industry leader, John Deere. Six billion dollars later, the deal was done.

Given the overlap in products and markets, you would think that the integration of these two companies would proceed swiftly, especially with those cost reductions so obvious. But New Holland was a company with a European parent, and its leaders were cautious about taking over an American enterprise on its own turf. Moreover, Fiat had paid a large premium for Case. That redoubled New Holland's trepidation. My old friend Paolo Fresco, the former vice-chairman of GE and at the time of the deal the chairman of Fiat, remembers the impact of the premium this way: "We didn't want to rock the boat or sink it with too many changes—we'd paid too much for the company to let that happen."

Fiat made the CEO of Case the head of the new company. In addition, most of the positions in the new organization were filled with Case managers, including COO and CFO.

Needless to say, the integration was rocky. The integration team did make one big decision—to keep two brands and two distribution systems. But most everything else was left up in the air.

When the market for farm equipment tanked in 2000, and with the integration stalled, the merged company tanked with it. In crisis mode, Fiat sent a new CEO, Paolo Monferino, to the United States, and he launched the integration the way it should have been on day one—quickly and decisively. The then-CEO of Case, Jean-Pierre Rosso, was made chairman. Ironically, Fiat had been afraid of making that change, but once it did, its managers quickly saw that Jean-Pierre was a perfect fit for the job and that he was happy to fill its role. He was strong with customers and an excellent industry statesman. All that timidity had been unnecessary!

When Congress passed the Farm Bill in 2002, the fully integrated CNH Global N.V., as the company was renamed, was positioned to take advantage of the market upsurge. But as Paolo Fresco notes, "We lost at least a year and maybe more because of our cultural uncertainty."

The Case New Holland story is not unique.

Back in 2000, GE tried to buy Honeywell—a deal, as some might recall, that never received European Union approval. But in the seven months that we awaited the regulatory OK, teams from both sides worked hard to merge the two companies.

Part of that process meant looking closely at the progress of Honeywell's own merger with AlliedSignal in 1999. The two companies had been together for a year at that point, so we expected to see notable progress.

Instead we were shocked to find that AlliedSignal and Honeywell managers were still "in discussions" about the merged company's values and behaviors, and both sides were still pining for the way they used to do things. The AlliedSignal people had an aggressive, numbers-driven culture. Honeywell's managers, however, liked their company's more consensus-based approach. The merged company's CEO, Mike Bonsignore, was disinclined to make a choice between the two ways of working. And so, well after the deal was signed, they still had two distinct companies operating side by side, with little integration.

Integrating at the right speed and with the right level of force-fulness will always be a balancing act. But when it comes to this pitfall, at least you know when you're off track. If ninety days have passed after the deal is closed and people are still debating important matters of strategy and culture, you've been too timid. It's time to act.

> The fifth pitfall is the conqueror syndrome, in which the acquiring company marches in and installs its own managers everywhere, undermining one of the reasons for any merger, getting an influx of new talent to pick from.

If acquirers are often too timid when it comes to integrating culture and operations, just as often they are too provincial when it comes to people selection.

By too provincial, I mean many acquirers automatically assume their people are the better players. They might be, but then again, they might not. In a merger, you have to approach your new personnel situation as if a headhunter had just delivered you a list of fresh players for about every position on your field. If you simply stick with the going-in team, you could lose better players for no good reason.

Oh sure, there's a *reason* for this behavior, but it's not good—it's just familiarity. Your own people are the devil you know—and they know you back. They understand your business and its culture. They know how work gets done *your* way.

To compound matters, it is simply harder to let go of friends than strangers. You know their families. You've been through good times and bad. You may have once told them they had long-term potential with the company. Some may have even worked on the deal.

It's hard to say, "You're not good enough anymore."

But you just have to remember, one of the great strategic benefits of a merger is that it allows acquirers to field a team from a bigger talent pool. That's a competitive advantage you cannot let pass. Just be very fair in your severance package and face into the deed, even if it means saying good-bye to "your own."

Without doubt, avoiding this pitfall can be challenging.

I cannot count the number of times we swooped into a deal and installed a GE manager in every leadership position. Most of the time, we were blissfully unaware of the potential that we had lost, but one time in particular, we couldn't be. The cost was too high.

It happened in 1988, when GE acquired a plastics business based in West Virginia from BorgWarner. It was the perfect bolt-on deal, or so we thought. The business we bought included an ABS engineering plastic product line. We had an engineering plastics business of our own, albeit in the higher-end products Lexan and Noryl. The GE Plastics team saw one immediate cost synergy. All they had to do, they figured, was to get rid of the BorgWarner sales force and push BorgWarner products through GE channels.

But there was a problem with the plan. Our sales force was a group of sharp, button-down types, accustomed to making a technical sale, convincing engineers to switch from metal to plastic. The BorgWarner sales force was a different breed. They sold their less expensive, more commodity-like product to purchasing agents the old-fashioned way—"belly to belly"—relying on personal relationships and hefty expense accounts.

———————————

Fight the conqueror syndrome. Think of a merger as a huge talent grab.

———————————

Our people weren't very good at that.

It was a disaster. We lost 90 percent of BorgWarner's sales force thanks to our conquering mind-set, and our ABS market share dropped about fifteen points. The acquisition stumbled, and it never did reach its full potential. ABS eventually turned out to be a worthwhile addition to the GE market basket, but at far too high a price.

We should have known better. Two years earlier, we had gotten the people selection process right when we acquired RCA.

On every level, the RCA deal was a win for us. With the acquisition of NBC, it met one of our strategic goals of moving into services, and at the same time, it strengthened our manufacturing base with the addition of three businesses we were already in, semiconductors, aerospace, and TV sets.

In all three of these industrial cases, we took advantage of the enhanced talent pool made possible by the acquisition and picked RCA leaders to lead the merged organizations.

GE's TV manufacturing business, for instance, was being run at the time of the deal by a smart young CEO who had come into the company through our business development staff. He was an MBA and former consultant, and although he had a bit of a swagger that he needed to be coached out of, his results were OK, and we generally thought he had long-term potential as a leader, which we'd told him more than once.

RCA's TV business also had a very good CEO in place—he was an old industry hand, with savvy and experience that our guy was clearly lacking. He too had satisfactory performance and was a clear candidate to run the larger, merged TV business. We could have picked either CEO.

But then there was Rick Miller. Rick was the CFO of RCA, and he was a big leaguer—smart, fast, full of creativity and energy. GE already had a great CFO, and it looked like Rick would need to be let go as a result.

As much as we wanted to help out our manager in TV by giving him the job, it just didn't make sense. We ended up suggesting that both the GE and RCA leaders find new jobs over the coming months, and gave Rick the CEO position. The two who left got great jobs elsewhere.

One last thought on people selection: in the most effective integrations, it starts during negotiations, in fact, before the deal is even signed. At JPMorgan Chase and Bank One, for instance, twenty-five of the top managers were selected by the time the merger was closed. That's on the far extreme of a best practice, but it is something to strive for.

The main point is, fight the conqueror syndrome. Think of a merger as a huge talent grab—a people opportunity that would otherwise take you years of searching and countless fees to head-hunters. Don't squander it. Make the tough calls and pick the very best—whatever side they're on.

The sixth pitfall is paying too much. Not 5 or 10 percent too much, but so much that the premium can never be recouped in the integration.

This pitfall is as old as the first marketplace. People are people; when they want something that someone else wants, all reason can disappear. Again, blame deal heat. This dynamic happens at yard sales, and it happens on Wall Street.

I'm not talking, by the way, about overpaying by a few percent-

> If you miss a merger on price, life goes on. There is no last best deal.

age points. That kind of premium can be made up for in a well-executed integration. And in fact, leaving a little money on the table can be helpful if it prevents the residual acrimony that can slow an integration.

I am talking, instead, about overpaying by so much you will never make it back.

The most egregious recent example of this dynamic has to be the Time Warner–AOL merger, in which a giant of a media company, with real assets and products, spent billions upon billions of dollars too much on a distribution channel with unclear competitive benefits. Amazingly, at the time, there was such excitement about an illusory notion called "convergence" that just about everyone jumped on the bandwagon. It was only after the failure of the deal was obvious that Ted Turner, a board member who was instrumental in promoting it, acknowledged on national TV that he had never liked the deal in the first place. By then, such "cool-headedness" was too late for Time Warner shareholders.

Of course, 2000 was a time when everybody was overpaying for everything. In the publishing industry, for example, the German media giant Gruner + Jahr paid an estimated $550 million for two properties, *Inc.* and the New Economy magazine *Fast Company*. At the time, the purchase scared the daylights out of other business magazines. But during the recession that followed, the premium could only be seen for what it was—excessive. No integration in the world would ever make up for it, a fact to which a crowd of deposed Gruner + Jahr executives would likely attest.

There is no real trick to avoiding overpayment, no calculation you can use as a rule of thumb to know when a sum is too much.

Just know that, except in very rare cases of industry consolidation, if you miss a merger on price, life goes on. There will be another deal.

There is no last best deal—there's just deal heat that makes it feel that way.

> The seventh pitfall afflicts the acquired company's people from top to bottom—resistance. In a merger, new owners will always select people with buy-in over resisters with brains. If you want to survive, get over your angst and learn to love the deal as much as they do.

In October 2004, there was a glowing article in my hometown paper, the *Boston Globe,* about a "thriving survivor" named Brian T. Moynihan. Brian started his career at Fleet Bank in its mergers and acquisitions division, then over fifteen-plus years, rose through the ranks to run its wealth management business, which is what he was doing when Bank of America bought Fleet in April 2004.

In the months after the merger was announced, many executives at Brian's level were shown the door—not Brian. He was promoted to run Bank of America's entire wealth and investment management division. In fact, Bank of America was so committed to Moynihan, it moved a hundred or so of its wealth managers from North Carolina to Boston to accommodate his leadership.

"It remains precisely unclear why Moynihan emerged on top while colleagues fell," the *Globe* said.

It wasn't unclear to me. All you had to do was look at a quote

> **Resisting a deal, no matter how scared, confused, or angry you are is usually suicidal to your career, not to mention your emotional well-being.**

in the same article from Alvaro de Molina, Bank of America's president of global corporate and investment banking.

Brian, he said, "was an immediate partner."

Which brings me to the one huge pitfall common to people at acquired companies: resistance. Resisting a deal, no matter how scared, confused, or angry you are is usually suicidal for your career, not to mention your emotional well-being.

Now, I don't know if Brian Moynihan ever felt scared, confused, or angry about the Fleet–Bank of America merger. And in a way, it doesn't matter because he clearly didn't show any of these emotions. Instead, he showed exactly what you should show if you want to survive a merger—enthusiasm, optimism, and thoughtful support.

Why? Because for an acquirer, there is nothing worse than laying down a boatload of money for a company, then walking through the front door to be greeted by a bunch of sour faces and bitter attitudes.

Who needs it?

Yes, some resistance to change is normal. But if you want to keep your job in a suddenly bigger talent pool, and frankly, if you want to enjoy work, *don't act like a victim!* Get behind the deal, think of ways to make it work, adopt the biggest, most can-do attitude you can muster. Tell yourself the good old days are over—and the best are yet to come.

I understand that not everyone can get their heads around this notion, but there is a price to pay if you don't.

Bill Harrison recalls meeting with a very talented manager from JPMorgan Chase who was one of the premier "sour faces" after the merger.

"For Christ's sake, man, you're so good, we really want to keep you," he told him, "but if you can't act in a more positive way and embrace this change, you're not going to make it."

The inevitable ending to this story is that the manager was, as Bill puts it, "like most people—no good at hiding his feelings." He left within a few months.

In mergers, managers will always pick the people cheering for the deal, even if they are not as talented or knowledgeable as the people pouting. When there are two people to do the same job, if their abilities are anywhere near each other, the upbeat, pro-merger candidate wins.

I have an old friend who worked for almost his entire career at a large insurance company, ending up with the top job in marketing, PR, and community relations. This executive was very close with the company's CEO, a relationship that afforded him all sorts of entrée into the executive decision-making process. He was the CEO's right-hand man, confessor, and sounding board, even though his title wouldn't suggest such impact.

Then, a few years ago, my friend's company was acquired by a financial services company halfway across the country, and his pal the CEO was "promoted" to chairman, with a two-year exit strategy.

I wasn't completely surprised when a month later, my friend called and asked to meet me for a drink, the sooner the better. When I saw him a few days later, he was completely forlorn.

"I am of no value to the company anymore. They kicked my boss upstairs; he's out of the game. My new boss is far away at headquarters, and he and I are not clear yet about just who is going to do what. I hate the situation I'm in."

To make a long story short, I advised my friend to befriend his boss and find as many ways as possible to make the merger a success. If he was as good at his job as he claimed, the new CEO would notice soon enough. In the meantime, it would be dumb to get booted for sulking.

My main message was, I suppose, "Swallow your pride, prove your worth, and start again."

A year has passed, and my friend has never been happier professionally. He carved out a new position for himself overseeing the integration of three overlapping businesses, took on the responsibility of advising the new head of marketing, and finally found a great, high-impact role working with the organization's new advertisers on a branding campaign.

"I don't know why I took it so hard," he said recently. "I'm always telling people that change is good, and then I let change freak me out. The hardest part was talking myself out of the hole. In truth, I had to fake it for a while, but one day I finally got over myself and stopped being a pain in the ass."

That's good advice to remember next time you want to bitch about the deal, your new bosses, and the tragedy of your fate. You and your bad attitude can be replaced—and will be if you don't learn to love the deal like the acquirers do.

Mergers mean change.

But change isn't bad. And mergers, in general, are very good. They are not only a necessary part of business, they have the potential to deliver profitable growth and put you in a new and exciting strategic position at a speed that organic growth just cannot match.

Yes, mergers and acquisitions have their challenges, and all kinds of research will tell you that more than half don't add value. But nothing says you have to fall victim to that statistic.

Don't let deal heat get you, and avoid the seven pitfalls—then reap the rewards of what happens when 1+1 = 3.

Six Sigma

BETTER THAN A TRIP
TO THE DENTIST

IN THE PREVIOUS TWO CHAPTERS of this book, we've looked at one of the more exciting aspects of business—growth—both through starting something new and through mergers and acquisitions.

In this chapter, we're leaping to the other end of the spectrum to talk (briefly, I promise) about what can be one of business's most dreary topics, Six Sigma.

Now, I am a huge fan of Six Sigma, the quality improvement program that GE adopted from Motorola in 1995 and continues to embrace today.

Nothing compares to the effectiveness of Six Sigma when it comes to improving a company's operational efficiency, raising its productivity, and lowering its costs. It improves design processes, gets products to market faster with fewer defects, and builds customer loyalty. Perhaps the biggest but most unheralded benefit of Six Sigma is its capacity to develop a cadre of great leaders.

Simply put, Six Sigma is one of the great management innova-

> Done right, Six Sigma
> is energizing and
> incredibly rewarding.
> It can even be fun.

tions of the past quarter century and an extremely powerful way to boost a company's competitiveness. These days, with Six Sigma being increasingly adopted by companies around the world, you can't afford not to understand it, let alone not practice it.

And yet, Six Sigma causes enormous anxiety and confusion.

Over the past several years, in virtually every Q & A session in country after country, someone in the audience has asked me a tortured Six Sigma question. You can see the interest level in the audience plummet and eyes glaze over, as people brace themselves for a long-winded technical lecture, complete with several graphs and charts.

I'm exaggerating a bit, of course, but it is fair to say that for many people, the concept of Six Sigma feels like a trip to a dentist. But Six Sigma couldn't be less like a root canal or any other awful procedure. Done right, it is energizing and incredibly rewarding. It can even be fun.

You just have to understand what Six Sigma really is.

There is nothing technical in what I am about to say. If you want to learn about the statistical premise behind the concept, or learn what it takes to become qualified in Six Sigma, an industry of books, videos, and training programs eagerly awaits you.

But for our purposes, I'm going to be very simple about what Six Sigma means and what it does. I call this "Six Sigma for Citizens," meaning those people—like myself—who'd like to hear the "elevator speech" version of what Six Sigma is all about and why it matters so darn much. This explanation is not meant to satisfy scientists and engineers, who actually *do* need to know about the statistical basis of Six Sigma in order to incorporate it into the design of experiments and complex equipment.

Here goes:

Six Sigma is a quality program that, when all is said and done, improves your customers' experience, lowers your costs, and builds better leaders.

Six Sigma accomplishes that by reducing waste and inefficiency and by designing a company's products and internal processes so that customers get what they want, when they want it, and when you promised it. Obviously, you want to make your customers more satisfied than your competitors do, whether you run Upper Crust Pizza or manufacture the most powerful jet engines. In the strategy chapter we talked about customer loyalty, and we used the word *sticky* to describe what you want. Well, a huge part of making your customers sticky is meeting or exceeding their expectations, which is exactly what Six Sigma helps you do.

One thing that is sure to kill stickiness is inconsistency in services or products.

Consider this hypothetical. You make spare parts and promise ten-day delivery.

Over the course of three deliveries, your customers receive their parts on day five, day ten, and day fifteen. On average, ten-day delivery.

Over the course of the next three deliveries, they receive their parts on day two, day seven, and day twelve. An average of seven days, a seemingly big improvement in the customer experience. But not really—you might have had some internal process or

> A huge part of making your customers sticky is meeting or exceeding their expectations, which is exactly what Six Sigma helps you do.

cost improvements, but the customer has experienced nothing but inconsistency!

With Six Sigma, your customers would receive all three of their deliveries on day ten, or in the worst case, on day nine, day ten, and day eleven.

Six Sigma, in other words, is not about *averages*. It's about *variation* and removing it from your customer's interface with you.

To remove variation, Six Sigma requires companies to unpick their entire supply and distribution chains and the design of their products. The objective is to wash out anything that might cause waste, inefficiency, or a customer to get annoyed with your unpredictability.

So, that's Six Sigma—the elimination of unpleasant surprises and broken promises.

SIMPLE, COMPLEX, OR NOT AT ALL

From 20,000 feet, Six Sigma has two primary applications. First, it can be used to remove the variation in routine, relatively simple, repetitive tasks—activities that happen over and over again. And second, it can be used to make sure large, complex projects go right the first time.

Examples of the first kind of application are a multitude. Call centers from South Dakota to Delhi use Six Sigma to make sure the phone is answered after the same number of rings for each incoming inquiry. Credit card processing facilities use it to make sure people receive accurate bills on the same day every month.

The second application of Six Sigma is the territory of engineers and scientists involved in multipart endeavors that sometimes take years to complete. If you're spending hundreds of millions of dollars on a new jet engine or a gas turbine, you cannot afford to figure out process or design inconsistencies late in the game. Six Sigma is incredibly effective in discovering them on the drawing board, i.e., the computer screen.

Obviously, the amount of Six Sigma training and education required depends on where and how you intend to apply it.

For the first application—simple, repetitive activities—the level of training and education is certainly manageable. In order to discover the root causes of inconsistencies, people need to know what kind of information to gather and how to analyze it. The rigor of this type of training has a terrific side effect. It builds critical thinking and discipline. That's one reason why we noticed that every time a business dove into Six Sigma, not only did its financial performance improve, so did its management ranks. They all became better leaders.

The second application is different. It involves a sophisticated level of training and statistical analysis. I myself have never had this kind of training, but I know from GE's very positive experience with jet engines and turbines that it works.

Make no mistake: Six Sigma is not for every corner of a company. Jamming it into creative activities, such as writing advertising copy, new marketing initiatives, or one-off transactions like investment banking, makes little sense and causes a lot of wheel-spinning. Six Sigma is meant for and has its most meaningful impact on repetitive internal processes and complex new product designs.

SO WHY THE PANIC?

At this point, you might be wondering: if Six Sigma is so straightforward, why does it cause so much anxiety and confusion?

> **"We're off to a good start. We've hired several statisticians, and we're looking for more."**
> **I thought to myself:**
> **This poor guy has really drunk the Kool-Aid!**

Probably because of the way it is initially presented to people. In many cases, senior management hires outside experts—scientists, statisticians, engineers, or Six Sigma consultants—to preach the new gospel. These experts, well-intentioned though they are, proceed to freak everyone out with complex PowerPoint slides that only an MIT professor could love. To make matters worse, they often present Six Sigma as a cure-all for every nook and cranny of a company. No activity is spared.

Several years ago, the CEO of a well-known consumer goods company visited me to get my take on Six Sigma. "We're off to a good start," he said. "We've hired several statisticians from places like Carnegie Mellon, and we're looking for more."

I thought to myself: This poor guy has really drunk the Kool-Aid!

Not using those words, I told him as much. The statisticians might be great, I said, but for the relatively straightforward projects he was looking at, he needed everyone in the company to understand Six Sigma. The brand-new experts were only going to scare people.

He said he'd think that over, but I think he was just being polite. He saw Six Sigma as the purview of experts, not in the blood of his company.

In time, most people come to understand Six Sigma and where to use it—and not use it—in an organization. Most of all, they also come to appreciate its competitive power after they've seen it in action for a few months. At which point, they usually become Six Sigma missionaries themselves.

So next time you hear Six Sigma mentioned, don't run for cover. Once you understand the simple maxim "variation is evil," you're 60 percent of the way to becoming a Six Sigma expert yourself.

The other 40 percent is getting the evil out.

YOUR CAREER

16.

The Right Job

FIND IT AND YOU'LL NEVER REALLY WORK AGAIN

IT'S SAID that you can only live life forward and understand it backward. The exact same thing is true about careers.

Every time I ask successful people about their first few jobs, the immediate reaction is almost always laughter. The chairman and CEO of Procter & Gamble, A. G. Lafley, thought he was going to be a professor of Renaissance history. That career plan evaporated when he dropped out of grad school to join the navy for two years, and then spent six more running grocery and specialty stores near a navy base in Tokyo.

Or take Meg Whitman. She started her career as a management consultant, then joined Disney to open its first stores in Japan, then moved to Stride Rite to revive its Keds brand, then took over the ailing floral company FTD, and then moved to Hasbro to run its PlaySkool and Mr. Potato Head divisions.

It makes perfect sense that Meg Whitman would end up as the CEO of eBay, the retailer of absolutely everything, doesn't it? But you know there was nothing specifically *planned* about her career. EBay didn't even exist until a few years ago!

The point is: it is virtually impossible to know where any given job will take you. In fact, if you meet someone who has faithfully followed a career plan, try not to get seated beside him at a dinner party. What a bore!

Now, I'm obviously not going to tell you to let fate take its course. A great job can make your life exciting and give it meaning. The wrong job can drain the life right out of you.

But how do you find the right job?

The first answer is simple: you endure the same gummy, time-consuming, up-and-down, iterative process that all working people go through. You take one job, discover what you like and don't like about it and what you're good and bad at, and then, in time, change jobs to get something closer to the right fit. And you do that until one day you realize—hey, I'm finally in the right job. I like what I'm doing, and I'm making the trade-offs I'm willing to make.

Yes, trade-offs, because very few jobs are perfect. You may love your work with every fiber of your being but wish the money were better. Or you may only like the work, but love your colleagues. Regardless of its dimensions, the right job for you exists.

My goal in this chapter is to make finding that job a somewhat shorter and, hopefully, less mysterious process.

How?

Luckily, most jobs send out signals about how right they are for you—or not. Those signals apply to jobs at every level of an organization; you can be right out of school, a middle manager trying to move up, or a senior executive looking for a top job. Of course, there are special situations in the job search process that require separate consideration—finding your first job, finding a job if you're stuck in a situation, and finding a job after you've been let go. We'll consider those at the end of this chapter.

But first, let's look at the general signals—both good and bad—of job fit.

IMAGINE YOU ARE CONSIDERING A NEW JOB . . .

SIGNAL	TAKE IT AS A GOOD SIGN IF . . .	BE CONCERNED IF . . .
PEOPLE	You like the people a lot—you can relate to them, and you genuinely enjoy their company. In fact, they even think and act like you do.	You feel like you'll need to put on a persona at work. After a visit to the company, you find yourself saying things like, "I don't need to be *friends* with the people I work with."
OPPORTUNITY	The job gives you the opportunity to grow as a person and a professional, and you get the feeling you will learn things there that you didn't even know you needed to learn.	You're being hired as an expert, and upon arrival, you will most likely be the smartest person in the room.
OPTIONS	The job gives you a credential you can take with you, and is in a business and industry with a future.	The industry has peaked or has awful economics, and the company itself, for any number of reasons, will do little to expand your career options.
OWNERSHIP	You are taking the job for yourself, or you know whom you are taking it for, and feel at peace with the bargain.	You are taking the job for any number of other constituents, such as a spouse who wants you to travel less or the sixth-grade teacher who said you would never amount to anything.
WORK CONTENT	The "stuff" of the job turns your crank—you love the work, it feels fun and meaningful to you, and even touches something primal in your soul.	The job feels like a job. In taking it, you say things like, "This is just until something better comes along," or "You can't beat the money."

A WORD ABOUT PAY

Before we talk about each of these signals in more detail, a few thoughts about money, the elephant in the middle of the room during any job discussion.

There is nothing worse than a guy who has made some money along the way opining that money shouldn't matter to people who are picking a job. So I won't do that. In fact, I'll tell you that *of course* money matters—it matters a lot.

When I took my first job, I had several offers, but the one from GE was $1,500 a year more than any other. Coming out of graduate school, I was broke. That $1,500 felt huge, and it made a difference in my decision. A year later, I got my first raise from GE. When I found out that it was exactly the same amount as everyone else in my unit, my fanatical belief in merit pay made me say, "Forget this place!" But I didn't quit until I found another job at a chemical company in Skokie, Illinois, which was going to pay me 25 percent more. I ultimately ended up being persuaded to stay with GE, but I wouldn't have if the company hadn't matched my salary offer in Skokie.

Because there is no way to disentangle money from decisions about job and career, the best you can really do is come to terms with how much money matters to you. Just remember, it can feel very noble to say that you don't care about being rich; it's another thing to live with that decision over the years, especially as mortgages and tuitions start to pile up.

There is nothing inherently wrong with wanting money or feeling indifferent to it or anything in between. But if you're not honest with yourself about those feelings during the first years of your job journey, you'll end up doing a lot of second-guessing later.

Now on to the signals of job fit, which have been listed in no particular order, since they all count.

PEOPLE

That said, the first signal concerns people, because everything else about a job can be perfect—the task, pay, location—but if you do not enjoy your colleagues on a day-to-day basis, work can be torture.

This may seem obvious, but I am surprised how often I meet people who have taken jobs in companies where they do not share the organization's overall sensibilities. By that, I mean a range of values and personality traits and behaviors, from how intense people act, to how comfortable they are with confrontation, to how candid they are about performance, to how much they laugh at meetings.

If you join a company where your sensibilities don't fit in, you'll find yourself putting on a persona just to get along. What a career killer—to fake who you are every day.

I know a woman—we'll call her Claire—who is an MBA who became a manager for a nonprofit after graduation. At first, Claire thought she had the perfect job—she could use her business skills to run an organization and still "make the world a better place," to use her words.

But several years later, Claire was at her wit's end. Her colleagues made every decision at a snail's pace. "It doesn't make any difference if we are picking where to have lunch or coming up with a marketing plan," she recounted. "Nobody can ever feel 'not heard.' Everybody has to reach consensus. It's driving me crazy! This organization has all the right intentions, but nothing ever gets done."

Finally, Claire decided that she could no longer tolerate the

> You need to find "your people," the earlier in your career the better. No job is ideal without the presence of shared sensibilities.

sensibilities mismatch she felt in a nonprofit environment, and she began to search for a consulting job in the private sector. She identified one firm in particular that was known for its pro bono work, and she consoled herself with the notion that she could work there and still keep one foot (or toe) in the "virtuous" world.

The problem was, the firm wouldn't hire her. "You haven't worked at the same speed or with the same kind of intensity we require," they told her. "We need someone who can hit the ground running." Basically, they said, "We need someone like us."

Claire is still at her nonprofit job, resigned to stay there and make the best of it. The sad thing is, she said, "I found 'my people' at that consulting firm," but it was too late. "They just didn't see I could be like them."

You too need to find "your people," the earlier in your career the better. Even if a job seems ideal in every other way, without the presence of shared sensibilities, it's not ideal for you.

OPPORTUNITY

The second job-fit signal concerns opportunity, as in, how much does the job offer you to grow and learn?

Without doubt, it can be very appealing to take a job where you suspect you will have no problem hitting it out of the park. Surefire success has its rewards—in the soul and the pocketbook.

But any job you take should feel somewhat challenging going in. It should make you think, "I can do most of the work, but there are certainly skills and knowledge this job requires that I don't have yet. I'm going to learn something here."

In other words, any new job should feel like a stretch, not a layup.

Why? Because stretching, growing, learning—all these activities keep you engaged and energized. They have the effect of making work more interesting, and they keep your head in the game.

Yes, a stretch job increases the possibility of you screwing up. That's why you should also make sure you join a company where learning is truly a value, growth for every employee is a real objective, mistakes aren't always fatal, and there are lots of people around whom you can reach out to for coaching and mentoring.

Incidentally, stretching doesn't—and shouldn't—just happen at the beginning of a person's career.

Take the case of Robert Bagby, who runs the brokerage firm A.G. Edwards. Bob says that he has twice taken on real stretch jobs—twenty-six years apart. The first time was when he began as a broker for another firm in Kansas City. The second time was in 2001, when he was named chairman and CEO of A.G. Edwards.

"At first, being a broker—my God, I had no idea what I was doing or why I had taken the job," Bob said recently. "The phone was like a dangerous weapon. I was afraid to touch it." Within a few months, though, Bob had learned enough new skills to start to excel. He came to love the brokerage business, and soon enough, his territory expanded and promotions started rolling in.

He didn't feel out of his element again until the A.G. Edwards board picked him for the top position.

> Any new job should feel like a stretch, not a layup.

"It was that same feeling again," Bob says. "There's no pretraining to be a CEO. All your past history, and all your past successes, they don't really matter anymore. You have to earn your respect all over again."

Bob's promotion to CEO couldn't have come at a more challenging time. The Internet bubble had burst, and the market was collapsing after 9/11. Bob had to oversee the firm's first workforce reduction and redirect its culture.

"I'd say it took a year for me to get on solid footing again," he said. "Things are really back to normal—it's fun now."

Bob's story, like so many others, illustrates that you shouldn't be afraid of a job that feels too big at the outset. If you're any good—which is why you were hired or promoted in the first place—you'll grow into it, and be better for the experience.

OPTIONS

If the opportunity signal is about finding a job that allows you to grow and stretch while you are there, the options signal is about finding a job that helps you if you leave.

Working for some companies is like winning an Olympic medal. For the rest of your career, you are associated with great performance and success. The consulting firm McKinsey & Company is like that. Because it is known to hire the world's top MBAs for their intelligence and intensity, and because of its reputation for intensive training, its alumni always get attention in the job market. By the same token, when I was in my early days of hiring in Plastics, we were always trying to hire people away from DuPont, and we considered it a real coup when we did. It may not have been true, but we had it in our heads that if you got a DuPont engineer, you were getting the most cutting-edge knowledge of processes and techniques.

Microsoft, Wal-Mart, and Johnson & Johnson also have enormous "employee brands," which is to say, their people get a real credential just by working there for a few years. Even putting my biases aside, GE is also in this category. Today, five of its former employees are CEOs in the Dow Jones 30. Many more are currently CEOs of Fortune 500 companies, and thousands more are executives at companies around the world.

> Working for some companies is like winning an Olympic medal. For the rest of your career, you are associated with great performance.

Obviously, you cannot let the employee brand phenomenon totally drive your job decisions. You could end up at a highly respected company only to discover your boss is terrible or your job responsibilities are limited. But these kinds of situations are less likely at the kind of good companies we're talking about.

You may be thinking that I am writing off small companies with this advice. Not true. Some small companies offer experiences and exposure that cannot be beat. You get a chance to manage people earlier in your career, run projects or units sooner, not to mention negotiate acquisitions and work more closely with the CEO and the board. When you're ready to move on, you won't have the credential of a prestigious company, but you will have a lot of mileage. That really counts at all kinds of places—especially other small companies, venture capital firms, and entrepreneurial start-ups.

There is a second part of the options signal.

Some companies open—or close—doors for you because of their reputation. Others do that because of their industry.

Back in the 1960s, being in plastics was a ticket to the future. The industry was booming, with new applications being developed every day. In the '70s, because of the energy crisis, you had job offers coming out of your ears if you had a degree or work experience in geology. And of course, people who got involved in high technology and finance in the late '80s and '90s had a good, long run of it.

At speaking engagements, I am often asked what industries I would recommend to college grads and MBAs today. I tell them to look into companies doing business at the intersection of biology and information technology. And I suggest they learn everything they can about China because it will permeate every aspect of business in their lifetimes.

This reminds me of something said by a very successful executive I know of who served in the air force before he began his business career. He is frequently contacted by headhunters, and he says his first questions about a potential job are just like those he asked as a fighter pilot assessing situational awareness.

"When I was on a mission, I would always ask, 'What's our altitude? What are the weather conditions ahead? Where is the enemy?' I think it's the same thing in business," he says. "You need to know the same kinds of things about a job or an industry. Are you getting yourself into a turnaround situation? Are the economics fatal? How tough is the competition? Has the industry peaked, or is it just getting off the ground? Are the expectations of me reasonable or am I walking into a time bomb?"

Every job you take is a gamble that could increase your options or shut them down.

Now, you can ask these questions and find that the job you like has a problematic future. The airline industry has very tough economics and relatively low pay, especially for managerial positions. The hospitality and publishing industries are likewise not very flush.

Still, some people just love the romance of air travel, the adventure of the hotel business, and the excitement of creating books. If you are one of them, of course you should enter these fields; just do so with your eyes open. Every job you take is a gamble that could increase your options or shut them down.

OWNERSHIP

A few years ago, a manager I know was visited in her office by the son of a business acquaintance. He was about to graduate from Harvard, and he needed career advice about two worlds she was very familiar with—investment banking and management consulting.

The student, hair combed neatly and dutifully dressed in a suit, came prepared with a list of questions. What was the difference, he asked, between the major consulting firms? What kind of assignments could he expect during his first year on Wall Street? And so on.

The manager had worked in consulting before joining a consumer goods company and had many acquaintances in investment banking, and so she answered each question thoroughly. She watched as the senior took careful notes, but she could tell he wasn't particularly curious about anything she said.

In fact, after a half hour or so, he thanked her politely and stood to leave.

As he was doing so, he tucked his pad inside a folder, which the manager noticed was completely covered with intricate drawings of cars.

"Wow, those are amazing! Who did them?" she asked.

Suddenly, the senior was filled with energy. "I did—I'm always drawing cars," he said. "My dorm room is covered with posters and paintings of cars—I subscribe to *every* car magazine! I've been obsessed with cars since I was five years old. My whole life, I've wanted to be a car designer. That's why I'm always going to car shows and NASCAR races. I went to Indianapolis last year—I drove there!"

The manager shook her head in disbelief.

"You've got to go work in Detroit," she said. "Why in the world are you thinking about consulting or banking?"

The senior deflated as quickly as he had come to life. "My dad says the car business is not what I went to Harvard for."

For the next few minutes, the manager tried to change the student's mind, but she quickly realized she was getting drawn into family dynamics that were none of her business. She was not surprised a few months later when she bumped into the young man's father and he proudly told her that his son was working eighty-hour weeks at a Wall Street firm.

Look, over the course of our careers, we all take jobs to meet the needs or dreams of other people—parents, spouses, teachers, or classmates.

That's not necessarily wrong, unless you don't realize you're doing it. Because working to fulfill someone else's needs or dreams almost always catches up with you. I know someone who literally became a doctor because his entire childhood his mother—a Polish immigrant who loved the American Dream—introduced him by saying, "And here's my doctor!" He didn't hate the profession, but you've never met anyone more eager to retire.

Similarly, there are countless stories of people who take jobs because their spouses want them to travel less. Then what invariably happens is that the compromising partner loses out on a promotion because of curtailed mobility. Sometimes, blame gets flung everywhere. Other times, it just sits there and simmers.

The hard reality is that there is no foolproof way out of the ownership bind. Especially as you get older, life and relationships can be complicated. Very few people have the total freedom and independence to take a job just for themselves. There are tuitions to pay, spouses with their own careers, and yes, inner voices saying what you should do

> Working to fulfill someone else's needs or dreams almost always catches up with you.

with your life, even when you're long past being a college senior.

That is why the only real defense against job ownership back-firing is to be explicit with yourself about the person (or people) for whom you are taking your job.

Over the course of your career, your Detroit will surely call you at one point or another. If you can go, that's great. If you can't, make peace with the reasons why.

WORK CONTENT

This signal comes last in our chart, but it could just as easily come first.

Every job has bad days or rough periods, and yes, there will be times when you work mainly to make ends meet. But in the very best job scenario, you love the work—at least *something* about it. It just excites you. The customers, the travel, the camaraderie at the Tuesday morning sales meeting, whatever—something about the job makes you want to come back day after day. Sometimes it is the sheer challenge of the job that turns your crank.

Take the case of Joel Klein, the chancellor of the New York City Department of Education. (I've gotten to know Joel through my work with the school system's Leadership Academy for new principals.) It is no exaggeration to say that Joel could have any number of prestigious, high-paying jobs as a corporate general counsel or CEO. As the assistant attorney general in charge of the U.S. Department of Justice Antitrust Division in the 1990s, he took on Microsoft in a highly publicized battle, and later was chairman and CEO of the U.S. division of Bertelsmann, the global media company.

There is no glamour and very limited glory in the school reform job Joel accepted in 2002. It goes without saying he took a massive pay cut to become chancellor, but in taking the job, Joel also agreed to deconstruct an insanely bureaucratic system with about a million students in more than 1,300 schools and a $15 billion budget. He immediately encountered entrenched interests, including fierce union leaders who were hell-bent on keeping the status quo, but in the face of that, he remained steadfast. Virtually every day, Joel appears in one of the New York papers, and because everyone has an opinion on education, he is often the subject of editorials, both laudatory and critical.

Joel could not love his work more.

"Sometimes I ask myself, 'What am I doing here? I could be eating a very nice, civilized lunch in a corporate dining room right now, and instead I'm in a high-crime school trying to get staff to work together to enforce our discipline code,'" Joel once told me. "But I grew up in public housing in Queens, and I'm a product of inner city New York public schools. I owe a lot to the principals and teachers who invested their lives in the system and changed my life and the vision of my opportunities. I'm lucky enough to be in a position to give something back. I don't want to sound pompous, but this work feels more important than anything I've ever done."

> **If a job doesn't excite you on some level—just because of the *stuff* of it—don't settle.**

On a much smaller scale, I know what he means about a job feeling meaningful. My work always felt really significant, even when (in retrospect) it was hardly that. I'll never forget when I was a teaching assistant at the University of Illinois and I was asked to present my PhD thesis on dropwise condensation to an international conference on heat transfer that was being held in Boulder, Colorado. You would have thought I was in the running for the Nobel Prize. I was a nervous wreck before my lecture and practiced for weeks. When the big day arrived, I spoke—and received the polite applause I deserved. That didn't stop me from rushing to the phone to call my mother in a state of complete exhilaration.

To tell you the truth, I still remember the excitement of that day!

Luckily, finding a job that touches your core is not hard. Such jobs are everywhere—every piece of work has the potential, since it only has to feel important *to you*. Shortly after I retired from GE, we were in Montreal, eating dinner at a small French restaurant, where we fell into conversation with a fellow tourist. Within a few minutes, we learned that this fellow was "the first mercury-free dentist in Quechee, Vermont." You could feel the pride bursting out of his chest. I didn't want to suddenly start a second career as a dentist, but his enthusiasm sure was infectious.

As I said before, every job has its ups and downs. But if a job doesn't excite you on some level—just because of the *stuff* of it— don't settle. And don't worry either about knowing when you find a job with meaning.

You'll feel it.

THOSE SPECIAL CASES

The job fit signals can be applied across pretty much all job situations, but a couple of special cases call for more specific discussion.

The first is finding your first real job. For a few lucky people, this process is relatively straightforward. They've got great grades from a quality school and some impressive work experience along the way. These new graduates, out of college or recent MBAs, usually have plenty of options, and I hope the signals in this chapter will be helpful in choosing wisely.

Many people, however, do not get their pick of first job assignments. Their school record is only OK, their job experience not particularly special. That puts them in a position where they have to sell themselves to an audience that ranges from skeptical to downright negative.

If you're in that category, my strong advice is just be real and come clean.

There is nothing less appealing than an applicant with a so-so record overselling himself with a lot of bravado or overeagerness. It's just so phony, and experienced managers can smell the fakery a mile away.

The best thing you can do is tell your true story. "OK, I know my grades aren't that great," you might say. "I spent a lot of time playing intramural sports and, to be honest, a lot of time with my friends. I definitely could have studied more, but I had other priorities, which probably weren't the best ones. The reason you should still hire me is because I never give up on a challenge, I work hard, I believe in your product, and I admire your company, and I know I can contribute here."

> Authenticity may be the best selling point you've got.

While you're telling your true story, act like your true self. If you are generally outspoken and funny, don't act stiff and serious during your interviews. If you are a nerd, don't try to act slick. The company should know what it's getting, and you should show them, so you see how they react. I know of an MBA who tripped over a doorjamb on her way into an interview with three executives at a prestigious consulting firm. After scrambling back to her feet, she shook hands with her interviewers, saying, "And I'm Grace, the ballet teacher."

None of them cracked a smile, nor did they try to put her at ease after what was obviously an embarrassing moment. She ended up being offered the job; she declined.

"They saw the real me, and I saw the real them," she recalls.

My main point is, when going after your first job, live in your own skin and be comfortable there. Authenticity may be the best selling point you've got.

The second special job situation is when you are stuck in a position and see no way out. There are a slew of ways to get stuck in a job. There is nowhere to move up, since your boss isn't going anywhere, and he has no interest in pushing you for a job in another division. You've been passed over for a promotion, and you've been told you are fine where you are, but you're not moving on anytime soon. Your company promotes people only after a certain period of time—which is a long way off. You love your job but the money is bad, or the money is great but your job is lousy.

This list alone could make you want to scream.

And that's the problem with being stuck. Frustration builds and builds until people generally do something stupid—they quit.

Don't do that. It is much, much easier to get a job *from* a job. I would even go further and say, not only should you stay put, you should work harder. Nothing will get you a new job faster than terrific performance in your old one.

Gerry Roche, senior chairman of Heidrick & Struggles, and one of the most respected headhunters in the United States, says that even if you feel stuck, if you are performing well, two outside observers are likely to know—headhunters and competitors.

"Great performers are like the masts of the tall ships," Gerry said to me recently. "We can see them over the horizon, and we are always trying to bring them in—to our port."

By contrast, the worst kind of job seekers are those Gerry called "perennials."

"These types are never moving up fast enough or they can't stand their jobs, so they are always out there with their résumés and their phone calls, hounding us or hounding companies to hire them," he said. "These people pretty quickly get themselves labeled."

Obviously, if you're stuck, you need to put feelers out there to let people know you are thinking of moving. Just don't make it your purpose in life, or you'll undermine your effort, and worse, you'll take your eye off your best hope for getting unstuck—your performance.

The third special case is finding a job after you've been let go. Last year, I had lunch with a former GE executive (let's call him Charlie) who had once worked for me in a staff position before moving into operations. After several promotions, he landed in a job where he struggled for a couple of years to meet his numbers. Finally, in his early fifties, he was let go.

Charlie's career, however, hardly ended. After a few months, he became a partner at a high-technology company, starting part-time and quickly being drawn into a full-time role. From there, he was asked to join several corporate boards, and he also started teaching at a well-known business school.

Five years after being let go, he told me, his work was more fulfilling than ever.

I asked him how he'd come back so strong.

"Listen, I screwed up," he said. "My boss and I had agreed to clear-cut objectives, and I missed them. I waited too long to let go of two direct reports who weren't delivering. I didn't take costs out fast enough when the downturn was approaching. I was just too optimistic."

"I told my wife I was going to get it, and I did."

Charlie's rational response floored me because usually after people have been let go, they become very defensive.

Defensive—and depressed.

Both conditions, albeit natural and common, are what kill you when you go out to get a job again. An employer can pick up low self-esteem across the room, and people want to hire winners.

But how do you act like a winner when you feel like a loser?

I asked Charlie that question.

His approach, he said, was to draw on what he called his "reservoir of self-confidence"—his strong family and his store of positive feelings about himself and his achievements in the past. He used that internal capital to stay connected with business colleagues and to network for new opportunities. He also used it to stay active socially and in community activities.

"At first, maybe people were looking at me differently and talking about me because I wasn't working anymore," Charlie said. "I tried not to pay attention to that."

The goal, if you've been let go, is to stay out of what I have always referred to as "the vortex of defeat," in which you let yourself spiral into inertia and despair.

> The goal, if you've been let go, is to stay out of what I refer to as "the vortex of defeat," in which you let yourself spiral into inertia and despair.

Every manager in the world knows what "I resigned" or "I left for personal reasons" really means.

One reason why people often get sucked into the vortex is that they wait too long before they start looking for another job. This is a tricky matter. It makes a lot of sense to take some time off after you are let go—say, a month or two—to reflect and compose yourself. On the other hand, the longer you wait, the more likely you are to start doubting yourself, and the more likely it is that prospective employers will think something is wrong. You just don't want any hole in your résumé to be too gaping.

Prospective employers will, of course, ask you about why you left your last job. Come right out and say you were asked to move on. Every manager in the world knows what "I resigned" or "I left for personal reasons" really means.

Just as important, take responsibility for your departure, like my friend Charlie did in our conversation. His ownership of the situation made him infinitely more appealing than the typical kind of defense I heard a hundred times. "My boss was really difficult" or "They don't care about customers as much as I do" or my favorite, "It was all politics there. It never mattered what you did; all that mattered was who you knew."

Compare that to Charlie's approach—even recognizing that he is on the far end of rationality! When he got back into the job market, he didn't blame a soul but himself. He told interviewers what he learned from the experience, and what he would do differently in his next job. "I'm determined to be more externally focused from now on," he said, "and I will definitely move faster on underperforming people. One of my objectives is to prove I don't make the same mistakes twice."

If you've been let go, you never want to present yourself with a swagger. But you do need to project realism and optimism. Draw on your reservoir of confidence. Say what happened, say what you've learned, and never be afraid to ask, "Just give me a chance."

Someone will.

Due to my vintage, I belong to a very small club—people who have spent their whole careers at one company. When I got my degree from graduate school, in 1961, that was the norm. Today, statistics show that college graduates change companies multiple times in their first decade out and newly minted MBAs do the same.

I can't say if that's good or bad, it just is. People are very hungry to hurry up and find the right job.

Here are some thoughts, though.

First, finding the right job takes time and experimentation and patience. After all, you have to work at something for a while before you know if you can even do it, let alone if it feels right.

Second, finding the right job gets easier and easier the better you are. Maybe that sounds harsh, but it's just reality. At the end of the day, talented people have their pick of opportunities. The right jobs find them.

So if you really want to find a great job, choose something you love to do, make sure you're with people you like, and then give it your all.

If you do that, you're sure to have a great job—and you'll never really work another day in your life.

17

Getting Promoted

SORRY, NO SHORTCUTS

THE PREVIOUS CHAPTER of this book was about finding your right job. This chapter is about getting your next one.

Now, not everyone in business wants to get a bigger and better job, but a lot of people do. If you're among them, this chapter is for you, whether you are hungry for your first promotion or your fifth.

I was there once. When I started my career at age twenty-four, I had no idea where I was going or how I was going to get there, but I was filled with ambition.

The drive to make something of myself had started pretty young. I had my first job at age ten, as a caddy at a country club near my hometown of Salem, Massachusetts. Through high school and college, I held one job after another, from bartender to teaching assistant. By the time I graduated from the University of Illinois with a PhD in chemical engineering in 1961, I was eager for the real thing.

The job GE offered me seemed like a good deal. I would be working in the lab developing a new plastic, and if it succeeded, I saw a chance to get out in the field and sell it. Best of all, the job was in Massachusetts, and it paid the most of any offer—$10,500.

Believe me, I wasn't thinking about a *career* at that point. If I had, I would have surely taken the offer I had received from Exxon, where a chemical engineering degree really meant something. But forget it—Exxon was in Texas! At that point in my life, the fact that I had gone to school in Illinois already made me feel like I had traveled halfway around the world.

Over the next thirteen years at GE, I got four promotions. Each one felt terrific. I liked having more responsibility, making bigger deals, building bigger plants, and managing more people. It was really only in 1973 that it dawned on me that I had a shot at the company's top job—and that I wanted it too. In an act of complete cockiness, I put that down on my performance evaluation under the question about career goals.

Eight years later, I got my wish.

So, how did that happen? How does a person get promoted?

The first answer is luck. All careers, no matter how scripted they appear, are shaped by some element of pure chance.

Sometimes a person just happens to be in the right place at the right time, and he meets someone—at an airport or a party, for instance—and a career door swings open. We've all heard stories like that.

> All careers, no matter how scripted they appear, are shaped by some element of pure chance.

Sometimes we don't even know luck is good until well after the fact.

An old golfing friend of mine, Perry Ruddick, remembers being sorely disappointed when he was passed over for a promotion that was in France early in his career at the investment bank Smith Barney. He thought he had missed out on his best shot at making a name for himself in the company, not to mention the glamour of Paris in 1966.

As luck would have it, two years after Perry would have left for the assignment abroad, another position at the company came open in New York, and he got it. In his new role, Perry, then thirty-two, got to run the company's investment banking operations, and with a team of forward-thinking young bankers, he helped guide the company successfully through a challenging period of consolidation in the industry.

To make a long story short, Perry was vice-chairman of Smith Barney from 1985 until his retirement in 1991.

But luck can also break the other way. Sometimes careers stall for no reason at all except bad timing. At the very least, careers can zig and zag for reasons beyond your control, like an acquisition or divestiture, or a new boss with very different ideas about your future. Occasionally, you miss out on a promotion because of office politics or nepotism. Such setbacks can be terribly disheartening—enough to make you ask yourself, "Why the heck should I even try?"

Don't go there.

In the long run, luck plays a smaller role in your career than the factors that are within your control.

While I never sorted these factors out while I was working, I have thought a lot more about them lately because audiences ask so many career questions. They come in every variety:

■ "I like my staff job at headquarters, but I want to move into operations. What do I need to do to convince my boss I can make the change?"

■ "I don't have any chemistry with my mentor, but she's really important at my company. How can I get ahead when I don't have someone pulling for me?"

■ "I'm in manufacturing, but I want to move into marketing. Will I ever get out of the factory?"

Career concerns, incidentally, are not confined to any one country or type of industry. In China, with its nascent market economy and "egalitarian" culture, business people are fiercely curious when they ask: "What does it take to get ahead?" And the same question has come at me in Portugal, France, Denmark, and even Slovakia, where capitalism is less than fifteen years old.

I think the same answer applies everywhere.

Basically, getting promoted takes one do and one don't.

■ *Do* deliver sensational performance, far beyond expectations, and at every opportunity expand your job beyond its official boundaries.

■ *Don't* make your boss use political capital in order to champion you.

These imperatives are not everything, of course. There are four other dos and one other don't, and we'll look at them in turn, but first let's focus on the two big ones.

THE POWER OF POSITIVE SURPRISE

When most people think about delivering sensational performance, they imagine beating agreed-upon performance goals. That's all well and good.

But an even more effective way to get promoted is to expand your job's horizons to include bold and unexpected activities. Come up with a new concept or process that doesn't improve just your results, but your unit's results and the company's overall performance. Change your job in a way that makes the people around you work better and your boss look smarter. Don't just do the predictable.

I learned this lesson for myself my first year at GE, while I was still working in the laboratory, developing a new plastic called PPO. A vice president was coming to town, and my boss asked me to give him an update on our progress. Eager to impress both of them, I stayed late at work for a week, analyzing not only the economics of PPO, but of all the other engineering plastics in the industry. My final report included a five-year outlook, comparing the costs of products made by DuPont, Celanese, and Monsanto, and outlined a clear route to a competitive advantage for GE.

My boss and the VP were surprised, to put it mildly, and their incredibly positive response showed me the impact of giving people more than they expect.

I would see this dynamic again and again over the next forty years.

Take the case of John Krenicki, who made everyone around and above him look better by expanding his job's horizons.

GE sent John to Europe to manage its $100 million silicones business in 1997. It was by no means a plum assignment, but it gave John a chance to run his own show. The business, while No. 2 globally, was a weak No. 6 in the European market, mainly because its biggest cost—raw materials—had to be sourced from the United States. It just could not compete with the local players.

Back at headquarters, everyone would have been happy if John had grown silicones by 8 to 10 percent a year by pulling the usual levers: on-time delivery to existing customers, finding new ones, and developing new products. But John had bigger ideas. He proposed building a new plant in Europe to produce his key raw material.

The price tag was well over $100 million. We said, "No way."

But John couldn't accept that there wasn't a solution to his cost bind. He tried a long-shot approach. Expanding his job's horizons, he entered into talks with several of his European competitors in search of a partner who would bring local sourcing and technology expertise to the table in return for GE's global strength.

After a long year of negotiations, John found what he needed, a silicones joint venture with the German company Bayer, with GE holding a majority stake in the new company.

I recently asked him about this experience.

"It was just persistence, I guess," he said. "I knew we had to become self-sufficient somehow. If we had just kept doing things as usual, even if we grew the business by a reasonable amount, we would have never broken out."

Today, the European silicones business is No. 2 in the local market, and with a recent acquisition, its sales are more than $700 million.

As for John, he was promoted in 1998 to CEO of GE Transportation, and in 2003 to CEO of GE's $8 billion plastics business.

YOUR OWN WORST ENEMY

If exceeding expectations is the most reliable way to get ahead, the most reliable way to sabotage yourself is to be a thorn in your organization's rear end.

Of course, no one sets out to do that. But it happens, and every time it does, you force your boss to use his political capital in order to defend you.

At this point, probably most people are thinking, "Who me—make my boss use his political capital? Never."

Well, think again.

You can have the greatest results in the world, but if you don't live your company's values and behaviors, you run the risk of this happening.

> The most reliable way to sabotage yourself is to be a thorn in your organization's rear end.

Take the case of an extremely smart and capable employee I'll call James. We hired James into our business development program at headquarters. This two-year, up-or-out program was designed for MBAs who had been with consulting firms for three or four years and wanted to get off that track and into operations. To test them, we put them in short, intense field assignments, transferring GE's best practices from business to business. In most cases, one of our businesses would "steal" these MBAs from the program within a year and place them in meaningful operating positions.

James was about thirty-two when we brought him in from a top-tier consulting firm where he had worked since graduating from business school. He was European, articulate, and as I said, very bright, with excellent experience consulting in several industries. We figured at least three GE businesses would be fighting over him within six months.

A year came and went, and no one would touch him. I couldn't figure out why until I sat in on his first performance review with his boss and the HR team. There I learned that James came into the office at ten or eleven each day and left late, at 8:00 p.m. or so. Those were plenty of hours to put in, and that kind of schedule was fine—for an individual contributor. We had people in R & D who liked to work at night, for instance, and people in sales who came and went according to the needs of their customers in three time zones.

James's hours, however, were not going to make it in a company where line managers generally showed up at 8:00 a.m. or earlier, and every meeting and work routine revolved around that.

But James didn't seem to care about GE's routines. He had his own way of doing things.

I saw that dynamic up close when James called my assistant and asked for an appointment. When we got together, after a few minutes of chitchat about his career, the real reason for his visit became clear.

"Would it be OK," he asked, "if I flew my own plane to my meetings in the field?"

I told him he was nuts. "Do that *only* if you want to piss everyone off," I said. "Your hours have already gotten you in enough trouble. That kind of showing off is going to kill you around here. It's not our culture."

"But I'd pay for the gas!"

"This is not about *gas*!" I said.

Despite James's disconnect with our values, he did land a job in operations. Because of his brainpower, energy, and background, I put him in charge of a relatively small, troubled business we had acquired in Europe. Two American transplants hadn't worked out. Putting James there was a classic corporate "stuff job," in that I stuffed him (despite my misgivings) down the throat of the business.

It didn't work. GE's European business culture wasn't any more

> Eventually, he had to leave the company. In the end, there wasn't a person left with any desire to spend political capital on him.

amenable to James than its American one, and eventually he had to leave the company.

In the end, there wasn't a person left with any desire to spend political capital on him.

By contrast, take the story of Kevin Sharer, who started in the same business development program as James.

Before joining GE, Kevin had received a degree in aeronautical engineering from the U.S. Naval Academy, served a four-year stint on nuclear attack submarines, and worked for two years at McKinsey & Company. Without question, he was as smart as James in terms of IQ. He was also industrious and, like James, ambitious, the latter of these traits mitigated by his maturity. Kevin knew that GE valued teamwork; he was the ultimate team player. He showed up early, worked incredibly hard, and never looked for personal credit.

Kevin worked in business development for two years and spent the next three years in operations. By that time, he was so universally respected we made a huge bet on him by offering him a position as one of the company's one hundred vice presidents, running our marine and industrial turbine business.

Unfortunately, the same day that we tried to promote him, Kevin told us he had decided to leave for a huge opportunity at MCI. We tried desperately to keep him, but he was determined to run his own show. He left MCI a few years later to become COO of Amgen, and in 2000 was appointed its CEO. In the years since Kevin joined Amgen, the company's market capitalization has grown from $7 billion to $84 billion.

It was obvious from the beginning that Kevin was a star. He had everything going for him, starting with performance. And you can be sure no one ever had to expend a drop of political capital when they mentioned his name. No wonder his career has consisted of one promotion after another.

OTHER POLITICAL CAPITAL DRAINS

Along with transgressing company values, there is a related but more egregious way that you can use up your boss's political capital. It has to do with character—that is, with the kinds of behaviors that can make people ask, "Hold on, can I really trust this person?"

Take lack of candor. As I mentioned earlier in the chapter on candor, I'm not talking about boldface lying, but a tendency to withhold information. That behavior is far more common, and it frustrates teams and bosses to no end.

We had a manager in one of our larger businesses whose results were quite good, but after several early promotions, his career hit a wall. The reason was whenever he was in a business review or a deal proposal session, we had to pepper him with about thirty questions to get him to explain what was really going on. And even then, we didn't feel as if were getting the whole story. All we got was hemming and hawing and then a hesitant "It's OK now" or a cagey-sounding "We've got it under control."

At every HR review, I would ask his boss why this guy played his cards so close to the vest. "It's his personality" was the answer. "He's not a bad person. He just doesn't like to open up."

"What's he hiding?" I asked. "Because when he withholds information the way he does, he just comes across as if he's not telling the truth. And I know I'm not the only one who feels that way."

"Yeah, that's true. It bugs other people too. But he's not lying. He's just guarded."

"But we need to talk about the business openly."

"Yeah, I know it's frustrating. I'll tell him again."

And back and forth like that.

Eventually his boss got tired of the routine, and soon thereafter, the too-cagey manager was de-moted.

The point is: Don't make your boss ask the perfect question to get information from you. If you want your character to stand up for you and make life easy for your boss, open up and tell it like it is.

There's another behavior that will also force your boss to use po-litical capital because it really alien-ates people. It's wearing your career goals on your sleeve.

> Career lust shows itself in tearing down the people around you, insulting or disparaging them in order to make your own candle burn brighter.

With most people, ambition is a positive thing—it's fire in the belly, it's energy and optimism. It's pushing yourself and the organization forward so that everyone wins. Kevin Sharer had plenty of this kind of drive, and so do most people who suc-ceed.

Career lust looks different. It shows itself in tearing down the people around you, insulting or disparaging them in order to make your own candle burn brighter, as the old saying goes. It's covering up your mistakes or (worse) trying to blame them on someone else. It's hogging meetings, taking disproportionate credit for team success, and gossiping incessantly about people and events in the office. It's seeing the company's org chart as a chessboard, and making an open display of watching the pieces move.

If you've got this problem, your best hope is to repress it, fight it, and keep it out of sight. If you don't do that, when the time comes to be promoted, there won't be enough political capital in the world to save you. It's very hard to champion someone over the clamor of objecting coworkers.

FURTHERMORE . . .

We've just looked at the two biggest factors in getting you promoted—getting great results while expanding your job's horizons and not using up your boss's political capital.

That said, there are four other dos that certainly help too and one don't.

The dos are:

■ Manage your relationships with your subordinates with the same carefulness that you manage the one with your boss.

■ Get on the radar screen by being an early champion of your company's major projects or initiatives.

■ Search out and relish the input of lots of mentors, realizing that mentors don't always look like mentors.

■ Have a positive attitude and spread it around.

The don't is:

■ Don't let setbacks break your stride.

Let's look at the dos first.

Managing down. Every business advice book tells you to network with people within your company and industry. They tell you how important it is to build a mutually respectful bond with your boss. That's all good advice, and you should take it.

But to get ahead, you also need to tend to your subordinates with the same level of attention and concern.

The boss-subordinate relationship is easy to neglect. Your boss is in your face, and your peers are on your mind, while your subordinates generally do what you say.

> The boss-subordinate relationship is easy to neglect. Your boss is in your face, and your peers are on your mind, while your subordinates do what you say.

But be careful, because the boss-subordinate relationship can easily fall into two career-damaging traps. The first, and by far more common, occurs when you spend too much time managing up. As a result, you become too remote from your subordinates, and you end up losing their support and affection. The second occurs when you get too close to your employees, overstepping boundaries, and end up acting more like a buddy than a boss.

Either way can catch up with you.

Your goal in managing your relationships with subordinates is to try to walk the line between the two extremes. When the time comes for your promotion, the best thing employees can say about you is that you were fair, you cared, and that you showed them tough love.

I learned this lesson firsthand. In the final showdown for CEO of GE, I was strongly opposed by two powerful vice-chairmen, who supported their own candidates.

Unbeknownst to me, I was really helped by my direct reports. I found out later that they had advocated relentlessly for my promotion with Chairman Reg Jones, telling him I was tough but fair, and that I would push GE harder and faster than any of the other CEO finalists. I'm not sure all of them liked me—I was rough around the edges and pretty short on patience. But I guess they respected me for respecting them and building relationships with them not just when I needed them, but years before.

Getting on the radar screen. As I've said, the first and best way to get noticed is with results.

But you can also raise your visibility by putting up your hand when the call comes for people to lead major projects and initiatives, in particular ones that don't have a whole lot of popularity at the outset. At GE, two of those were globalization, which we launched in earnest in the 1980s, and Six Sigma, which was launched in 1995.

Wayne Hewett is a perfect example of a person whose career benefited from this dynamic. Wayne was a thirty-five-year-old manager when he took over the Six Sigma program in Plastics after running GE Plastics-Pacific. Using Six Sigma, he and his team drastically reduced product variation and stretched plant capacity 30 percent with little additional investment. Three years later Wayne was promoted to CEO of GE's $2 billion global silicones business.

Dan Henson is another case in point. Dan was running a GE Capital lending business in London when he had the courage to volunteer to spearhead Six Sigma throughout GE Capital, a business where a lot of people doubted it had any value. Dan found out exactly where Six Sigma applied, and equally important, where it did not. In two years, Dan achieved variation reduction in highly repetitive activities, such as credit card processing and mortgage insurance applications, and the results were impressive. Today, Dan is CEO of one of GE Capital's largest businesses, Vendor Financial Services.

GE is so big, if Wayne and Dan hadn't put themselves on the radar screen, who knows when they would have been made CEOs. Certainly, it would have happened eventually, but not nearly as quickly.

The best proof of the radar screen dynamic is in the numbers. Today, more than half of the senior vice presidents reporting to Jeff Immelt have worked in global assignments, and one-third of the company's approximately 180 officers have significant Six Sigma experience.

Amassing mentors. The third career do concerns mentors, a burning topic while I was at GE, and these days, wherever I speak.

People, it seems, are always looking for that one right mentor to help them get ahead.

But in my experience, there is no one right mentor. There are *many* right mentors.

I had dozens of informal mentors over the course of my career, and each one taught me something important. My mentors ranged from the classic older and wiser executive to coworkers who were often younger than I was.

Some mentoring relationships lasted a lifetime, others lasted just weeks.

One of the most meaningful mentors in my life never called himself my mentor, nor did I ever identify him that way. I thought of Si Cathcart, who was ten years my senior and a member of the GE board, as my friend. To my great sadness, he died in 2002.

Si was everything people look for in a great mentor—a person who cheered me on and challenged me in equal measure. His judgment about people was pitch-perfect, and I rarely made a big decision on hiring without running it by him first.

> There is no one right mentor. There are *many* right mentors.

During the toughest period of my career, when I was choosing a successor to recommend to the board, Si spent several hundred hours over the course of five years visiting all of the candidates and sharing his impressions with me.

Si, the longtime chairman of Illinois Tool Works, was on the GE board when I became CEO. We played golf often and chatted on the phone regularly. Si used both these venues to push my thinking up unseen alleys and around blind corners. "Are you sure that guy's not a phony?" he would ask. "Do you think that acquisition is still going to make you happy when the fanfare dies down?" Si always knew the right question to ask.

I had another great mentor in Dennis Dammerman, who was not only younger than me by ten years, but my subordinate as well.

I met Dennis in 1977, when I was named head of GE's consumer products group. I arrived in the job knowing basically nothing about insurance or financing, the main activities of GE Capital, one of the group's businesses. Dennis, whom I had hired as my financial analyst, had spent several years there.

For months on end, Dennis taught me something every single day. His patience was remarkable. Here was his boss asking him to define the simplest concepts—I barely understood types of debt in those days. After all, I had come from the manufacturing side of GE. When we wanted money, all we did was make a pitch to corporate, and if the proposal was good enough, they sent it. Suddenly, I was dealing with combined ratios, delinquencies, leveraged leases, and the like.

> Business is like any game, with players, a language, rules, controversies, and a rhythm. The media covers it all.

Dennis basically downloaded his brain into mine. He never called himself my mentor, but he was nothing less.

There were countless other mentors who helped me in my career, from the executive education teacher who tried to teach me public speaking when I was twenty-six, to the young woman in PR who tried to teach me the Internet when I was sixty. But let me just add to the list one more mentor that can work for everyone: the business media.

Business is like any game. It has players, a language, a complex history, rules, controversies, and a rhythm.

The media covers it all, and from every angle. From my earliest days in Plastics, I learned mountains about business just by reading every financial newspaper and magazine I could get my hands on. From them, I picked up what deals worked and which failed, and why. I followed people's careers. I tried to understand what kinds of strategic moves were criticized and which were praised. I kept up with different industries, from chemicals to medical technology.

And I used what I read. I learned, for instance, about PepsiCo's executive training program from an article in *Fortune* magazine. I was so impressed by PepsiCo's model—which used the company's own executives as teachers—that I built it into the foundation of our training program in Crotonville.

I didn't believe everything I read, of course, and the more I knew, the more I realized that some articles were off the mark in their analyses. Regardless, I still believe the business media is such a good teacher that I am always amazed when I meet a young person who doesn't just *consume* it. Don't let that happen—this mentor is right there for the taking!

My point is that mentors are everywhere. Don't just settle for the mentor assigned to you as part of a formal program. Those official mentors teach you the company ropes, but they're just a start.

The best mentors help you in unplanned, unscripted ways. Relish all that they give you in whatever form they come.

Don't be a downer. The fourth and final way to help yourself get promoted is as hard or as easy as you make it—have a positive attitude and spread it around.

Yes, it's nothing more sophisticated than that. Have a sense of humor, be fun to hang out with. Don't be a bore or a sourpuss. Don't act important, or worse, pompous. Smack yourself in the head if you start taking yourself too seriously.

In politics, people talk about each candidate's likability factor, which is just another way of saying "personality appeal." Both of those terms refer to something intangible, but they really matter—in politics and at work.

Obviously, being a congenial, upbeat person will not get you ahead by itself. You need everything else we've just talked about—great results, expanded job horizons, good character, visibility, mentors, and all the rest. But it is very, very hard to get ahead without being a positive person because, very simply, no one likes to work under or near a dark cloud. Even if the "cloud" is very smart.

I know it is not easy to always be upbeat. Life doesn't always go your way. But every time you feel yourself spreading gloom at work, think of Jimmy Dunne.

Jimmy was a senior executive at Sandler O'Neill & Partners, the investment banking firm that was located on the 104th floor of the World Trade Center's south tower. On September 11, sixty-eight of the staff's 177 employees were killed, including the company's founder, Herman Sandler, and its lead partner, Chris Quackenbush. Overnight, Jimmy became the CEO of a company that was literally and emotionally decimated.

Jimmy was, of course, grief-stricken by the firm's incalculable human tragedy, and distraught over the deaths of two of his closest friends, Herman and Chris. But today he will tell you that he knew one thing would prevent the firm from shutting down and the disaster worsening—a can-do attitude.

> You can win without being upbeat—if every other star is aligned—but why would you want to try?

"All I did after 9/11 was walk around, consoling people, talking about how we were going to survive and rebuild," he said recently.

As he hired to replace Sandler O'Neill's lost employees, Jimmy looked for people who were upbeat, positive, and as undaunted as humanly possible by 9/11. Skill mattered a lot; outlook mattered more.

"Success," Jimmy says, "is so much about attitude."

A positive attitude does not always come easy—and in cases like Jimmy Dunne's after 9/11, it comes unimaginably hard.

If it's natural for you, fantastic. If it isn't, fight to find it and wear it all over yourself.

You can win without being upbeat—if every other star is aligned—but why would you want to try?

ONE LAST DON'T

The final don't concerns setbacks.

Once or twice or more times than that, you will not get promoted. Don't let it break your stride.

Of course, you will feel terrible, maybe even bitter and angry. But work like hell to let those feelings go.

First, and by all means, do not turn your career setback into the office cause célèbre. What a way to alienate everyone—your boss, coworkers, and subordinates. If you want to complain about your career, do it at home, at a bar across town, or wherever you go to worship. The people at work, while they know a lot about your case, should not be drawn into your emotional experience.

More important, even if you are thinking of leaving your company, try to accept your setback with as much grace as you can muster, and even see it as a challenge to prove yourself anew. Such an approach will serve you well whether you stay or go.

No one makes this point better than Mark Little.

Mark was the quiet, self-confident, and well-liked engineering vice president of GE's Power Systems when, in 1995, the business ran into serious quality problems. As Mark puts it, "I had just gotten the job, and, basically, turbine blades were cracking all over the world. It was a mess."

Mark worked hard to get the business back on track, but when Bob Nardelli was promoted to run the entire Power Systems group, he decided Mark had neither the sense of urgency nor the engineering expertise for the job. He split the business and gave Mark engineering responsibility for just steam turbines, the much smaller and less important piece. Suddenly, Mark was in charge of one-third as many people and a product considered to be old, dull, and slow-growth.

"It felt like the end of the world," Mark said to me recently. "I thought it was unfair, and I was mad as hell. I felt like I hadn't created the problem, and I had done everything I could to fix it. Then I was punched in the stomach. I was angry and hurt, and I had to believe it was the end of my GE career."

But Mark did an amazing thing. He stuck his chin out and got back to work.

"I just figured I was going to prove everyone wrong," he said. "I wanted to show the whole world what we could do."

Over the next couple of years, Mark energized his team to revitalize the steam turbine product line. He introduced new technologies and put in process disciplines, driving costs down to new levels.

"I made up my mind that I was not going to show my people that I was mad and hurt. I was going to go in there every day and do what was best for me and my people and for GE. And that was to refocus the business."

In 1997, Mark's results were so terrific and his self-confidence was so restored that when the much-larger position of product manager for all turbines came open, he approached Bob Nardelli and asked for the job.

The answer was yes.

"I'd say the main reason I got the promotion was because I surprised everybody with my results, my attitude, and my perseverance. I just never gave up."

Today, Mark is the product manager not only for the turbine business, but for GE's hydro and wind businesses as well, a $14 billion enterprise.

To get ahead, you have to *want* to get ahead.

Some promotions come because of luck, but very few. The facts are, when it comes to careers, you mainly make your own luck. You will likely change companies, maybe even professions, more than a few times over the course of your working life. But there are some things you can do to keep moving ahead. Exceed expectations, broaden your job's horizons, and never give your boss a reason to have to spend capital for you. Manage your subordinates carefully, sign up for radar-screen assignments, collect mentors, and spread your positive attitude. When setbacks come, and they will, ride them out with your head up.

That may sound like a lot of stuff to do, but there are no real shortcuts.

Along the journey, you won't get every promotion you want when you want it. But if you take the "long way," eventually—and sometimes sooner than you expect—you'll reach your destination.

Hard Spots

THAT DAMN BOSS

I'VE NEVER KNOWN A PERSON who didn't light up at the memory of a truly great boss. And for good reason: great bosses can be friends, teachers, coaches, allies, and sources of inspiration all in one. They can shape and advance your career in ways you never expected—and sometimes they can even change your life.

In stark contrast, a bad boss can just about kill you.

Not literally of course, but a bad boss can kill that part of your soul where positive energy, commitment, and hope come from. On a daily basis, a bad boss can leave you feeling angry, hurt, and bitter—even physically ill.

If you're like most people, over the course of a forty-something-year career, you will have a handful of great bosses, many more that are pretty good, and one or two total jerks—people who are so consistently awful they make you want to throw it in and quit.

Bad bosses come in every variety. Some grab all the credit,

The world has jerks. Some of them get to be bosses.

some are incompetent, some kiss up but kick down; others bully and humiliate, have mood swings, withhold praise and money, break promises, or play favorites.

Occasionally, there are bad bosses who display several of these characteristics all at once.

How do these people ever get ahead?

Well, sometimes they happen to be very talented. They deliver the numbers or they're extremely creative. They can have shrewd political alliances or maybe even a family member in high places.

Bad bosses, incidentally, tend to have longer lives in some industries rather than others. On the creative side, very talented writers, artists, and producers who get promoted to run projects are often given a pass on bad behavior because they are "geniuses." Wall Street is also often a safe harbor for bad bosses. Top money-makers are often thought of as irreplaceable, and they know it, making some of them even more insufferable.

But never mind industry specifics. The world has jerks. Some of them get to be bosses.

This chapter is about what to do when one of them gets to be *your* boss.

Now, this chapter won't provide any hard-and-fast answers because each bad boss situation is unique. But it will walk you through a series of questions that hopefully will surface the right approach to your bad boss situation, "right" in the sense that it fits your goals in life and at work.

Before we look at those questions, though, let me state the overriding principle behind this chapter.

In any bad boss situation, you cannot let yourself be a victim. That theme has come up before in this book—most recently in the chapter on mergers and acquisitions—and, for many of the same reasons, it applies here too.

I realize that a bad boss (like a merger) may make you want to bitch and moan to your coworkers, whine to your family, punch a wall, or watch too much TV with a drink in your hand. He may make you want to surf the Web or call headhunters, looking for jobs anywhere but where you are.

All in all, he may end up making you want to feel very sorry for yourself.

Don't!

In any business situation, seeing yourself as a victim is completely self-defeating. And when it comes to your career, it's an attitude that kills all your options—it can even be the start of a career death spiral. I have a friend, a financial analyst at a Wall Street firm, who bounced from one crummy job to another after he had a falling out with his bad boss and quit in a huff. Out in the market, with no recommendations, all he had was an "I was screwed" story of woe to tell prospective employers. Ultimately, five years later, he ended up with the same job he had started from, only at a less-respected firm and at about 60 percent of the pay.

Obviously, you shouldn't always stay with a bad boss. Sometimes you need to get out. Regardless of your decision, avoid the pervasive victim mentality. You know what I mean. We live in a culture where parents sue fast-food restaurants for making their kids fat and cities spend millions of dollars a year to settle claims for injuries caused by uneven sidewalks and potholes.

Please!

Like every other unfortunate or unfair event that befalls you in life, working for a difficult boss is your problem and you must solve it.

> **In any bad boss situation, you cannot let yourself be a victim.**

To do that, ask yourself the following series of questions. The answers will help you navigate what is undeniably a painful situation. Painful—but yours to accept, fix, or end.

The first question is:

Why is my boss acting like a jerk? Sometimes the answer to this question is a no-brainer. Your boss is acting like a jerk because that's the way he is. He may be fine with customers and fairly reasonable with his own bosses and peers, but he treats everyone below him with the same kind of bad behavior—be it in the form of intimidation, belligerence, arrogance, neglect, secrecy, or sarcasm.

It is an entirely different situation if your boss is just impossible toward you.

In that case, you need to start asking yourself what you have done to draw his disapproval. That's right—you need to ask yourself if you are the cause of your boss's behavior. Generally speaking, bosses are not awful to people whom they like, respect, and need. If your boss is being negative to you—and mainly you—you can feel pretty confident that he has his version of events, and his version concerns *your* attitude or performance.

You've got to find out what's going on.

> Generally speaking, bosses are not awful to people whom they like, respect, and need. Think hard about your performance.

Start by asking yourself that question, but know that self-assessment is difficult, to put it mildly. Even with a huge amount of maturity and a cast-iron stomach, it is hard to see yourself as others do.

I know of an HR executive at a training center in the South who spent ten years administering 360-degree feedback programs and then delivering the conclusions to the individual being evaluated. "Seven out of ten people are completely stunned by what they hear," she said. "When they get their feedback, they think I've mixed up the forms. They are convinced their colleagues must be talking about somebody else."

The problem, the HR executive said, is that people generally overrate their performance on the job and their popularity with the team—most often by a factor of two or more.

Know that, then, as you conduct what is an admittedly difficult "mirror test." Think hard about your performance, and press yourself for the ways you may have fallen short. Think about why your colleagues might not consider you a team player. In a state of forced self-loathing, gauge your personal productivity, your face time in the office, your contribution to sales and earnings. Maybe you open a lot of deals but never close them. Maybe you close a lot of deals but boast too much. Maybe people weren't really "OK with it" when you blew a big account a few months back.

Finally, face into your attitude toward authority, because it just might be that the source of your problem with your boss is that you are, at your core, a boss hater.

Boss haters are a real breed. It doesn't make any difference who these people work for, they go into any authority relationship with barely repressed cynicism. Who knows why—upbringing, experiences at work or home, political bent. It doesn't really matter. Boss haters usually exude constant low-level negativity toward "the system," and when they do, their bosses feel it, and they return the favor.

I'll never forget a group of boss haters we had at GE headquarters in Fairfield, Connecticut—a half-dozen or so guys who ate lunch together in the cafeteria every day. They labeled themselves "The Table of Lost Dreams." Each of these employees was very talented. One had a real knack for turning just the right phrase. He had a background in journalism and worked in PR. Fortunately, the media found his cynicism appealing. Another was a labor-relations specialist who had a real affinity for the unions. His natural sympathies made him enormously effective in frontline negotiations.

All of the guys at the Table of Lost Dreams were very good at their jobs, and none of them managed anyone, so their defiance of conditions at the company was pretty much left alone. I wrote them off as harmless but effective curmudgeons who would have hated any work situation.

But tolerance is not usually what happens in these cases. Most of the time, leaders get sick of the undercurrent of whining and the energy-sapping effects of boss haters and manage them out—by showing them just what a bad boss really looks like.

Maybe this all sounds very unfamiliar to you—you're basically comfortable with authority, and the rest of your self-examination has you coming up empty-handed too. Now what?

It's time to find out what your boss is thinking.

Any kind of confrontation, however, is incredibly risky. Your boss may be waiting for just such a moment to dump you. In fact, he may have been hoping his negative vibes would eventually inch you into his office with the question, "So what am I doing wrong?" so that he can answer, "Too much for this to go on any longer."

Still, you have to talk. There is no way around it. Just remember, before you go into that meeting, be prepared and have options in the event that you come out of it unemployed.

Then, go do it. Don't be defensive. Remember, your goal is to uncover something your boss has not been able to explicitly tell you for whatever reason. Maybe he's conflict averse or he's just been too busy. Regardless, your objective is to extract from him the problem he has with your attitude or performance.

If you're lucky, your boss will come clean about your shortcomings, and together, you can work on a plan to correct them and get your performance or attitude back on track. Ideally, as you give it your all to improve, his attitude toward you will as well.

Ironically, you are less lucky if you find out that your bad boss is satisfied with your performance. If that's the case, he is being awful simply because he doesn't particularly like you.

Which puts you in the same position as the people who work for bad bosses who act the same way . . . just because that's the way they are.

For all of you, the next question is:

What's the endgame for my boss? Sometimes it's obvious that a bad boss is on the way out. His own bosses have signaled as much to the organization; or he himself makes it clear he can't wait to move on. In either case, survival is just a waiting game. Deliver strong results and have a can-do approach until relief arrives.

You are in a different boat if your bad boss is not going anywhere anytime soon.

More than a decade ago, I drew the chart below to categorize types of leaders, and to help me talk about who should stay and who should leave.

The chart split leaders according to their results—good or bad—and how well they lived GE's values, such as candor, voice, dignity, and boundarylessness.

TYPE 1:	TYPE 2:
Good values/ Good performance	Bad values/ Bad performance
TYPE 3:	TYPE 4:
Good values/ Bad performance	Bad values/ Good performance

Type 1 bosses, in the top left corner, are the people you want to reward and promote and hold up as examples to the rest of the company. Type 2 bosses, in the upper right corner, have to go, the sooner the better, and usually do.

Type 3 bosses, in the bottom left corner, really believe in the company's values and practice them in earnest, but just can't get the results. Those individuals should be coached and mentored, and given another chance or two in other parts of the company.

Most bad bosses are in the lower right corner—Type 4—and they are the most difficult to deal with. They often get to hang around for a long time, despite their awful behavior, because of their good results.

Most good companies usually know about these people and eventually move them out.

But every company, even the good ones, keeps some managers in this quadrant for longer than they should. It's such a dilemma for bosses at every level. They hear the grumbling down below, but they see the great numbers right in front of them.

Which leads to a kind of organizational inertia.

Take the case of a man I know of whom I'll call Lee, who ran a thirty-person division of an international communications company. Formerly a successful writer himself, Lee created a competitive, almost frantic, environment in the office, with the staff churning out more copy than divisions twice the size. At the same time, he held the team to extremely high standards of creativity, a major plus in the eyes of headquarters.

But Lee had a mean streak a mile wide. His humor could be cruel, and he particularly let loose on young, inexperienced employees. He also reveled in his intensely adversarial relationship with the division's unionized employees, which poisoned the atmosphere for everyone.

Lee held his staff in a kind of terrorized thrall. Many people liked the prestige of working in his high-performing division, but they hated his day-to-day nastiness. Top performers often stayed for only a year or less, but Lee was protected by the industry's laws of supply and demand. There was always another young, ambitious writer or artist ready to sign up.

And so, despite the constant turnover, the organization's top management let Lee stay and stay—until he suffered a heart attack. After he was gone, one of his former employees said, "It took an act of God to get rid of him."

Usually, a bad boss with great numbers doesn't have to die for senior management to replace him, but it can take a cataclysmic event to provoke action.

Take "Karen," a senior-level boss at a money management firm. Karen managed fifteen fund managers and their teams— about two hundred people combined. The company was known for its ruthless, hard-driving culture, and Karen epitomized it. She worked eighteen-hour days. She publicly denounced fund managers who underperformed, occasionally reducing people to tears in meetings, and routinely belittled the support staff, snidely referring to them as "the Danielle Steel fan club," since many were middle-aged women who read popular novels during their lunch breaks. When Karen's bosses were around, however, her persona became thoughtful and caring, earning her the nickname of Sybil, after a woman with multiple personality disorder who was the subject of a best-selling book.

For more than a decade, Karen's money managers posted impressive results, significantly outperforming comparable funds. But when the Internet bubble burst, the cost of her management approach began to show. Fund managers were heavily invested in high-growth stocks to make their numbers and avoid Karen's ire—in fact, their biggest holdings were in Enron, WorldCom, and Tyco.

When Karen was fired, senior managers made a big show of denouncing her management style. Many of her people shook their heads in amazement—it had been in evidence for years, but it took a disaster to make management confront it.

You may not work at a company that lets a bad boss hang around until a mess erupts. But it's possible great numbers will keep your bad boss around indefinitely.

If you feel that's the case, your next question should be:

What will happen to me if I deliver results and endure my bad boss? If you think that your organization, and in particular your boss's boss or someone in HR, understands your bind and sympathizes, you should feel pretty confident that eventually you will be moved up or sideways as a reward for surviving. While you're waiting, hang in there and give the job your all.

I was fortunate to have many great bosses during my career. They encouraged me, protected me, built my self-confidence, and gave me challenges that stretched my abilities. Reuben Gutoff, my boss for more than a decade when I was starting out, did all these. He kept the mammoth bureaucracy of GE off my back while I learned real-time how to build a business from scratch. I was able to travel the world in my twenties, setting up joint ventures and making small acquisitions.

It took seventeen years for me to bump into a bad boss. It wasn't that Dave Dance, a vice-chairman, was actually bad, it was just that I was in the running for the CEO job, and he strongly supported another candidate. Every day felt like a week. No matter what I did, I felt that Dave was rooting for me to fail. What

> What an awful feeling when your boss is not on your side.

an awful feeling when your boss is not on your side. I tried to stay out of his way—I hung out at headquarters as little as possible. I spent my time in the field with people I liked, doing what I liked to do, reviewing businesses.

My situation was a lot easier than it is for many people. I knew that it

> There is a reason why kids don't tattle on bullies. Unfortunately, the same principle applies in the office.

couldn't last more than a couple of years, and I also knew the potential reward if I endured, and it was big. You may not have that luxury.

But be careful. Uncertainty about the final outcome can make you do something foolish—that is, pull an end run. You may feel the impulse to sneak upstairs and talk to your boss's boss about the situation. That can be suicide. About 90 percent of the time, complaining about a bad boss to his boss circles right around to bite you on the rear. The big boss may have your best interests at heart when he scolds your boss for his behavior, but you can be absolutely sure that your life will only become more unpleasant afterward. There is a reason why kids don't tattle on bullies. Unfortunately, the same principle applies in the office.

There will always be an element of uncertainty to enduring a bad boss. You may surmise a happy ending or be promised one. But there are very few guarantees. All you know for certain in this kind of situation is that going to work every day isn't fun.

Which is why you need to ask the following:

Why do I work here anyway? Remember how, in the chapter on finding the right job, we talked about the inevitability of trade-offs? It is rare for a job to be perfect in every way. Sometimes you stay in a job for the money or the friends; sometimes you give up money and friends for the love of the work itself or the job's location or its lack of travel. Sometimes you stay in a job because the company has so much prestige, you know it will help you get a new job once you have a few more years of experience under your belt.

When you find yourself in a situation with a bad boss that isn't going to change anytime soon, you need to assess your trade-offs and ask, "Are they worth it?"

If the answer to this question is no, then start constructing an exit plan that gets you out the door with as little damage as possible.

On the other hand, if your boss situation offers some kind of long-term benefit that you understand and accept, you really have no choice. Focus on why you are staying, and put your bad boss in perspective. He isn't everything in your life—he is the one downside of a career or life deal you have made with yourself.

More than anything else, come to grips with the fact that you are staying with a bad boss by choice. That means you've forfeited your right to complain.

You can't consider yourself a victim anymore.

When you own your choices, you own their consequences.

■

In a perfect world, all bosses would be perfect.

That happens so infrequently that entire movies and books are written about bad bosses, not to mention lots of country-and-western songs.

When you get a bad boss, first find out if you are the problem. That's not easy, but in many cases, a bad boss is just a disappointed one.

If you're convinced you aren't the problem, ask yourself if your company is likely to keep a bad boss with good results. If the answer is yes, the only thing left to do is look at the trade-offs you are willing to make. Is your job worth the price of enduring a bad boss? If so, put up *and* shut up, to put a twist on the old saying.

If the trade-off is not worth it, leave gracefully.

And as you start your next job, remember exactly what made the bad boss bad and how it made you feel—so that when the time comes for you to be a boss, you won't do the same.

19

Work-Life Balance

EVERYTHING YOU ALWAYS WANTED TO KNOW ABOUT HAVING IT ALL (BUT WERE AFRAID TO HEAR)

IF EVER THERE WAS A CASE of "Do as I say not as I did," this chapter is it. No one—myself included—would ever call me an authority on work-life balance. For forty-one years, my operating principle was work hard, play hard, and spend some time as a father.

Had the concept been around at the time, I am sure I would have described my life as perfectly balanced. It felt like it had everything in it, all in the right amounts.

I grew up in an era and as part of a culture where you struggled to go to college and get a decent degree. During school, or very shortly thereafter, you got married and started having kids. Getting a job and working your ass off at it was considered the ticket to a good life.

I followed this pattern without a lot of thought. Luckily for me, I found work to be enormously exciting. I saw the weekends as a time to play golf and party with other young couples.

But looking back, it is clear that the balance I chose had consequences for the people around me at home and at the office. For instance, my kids were raised, largely alone, by their mother, Carolyn.

By the same token, from my earliest days in Plastics, I used to show up at the office Saturday mornings. Not coincidentally, my direct reports showed up too. Personally, I thought these weekend hours were a blast. We would mop up the workweek in a more relaxed way and shoot the breeze about sports.

I never once asked anyone, "Is there someplace you would rather be—or need to be—for your family or favorite hobby or whatever?" The idea just didn't dawn on me that anyone would want to be anywhere but at work.

My defense, if there is one, is that those were the times. In the 1960s and '70s, all my direct reports were men. Many of those men were fathers, and fathers were different then. They did not, by and large, attend ballet recitals on Thursday afternoons or turn down job transfers because they didn't want to disrupt their kids' sports "careers." Most of their wives did not have jobs with their own competing demands. In general, it was assumed that wives stayed at home to make everything run smoothly.

All that started to change, of course, in the '80s, when women started moving up in the workforce, and by late in the decade, I started to hear a lot more about work-life balance. It initially bubbled up in many of our management development classes at Crotonville, where managers started to describe the pressures they felt trying to manage travel and transfers in two-career households. Debate about the topic within GE became more intense in the early '90s, both at Crotonville and during meetings with the GE African American Forum, and it reached a new level of intensity later on during my meetings with members of the company's Women's Network.

These conversations forced me to confront something that I

had never really confronted for myself—the conflicts involved in managing two full lives—the one at work and the one after hours, be it caring for kids, volunteering at a homeless shelter, or running marathons.

While work-life balance was increasingly front and center during the 1990s, the debate about it has only intensified since my retirement in 2001. Today, no CEO or company can ignore it. In fall 2004, for instance, the *New York Times* ran a front-page, three-part series on work-life balance and job stress. That same week, *Fast Company's* cover story was entitled, "Still Worried About Work-Life Balance? Forget It. But Here's How to Have a Life Anyway." There is a whole consulting industry devoted to the subject, and too many books and Web sites about it to even estimate a number.

Not surprisingly, then, as I've traveled around the world for the past three years, I've gotten slews of work-life balance questions. The most common is, "How did you find time for all that golf and still become CEO?" but they run the gamut. Once, in Beijing, a man in the audience who looked to be in his thirties asked me, "How did you manage your children while you were managing GE?"

My answers to these questions have been of limited use, I'm sure. I say that I found time for golf because I didn't spend my leisure time on much else. As for my children, I didn't "manage" them, except to crack the whip on grades and play social director during my three weeks of vacation each year. Their happy lives today have a lot more to do with their mom than with me.

So, I'm clearly no expert on just how individuals should prioritize the various parts of their lives, and I've always felt that choice is personal anyway.

But I have dealt with dozens of work-life balance situations and dilemmas as a manager, and hundreds more as the manager of managers. And over the past three years, I've heard from many people—both bosses and employees—about this complex issue.

From all these experiences, I have a sense of how bosses think about work-life balance, whether they tell you or not.

You may not like their perspective, but you have to face it. There's lip service about work-life balance, and then there's reality. To make the choices and take the actions that ultimately make sense for you, you need to understand that reality:

> 1. Your boss's top priority is competitiveness. Of course he wants you to be happy, but only inasmuch as it helps the company win. In fact, if he is doing his job right, he is making your job so exciting that your personal life becomes a less compelling draw.

> 2. Most bosses are perfectly willing to accommodate work-life balance challenges if you have earned it with performance. The key word here is: *if.*

> 3. Bosses know that the work-life policies in the company brochure are mainly for recruiting purposes and that real work-life arrangements are negotiated one-on-one in the context of a supportive culture, *not* in the context of "But the company says . . . !"

> 4. People who publicly struggle with work-life balance problems and continually turn to the company for help get pigeonholed as ambivalent, entitled, uncommitted, or incompetent—or all of the above.

5. Even the most accommodating bosses believe that work-life balance is your problem to solve. In fact, most know that there are really just a handful of effective strategies to do that, and they wish you would use them.

PRIORITY MANAGEMENT

Let's look at these points one at a time, but first, a few words on what work-life balance really means.

It is no coincidence that work-life balance entered the public domain about the time that women—and especially mothers in dual-career households—started working in force. Suddenly, there was a whole group of people juggling two mutually exclusive and colliding demands: being great parents and great employees at the same time. Especially in the early days, the struggles to make everything work were messy and painful for many working moms, and their stories were filled with guilt, ambivalence, and anger.

Today, work-life balance remains largely the purview of working mothers, in that they are the people most likely to be grappling with the issue on a daily basis.

But without question, work-life balance as a concept has grown and expanded. It isn't just about how mothers can make time for all the demands in their lives. It's about how all of us manage our lives and allocate our time—it's about priorities and values.

Basically, work-life balance has become a debate about how much we allow work to consume us.

Now, you can be like me and my type, and make work your major priority. Or you can attempt a kind of literal balance, with work and life each getting 50 percent of your time, or you can go surfing 80 percent of your time and work 20. There are as many work-life balance equations as there are individuals.

But no matter what balance you choose, you'll have to make trade-offs. After all, as I've noted before in this book, it is a rare and lucky person who can have it all in life, all at the same time. Usually, that's not the case. Working parents who want to be very involved in their kids' lives, for instance, often have to give up some of their ambition. People who put business success first most likely have to give up some level of intimacy with their kids.

Work-life balance is a swap—a deal you've made with yourself about what you keep and what you give up.

I remember one Q & A session with about five hundred executives in Melbourne, Australia, where the moderator was Maxine McKew, one of the country's most respected newscasters. The session was moving along on all the usual business topics for about an hour when a woman in the audience stood and said, "Could you tell me, Mr. Welch, why must all women who succeed in business act like hard-assed, bullheaded men? When will we see the day that every female CEO doesn't have to be like Margaret Thatcher?"

I can't recall my exact answer, but I know I said something very politically incorrect right off the bat about how most women slowed down their career advancements by having children, and while I thought that was a worthy choice, it wasn't going to get them to the boardroom very quickly.

> **Work-life balance is a swap—a deal you've made with yourself about what you keep and what you give up.**

This comment enraged the questioner, who shot back, "Why must women give their lives up to get ahead while men do not?

Women should not have to make all the sacrifices—should they?"

Some of the men in the audience groaned, and one called out, "My wife did it." Another one shouted, "Hey, we all make sacrifices."

Up on stage, I shrugged. "I cannot give you a good answer to your question," I said. "I'm not sure that pausing on the corporate ladder is a 'sacrifice' to the mothers who make that choice."

> "I chose to put my career first," she said, "and I cannot blame anyone for my happiness or lack thereof."

Just then, Maxine stepped in. To be honest, I expected a real slam, but her answer surprised me.

"Women do give something up. It's biology," she said. "Let me tell you what I gave up. I wanted my career. And so I never had children. Maybe I would be able to do it with children now. Still, twenty-five years ago, when I was entering broadcasting, it just wasn't possible to achieve the highest levels and raise babies along the way. It was my choice. Of course I wanted children. But I chose to put my career first, and I cannot blame anyone for my happiness or lack thereof."

You could have heard a pin drop. In the silence, someone raised his hand and changed the subject with a question about the Australian economy.

I tell this story because you simply can't talk about work-life balance without acknowledging that it's so contentious because it's so personal—and so universal.

Everyone these days makes work-life balance decisions— from working mothers and fathers to single people who want to write a novel or volunteer to build homes for Habitat for Humanity.

Work-life balance means making choices and trade-offs, and

living with their consequences. It's that simple—and that complex.

Just remember, you are not in this alone. Your company also feels the impact of your choices and actions.

And with that in mind, let's take a work-life balance reality check from your boss's point of view.

---

1. Your boss's top priority is competitiveness. Of course he wants you to be happy, but only inasmuch as it helps the company win. In fact, if he is doing his job right, he is making your job so exciting that your personal life becomes a less compelling draw.

Clearly, most bosses want their employees to have great personal lives. Nobody wants their people hauling family or social problems into the office, where they can leak into the atmosphere and do nothing for productivity.

Then there's that matter of retention. Satisfied people tend to stay where they are and work with more enthusiasm. So all in all, good bosses don't want their people to feel unbalanced.

But more than that, bosses want to win—that's what they're paid for. And that's why they want all of you—your brain, your body, your energy, and your commitment. After all, they have a big game to win, and they can't do that effectively with absentee players—in particular, if the other team draws its players from countries like India and China, where work-life balance is not exactly a cultural priority.

The fact is: work-life balance concerns are actually a luxury—"enjoyed" largely by people who are *able* to trade time for money, and vice versa. You can bet your bottom dollar that the Korean grocer who just opened his shop in New York doesn't worry about whether he has time to get to the gym, just as you can be absolutely certain that 99 percent of the entrepreneurs in China's huge emerging competitive workforce don't wring their hands about working late every night.

Your boss is fully aware that most competitors in the global marketplace do not invite their people to decrease their productivity in the name of work-life balance.

That's why, when your boss thinks about meeting your work-life balance needs, he is guided by the question: How can I accommodate this person and still keep him or her totally riveted to the job?

The truth is, your boss wants 150 percent of you and, if you are good enough, he will do almost anything to get it, even if your family wants 150 percent too.

It's not that bosses *want* you to give up your family or your hobbies or any other interests. It's not that diabolical. They're just driven by the desire to capture all of your energy and harness it for the company.

In most cases, bosses see a good offense as their best defense against life's yearnings—and that offense would be to make work so exciting and so much fun that people don't actually want to go home for dinner, let alone play amateur chess or write the great American novel in their attic.

For many years, Gary Reiner

> It's not that bosses *want* you to give up your family or your hobbies. They're just driven by the desire to capture all of your energy and harness it for the company.

worked for me as the head of Business Development in Fairfield. Although he never advertised it, Gary had clearly made a work-life balance choice where time with his family played a large role. Every day he showed up early at the office, but he was a stickler about leaving at six, and he rarely engaged in the banter that slowed work down. He was about as cool and efficient as you could get.

But Gary was a star in every way. His performance in a corporate staff job year after year opened up huge operational opportunities for him, but he always said he liked what he was doing, his travel load was manageable, and he didn't want to move. That was OK with me. I loved what he was doing, and the whole company was benefiting.

But I worried, as I'm sure Gary did, about how long we could keep a staff person fresh and engaged. I didn't want Gary to leave GE or just check out mentally.

For the next decade, every time we launched a major initiative—from Services to Six Sigma to e-business—we asked Gary to take charge of organizing councils, comprised of leaders from each business, to transfer best practices around the company. Along the way, he took on the role as chief information officer for the company. Gary stayed put, but just about every couple of years, he expanded the scope of his job, bringing great value to GE while remaining true to his work-life balance choices.

Gary's story is an example of thousands like it that take place every day—a boss pulling out the stops to keep a star performer hooked and excited. I knew what Gary needed and what the company needed, and fortunately, with his intellectual curiosity, commitment, and energy, we found a solution where everyone won.

So every time you think about your work-life balance issue, remember what your boss is thinking about—and that's winning.

Your needs may get heard—and even successfully resolved—but not if the boss's needs aren't met as well.

> **2. Most bosses are perfectly willing to accommodate work-life balance challenges if you have earned it with performance. The key word here is: *if.***

Admittedly, there are bosses out there who think, "I never got any kind of special help with my work-life issues, and I'm not going to give any. Each person has to make it on his own."

Moreover, there are people who don't have children who frankly resent their coworkers who are parents who ask for a "special pass" because of their family responsibilities. I have heard these individuals say things like, *"They* wanted to have children. Now they want *us* to make it easy for them!"* That perspective is not particularly charitable, but I can understand where it's coming from.

Actually, the reality of the workplace is that there are very few special passes. Yes, bosses are agreeable to giving people the flexibility to come and go as they please—but only after they have earned it with their performance and results.

In fact, I would describe the way work-life balance really works as an old-fashioned chit system. People with great performance accumulate chits, which can be traded in for flexibility. The more chits you have, the greater your opportunity to work when and where and how you want.

You cannot talk about this chit system, however, without mentioning face time.

Face time is a big deal at most companies, especially when it comes to promotions. Despite all the technology that makes virtual work possible, most managers are simply more comfortable promoting people they've gotten to know in the trenches, people whom they've seen in meetings and hallways or lived with through a really tough crisis. Your work from off-site may be spectacular. You may be the most productive person on your team. Your current job may not even technically require you to come in to the office! But when push comes to shove at promotion time and qualifications are close, bosses will almost always give the job to the devil they know. And nothing makes a person familiar like showing up.

For an example of a typical chit system in action, let's take the case of Susan Peters.

Susan joined GE in 1979 at age twenty-six as an HR manager in Appliances. She quickly distinguished herself as a high-potential and was moved several times to give her new challenges. In 1986, three months after her daughter, Jess, was born, Susan was working in Pittsfield, and unexpectedly, her boss had to undergo serious back surgery and needed to be out for a long time. In a big step up, she was named head of HR over other more senior people. She hit the ball out of the park.

Next, Susan moved to Holland, then back to corporate headquarters, then back to Pittsfield. Two years later, we moved her to Louisville to head up human resources for the appliances business. In every job, her performance was terrific.

In 1998, we needed to fill the HR job in our medical business in Milwaukee, and we knew what to do: send Susan Peters. When she was called, everyone expected a fast and simple "OK, when do I start?"

Instead she said, "I just can't—I have family issues here that I have to resolve."

It was as if a bucket of cold water had been poured on our heads. We had never given a thought to Susan's personal life, and she had never brought it up. Even when we had sent her for eight weeks of training—four in Japan in 1992 and four in China in 1993—she hadn't made a peep about being away from her daughter or managing a dual-career household from the road. Suddenly here she was, asking for a break, and we were mortified.

Damn it, we thought, how many people like Susan Peters had we lost along the way because they took our silence about work-life as indifference?

We couldn't give Susan her break fast enough. By that point in her career, her pile of chits was about a mile high—far higher than she would have ever needed to reach out for assistance. We told her not to worry and stay put. Our main concern at that point was that she successfully resolve her family issues.

That took a couple of years. Never once in that time did anyone at the company mention Susan's new limitations in a negative context. Then, in 2000, Susan told us she was back in the game, and we quickly promoted her to head of HR at NBC. She is now the vice president of executive development for the whole company, based in Fairfield, making her the No. 2 HR executive at GE.

When you ask Susan about her career, she says, "Basically I learned that you can have all the work-life balance you want if you deliver. I'm not saying it wasn't hard at certain points. It was hard.

"When I went to Japan and China, my daughter was about seven—old enough to lay a real guilt trip on me. I cried my eyes out all the way over. But I had made a conscious decision about work-life balance, and part of that decision was to travel for my career.

"I knew I'd always have flexibility in my job when I needed it. I had earned it with commitment and performance over the years."

Contrast Susan's story to that of a friend of mine who managed a sixty-person unit of a fast-growing company.

A few years ago, she was approached by a member of her team—let's call her Cynthia—who had just had her second child. Cynthia asked if she could work at home on Fridays. The executive (a working mother herself) immediately said yes because she knew that Cynthia—an eight-year veteran of the company—would continue to deliver stellar results. She always had. In fact, she was one of the hardest-working, most organized, and productive members of the staff.

After a week or two, word got around the office that Cynthia was working from home on Fridays. Soon enough, my friend was approached by a young guy—we'll call him Carl—who had been at the company for about a year with no distinguishing results. He too wanted to work at home on Fridays. "I want to perfect my yoga practice," he explained.

When my friend said no, the conversation got very awkward. "You're imposing your values on me," Carl said. "You're saying that mothering has more value than yoga. But I'm never going to have children. Who are you to say that my yoga is less meaningful in my life than Cynthia's children are in hers?"

"Sorry, but that's the decision I made!" the boss shot back.

Later, when the confrontation hit the office gossip mill and distracted Carl's coworkers for a week with minidebates over fairness and values, my friend came to regret the fact that she hadn't been more direct in her answer. Carl couldn't work at home on Fridays because he hadn't demonstrated he could do the job at the office Monday through Thursday!

Despite her own personal circumstances, my friend's decision *hadn't* been about yoga versus babies. It hadn't been about values at all. It had been about results. Carl didn't have any chits.

What does this mean for you? It means that as you think about work-life balance, know that to get it in most companies, you have to earn it. That process will take time.

One last thing to know about the chit system. To people just entering the workforce, it often seems unfair. Why, they wonder, do you have to *wait* to get the freedom and flexibility you want? But more experienced people tend to get it—in fact, many see the give-and-take of chits as perfectly equitable.

Finally, bosses like it too. For them, it's a win-win deal.

> **3. Bosses know that the work-life policies in the company brochure are mainly for recruiting purposes, and that real work-life arrangements are negotiated one-on-one in the context of a supportive culture, *not* in the context of "But the company says . . . !"**

A company brochure can be a sight to behold, with its glossy photos and long lists of lifestyle benefits, such as job sharing and flextime.

But most people know that the last time you look at the company brochure is the first day at work, when you fill out your insurance paperwork in the HR office. In fact, most savvy people realize pretty quickly that most brochure work-life balance programs are primarily a recruiting tool aimed at new candidates.

Real work-life balance arrangements are negotiated by bosses and individuals on an as-needed basis, using the performance-for-flexibility chit system we just talked about.

That chit system requires a special environment.

It requires a supportive organizational culture where bosses are encouraged to strike creative work-life deals with high performers, and high performers feel entirely comfortable talking with their bosses about their work-life challenges.

In such a culture, bosses have the freedom to reward results with flexibility. They don't have to clear work-life arrangements with HR, nor do they feel forced to adhere to formalized work-life policies that actually might limit their ability to win, rather than enhance it.

Remember the case of the boss who had the employee who wanted to work at home Fridays to practice yoga? In the end, when the news of the incident reached senior management, she was told to agree to his request. It was company policy to "offer equal opportunity for flexible working arrangements." Merit had nothing to do with it!

It should come as no surprise that this yoga employee didn't last another year at the company. With just four days at the office, his performance continued to deteriorate. And just as damning, he got branded by managers within the business unit as a "But the company says . . . !" kind of employee.

You know the type. They bank vacation days. They hand in slips of paper noting how many half-days or holidays they've worked. They remind bosses and colleagues of company policies regarding overtime. They are little technocrats who show time and time again that they are not working for fun or the passion to win. They're just logging hours.

If you want real work-life balance, find a company that accommodates it as part of its everyday business.

No wonder they don't have many chits in the bank. By operating outside the culture of one-on-one negotiated arrangements, these rule-book types screw themselves right out of the "rights" they claim they are owed!

The point here is, don't get carried away by the work-life policies and programs advertised in virtually every corporate brochure. If you want real work-life balance, find a company that accommodates it as part of its everyday business.

> 4. People who publicly struggle with work-life balance problems or continually turn to the company for help get pigeonholed as ambivalent, entitled, uncommitted, or incompetent—or all of the above.

In September 2004, the *Financial Times* published a story about Vivienne Cox, who at age forty-five was appointed head of the power, gas, and renewable energy division of BP. The paper noted that the promotion made Ms. Cox one of the most powerful businesswomen in the world.

It also noted that she had two small children and that she never talked about their impact on her ability to work. Vivienne Cox, the newspaper said, "is part of a generation of high-achieving women who just want to get on with the job."

There are, without doubt, tens of thousands of Vivienne Coxes. And surely in total there are millions of successful working people, mothers and otherwise, who have full and busy personal lives—achieved without griping about how hard balance is and how much help they need from their companies to attain it.

The fact that these people exist makes it very hard, in the real world, to be a work-life moaner.

And that's why most work-life moaners eventually get marginalized. Sometimes it takes a while because companies want to be politically correct, and they tiptoe around people who publicly identify themselves as work-life poster children. But with time, people who can't seem to get their work-life challenges in order or continually ask the company for special arrangements get held back or pushed aside.

Not surprisingly, work-life moaners tend to be a phenomenon of below-average performers.

Here's my theory on why.

You almost never hear people in the top 20 percent of any organization complaining about work-life balance. That fact is surely linked to their intrinsic abilities. At home, as at work, they are so smart, organized, and competent that they have figured out and implemented sustainable solutions. They have installed, as Susan Peters calls them, "home processes" of backup resources and contingency plans that take a lot of the uncertainty out of juggling situations.

Below-average performers, by contrast, have three strikes against them. First, they tend to be less expert at organizing their time and sorting through priorities, not just at work, but at home. Second, because of their middling performance, these people have been told they have limited chances of advancement. That lowers their self-confidence and raises their ambivalence. And finally, they're not as financially secure as people in the top 20, giving them fewer resources to buy work-life balance with nannies or personal trainers or whatever. Put all three dynamics together, and it's no wonder underperformers struggle publicly with work-life dilemmas and ask for help so often.

As the HR director at a New York company told me, "It's always my weakest people who want the most flexibility from the company. That's frustrating—to put it mildly." (Not surprisingly, he also said, "Don't use my name if you quote me on this!")

So before you open your mouth a fifth time to ask for limited travel and Thursday mornings off, or occupy your boss's time with concerns over your child-care arrangements, know that you are making a statement, and no matter what words you use, it sounds like, "I'm not really into this."

> **5. Even the most accommodating bosses believe that work-life balance is your problem to solve. In fact, most of them know that there are really just a handful of effective strategies to do that, and they wish you would use them.**

Look, only you can figure out your values and priorities. Only you know what trade-offs you are willing to make, and only you can envision their consequences. Only you can organize your schedule and your life, at work and at home, for the balance you have chosen.

That is why, at the end of the day, most bosses correctly believe work-life balance is your problem to solve, not theirs.

Now, some managers are very adept at helping their people go through the process of sorting out priorities and selecting trade-offs, and even in coming up with scheduling solutions that work equally well for their employees and the company. In fact, they see that activity as an integral part of their jobs.

But helping people find work-life balance is really a special skill. Not every manager has it, and not every manager wants it. Some managers feel, "What the heck am I supposed to be now, a mother and a therapist? Forget about it!"

But many do not. In my speaking and consulting engagements over the past several years, I'd estimate about half of all managers want to actively work with their employees to help them achieve some form of balance. That's a lot more than five years ago.

There can be no question that negotiating work-life balance arrangements adds a layer of complexity to a manager's job. But your manager should welcome the challenge. It gives him another tool to motivate and retain great performers, just like salary, bonuses, promotions, and all other kinds of recognition.

But along the way, you can and should help yourself. The work-life balance debate has now been out there long enough that a handful of best practices have emerged. Most experienced bosses know about these techniques. In fact, many use them, and they wish you would too.

Here they are.

Best practice 1: Keep your head in whatever game you're at. We've already established that work wants 150 percent of you, and so does home. To alleviate angst and distraction, and to enhance your performance no matter what you are doing, be focused on where you are and whom you are with.

In other words, compartmentalize.

No one wins when you routinely run your family's carpool logistics from your office phone or e-mail customers from the soccer field.

Compartmentalizing isn't easy, obviously. Sometimes you must call a customer from the gym or check on a sick child between meetings. But the more you blend your life, the more mixed up, distracted, and overwhelmed you feel and act.

Technology is a real two-edged sword on this. On the one hand, you can be home for dinner three nights a week when you have the ability to check e-mail on your BlackBerry from 8:00 to 10:00 p.m. On the other, you can give yourself a real ulcer by encouraging your office to call your cell phone while you are skiing.

The absolute ideal is to draw crisp boundaries around your activities. Then, when you are at work, keep your head in work completely, and when you are at home or play, keep your head there, and only there. I realize this is something of a fantasyland. There will always be pressures on whatever rules you set, but the smaller and less frequent the interruptions are, the more balance you will actually feel.

Best practice 2: Have the mettle to say no to requests and demands outside your chosen work-life balance plan. Eventually, most people come up with a work-life balance arrangement that works for them. The trick is sticking to it.

That takes discipline. Saying no is hard, especially for business-people who have gotten ahead precisely because they have said yes so often. I will always be impressed by Bill Woodburn, who was running GE's industrial diamond business in the 1990s. We asked him to run a division several times that size, but he had the clarity about his priorities to say no, despite our efforts to persuade him. He had a daughter with two years to go in high school, and he didn't want to uproot her. Today, Bill's daughter has long since graduated, and he has been promoted twice. He's now president and CEO of GE's infrastructure business.

Usually, however, you don't need to say no to something as large as a promotion to get the balance you want. You just need to say it to smaller stuff—a request that you join yet another non-profit board, a plea to coach yet another kids' sports team, and the like.

If you say yes to everything, you won't get balance. You'll get *off* balance.

Saying no is incredibly liberating. Try it on anything and everything that is not part of your deliberately chosen work-life plan.

Best practice 3: Make sure your work-life balance plan doesn't leave you out. A really killing dynamic in this work-life balance thing is the everyone's-happy-but-me syndrome. Very competent people figure out a perfect work-life balance plan that

If you don't fulfill your own joy with your work-life plan, one day you'll wake up in a special kind of hell, where everyone is happy but you.

allows them to deliver enough of themselves to the workplace, enough of themselves to family, and enough of themselves to one or two volunteer organizations.

The problem is, this perfect plan creates a kind of fun-free vacuum for the person at its center.

Of course, work–life balance involves making trade-offs, and decent people are obliged to deliver on their commitments to home and work. But if you craft a work–life balance plan where you are having no fun, chances are you won't be able to sustain it.

You have to make sure your work–life balance plan fulfills your dreams and passions. If that means working a lot, do it. If that means being home every night, let that happen too. Yes, you have to be responsible to those around you, but you can't live someone else's concept of your life in the name of balance.

Well, you can, but you shouldn't. It almost always back-fires.

We all know outwardly happy-looking people who juggle huge career and family demands only to suddenly stop and make drastic changes to their lives. They've just had enough of hanging on by their fingernails.

One person we met recently at a cocktail party explained her decision to "throw it in" this way: "I hadn't really had a good laugh for fifteen years. I hadn't read the newspaper with a cup of coffee or played with the dog or called an old friend. It felt like every single minute, I was struggling with logistics in order to meet everyone's needs but my own.

"Technically, I was a good enough wife and mother, and I was good enough at my job. Everyone else was OK, but I was miserable. I had to quit or I was going to collapse."

Today, this woman works from home. Her family has less money, and she will tell you she misses her old life as a professional. But at least she can breathe—and laugh.

Work-life balance is not a decision you make alone. You have to confront how your choices affect a myriad of others.

But if you don't fulfill your own joy with your plan, all the balance in the world is just duty. One day, you'll wake up and find yourself in a special kind of hell, where everyone is happy but you.

And that doesn't do anyone any good.

When you get right down to it, there are only a few things you need to know if you want, as the title of this chapter says, to have it all.

Outside of work, clarify what you want from life.

At work, clarify what your boss wants, and understand that, if you want to get ahead, what he or she wants comes first. You can eventually get what you both want, but the arrangement will be negotiated in that context.

Make sure you work in a supportive culture where performance matters and you can earn flexibility chits with great results.

Earn a lot of chits. Redeem as needed; replenish often.

Achieving work-life balance is a process. Getting it right is iterative. You get better at it with experience and observation, and eventually, after some time passes, you notice it's not getting harder anymore. It's just what you do.

TYING UP
LOOSE ENDS

20

Here, There, and Everywhere

THE QUESTIONS THAT
ALMOST GOT AWAY

BACK IN THE INTRODUCTION, I said that I was inspired to write this book by the questions I received traveling around the world over the past several years. Most of those questions, and my answers to them, ended up fitting into the nineteen chapters preceding this one.

A few questions, however, just couldn't be wedged into one topic area or another, be it leadership, hiring, change, strategy, or work-life balance. They were too broad, narrow, specific, or unusual. They just defied categorization.

And yet these questions actually call to mind several of the themes that run through this book—the importance of candor and positive energy, for instance, the effectiveness of differentiation, the importance of voice, the power of authenticity and meritocracy, and the absolute necessity of change and never letting yourself be a victim.

So I'm going to end this book with the "questions that almost got away," hoping that they cover any territory I've missed, and perhaps even remind you of some of the major signposts of the territory we've covered so far.

This question was posed at a working dinner in Mexico City, attended by about thirty CEOs from various industries:

We spent the last ten years bringing our company up to speed with training and process improvements, and with our low-cost labor, we were extremely competitive. But now we're getting killed by China. How can we stay alive?

I've heard some form of this question everywhere—except China, of course.

When I was in Dublin in 2001, for instance, a couple of months after Gateway announced it was closing up shop, an Irish technology executive anxiously asked, "Does this mean the end of the long boom for us?" In Milan in 2004, I spoke with a German manager who wondered if his company's only hope was to sell out to an Asian company that wanted his European distribution capability. At a conference in Chicago the same year, a machine parts manufacturer based in Cleveland described in agonizing detail how the Chinese kept lowering and lowering the price of their competing products. "Will there be any manufacturing jobs left in Ohio?" he asked.

There is no easy answer to the China question. Yes, you hear about China's problems—its scarcity of middle managers, for instance, and the massive number of poor farming families moving into unprepared cities with not enough jobs to support them. Lumbering, bureaucratic state-owned enterprises still make up most of its economy. And the country's banks are saddled with bad loans.

But for China, these aren't mountains to be scaled, they're blips to be flattened by the giant, high-speed bulldozer that is its economy. Increasing prosperity from spectacular economic growth over the past twenty years has given the Chinese enormous self-confidence. But China has so much more: a massive pool of low-cost, hardworking laborers and a rapidly expanding number of well-educated engineers.

And then, there's its work ethic, which may be its single biggest strength. Entrepreneurship and competition are baked into the Chinese culture. Consider the executive who hosted me during a weeklong visit to Shanghai and Beijing last year. She said she's at the office from 7:00 a.m. until 6:00 p.m., goes home for dinner to join her husband and son until 8:00 p.m., and then returns to work until midnight. "This is very typical here," she said, "six days a week." And she works for a U.S. multinational!

So, faced with the inevitability of China, what do you do?

First and foremost, get out of the tank. The sense of bleakness that I heard from Mexico to Milan and across the United States is perhaps understandable, but it doesn't get you anywhere.

It's not as if the developed economies of the world are in shambles. The developed world has large consumer and industrial markets, all thirsting for products, with great brands and distribution mechanisms to serve them. Its economies have open and mature legal systems. They are transparent societies, with democratic governments and good education and social systems. Its businesses have fully developed management processes. The United States has the added advantage of a large, thriving venture capital market with the capability to provide seed capital for just about any good idea.

The list of the developed world's competitive advantages could go on and on.

So think positively. At the very least, a can-do attitude is a place to start.

Remember my description of the Japanese threat in the early '80s? At times it felt like we were dying, and everyone seemed to agree. Journalists and political pundits predicted the imminent demise of industrial companies like GE, and you couldn't blame them, given the circumstances. Inflation was double digit, and the prime rate peaked at more than 20 percent. In Syracuse, we were making TV sets that cost more coming out of the factory than the Japanese were selling them for in a mall less than two miles away.

It sure felt like the worst of times.

But that's the point, really. In the heat of battle, it always feels like the worst of times. Low-cost competitors are not new. Hong Kong and Taiwan have been in the game for over forty years, and Mexico, the Philippines, India, and Eastern Europe have been a factor for some time. Even in the late '90s, when the wind was at everyone's back and making money was easier than it had been in decades, work felt really hard. Big companies were labeled dinosaurs, and it became conventional wisdom that technology start-ups would soon rule the world. In fact, it was said whole industries were going to be obliterated by the Internet.

Then the bubble burst. Many of those little companies that were going to rule the world disappeared. Others, like eBay and Amazon, not only survived, they thrived. But so did the so-called dinosaurs—because they changed. They grabbed the new technology and transformed themselves, emerging stronger than ever.

And change is what China demands of us now.

How?

First and most obvious, bring out the three old warhorses of competition—cost, quality, and service—and drive them to new levels, making every person in the organization see them for what they are, a matter of survival.

Take costs. Everyone needs to be searching everywhere, inside the company and out, for best practices. Hard calls need to be made about where and how every single process should be performed to ratchet up productivity. Don't think about reducing costs by 5 to 10 percent. You have to find the ways to take out 30 to 40 percent. In most cases, that's what it will take to be competitive in the China world.

> First and most obvious, bring out the three old warhorses of competition—cost, quality, and service—and drive them to new levels.

On quality, you just can't have a ship-and-fix mentality. Getting it right 95 percent of the time is not good enough. Use Six Sigma or any methodology you like. But get rid of defects.

Service is the easiest advantage to exploit. China is thousands of miles away from most developed markets. Remember Gary Drug, the tiny pharmacy in our neighborhood where not only do they know your name, they deliver to your house within an hour? It's standing strong against its China—the big, shiny chain-store pharmacy three blocks away. And think about the Mexican CEO who asked this question to start with. His country's proximity to the United States gives it a huge advantage in response time.

Again, your challenge is not just to improve. It is to break the service paradigm in your industry or market so that customers aren't just satisfied, they're so shocked that they tell strangers on the street how good you are. FedEx and Dell come to mind as examples of this.

While you have to innovate to improve cost, quality, and service, go beyond that. Take a new, hard look at your market. Search out untapped opportunities; find new niches. Just don't keep pounding out the same stuff.

That market you're serving may seem saturated, but it is filled with plenty of demand for exciting new products, services, or technologies. That's what Procter & Gamble discovered recently.

There was no company more set in its ways than P&G. But in less than five years, the company instilled a whole new vigor into its innovation efforts. It broke its NIH syndrome and scoured every corner of the world for "garage" inventors with cutting-edge ideas. And they didn't stop there. Their search for new ideas led them to create networks into other companies, suppliers, universities, research labs, and venture capitalists. They took some of the ideas they found and fine-tuned them, and used still others to reinvent their existing products. For instance, P&G took the tried-and-true electrostatic technology used to paint cars and applied it to its cosmetics business—transforming the way its makeup products go on the skin. With a new can-do attitude, the company also revitalized in-house R & D. The result was products like Crest Whitestrips and the Swiffer cleaning products, which literally invented whole new mass-market categories.

And finally, while you are innovating and searching for new products, markets, and niches, come to terms with the fact that China can be much more than just a competitor.

Think of China as a market, an outsourcing option, and a potential partner.

> You can look at China and feel victimized.
> Or you can look at it and be excited about conquering the challenges and opportunities it presents.

Unlike Japan in its early development, China's huge market is relatively open to direct investment. Many can go it alone there, ideally selling their product in the Chinese market while sourcing product for their home market.

Alternatively, you can join forces with a local business. Needless to say, Chinese joint ventures aren't easy. In my experience, to make them happen you have to make sure the Chinese partner feels as if it has gained a lot, perhaps more than you. But there are ways to craft win-win deals. When GE Medical formed a joint venture in 1991, its Chinese partner brought great local market know-how. That was a big factor in the new company's achieving the No. 1 market share in imported GE high-end imaging products. At the same time, the joint venture's Chinese engineers designed and built low-cost, high-quality products that were exported through GE's global distribution network.

Now, I don't want to sound like a Pollyanna about China. Its presence is a real game-changer in business today. And even if trade restrictions get enacted, its currency is allowed to fluctuate, and intellectual property laws are passed, no political solution in the world is going to make it go away.

But China is a classic case of the glass half empty or half full, isn't it?

You can look at the situation and feel victimized. Or you can look at it and be excited about conquering the challenges and opportunities it presents.

Pick the latter. You can't win wringing your hands.

This question was posed by an audience member in London, at a conference attended by about three thousand middle and senior managers:

Norway just passed a law mandating that half of every corporate board be comprised of women. What is your opinion of that?

It's ridiculous.

Obviously, I'm not against women directors. They've made major contributions to thousands of boards around the world. In fact, one of the best directors I've ever known is a woman who served on the GE board, G. G. Michelson, the former director of human resources at R. H. Macy & Co. and past head of Columbia University's board of trustees, whose people insights and general wisdom guided me for two decades.

Nevertheless, I just don't like quotas in the boardroom or in the office. Winning companies are meritocracies. They practice differentiation, making a clear distinction between top, middle, and bottom performers. This system is candid and fair, and it's the most effective way for an organization to field the best team.

Quotas undermine meritocracies. They artificially push some people ahead, independent of qualifications. That can be demotivating to the top performers who are passed over, and it doesn't do much for results, either, when unprepared people are thrust into important jobs.

So what does work?

Return for a minute to the "Getting Promoted" chapter; its advice is color- and gender-blind. If you want to get promoted, your best bet is to overdeliver on your results, manage your subordinates as carefully as you manage your boss, get on the radar screen by supporting major initiatives early, relish the input of lots of mentors, and always, always have a positive, high-energy approach to life and work. At the same time, don't make your boss use his or her political capital to champion you. And when setbacks occur, and they will, don't let them break your stride.

I'm not saying women and minorities haven't had a tough go of it in the business world. They have, and they do need mechanisms to give them a higher profile in the system.

One such mechanism is diversity groups, like GE's Women's Network or its African American Forum. These groups have created an opportunity for successful women and minority executives to serve as role models. Just as important, they provide a setting to talk about the ways women and minorities can increase their experience and skills, and thus their visibility in an organization. They promote the concept that success is a function of talent, energy, and drive—just as meritocracies are.

> The only quota that I ever thought worked was the exposure quota.

But the whole subject of diversity is more nuanced and complicated than I am making it out to be.

At GE, the African American Forum was a grassroots effort that started in 1990. It was bumping along without a lot of momentum until a senior vice president, Lloyd Trotter, grabbed it by the neck and gave it a whole new energy with seminars, conferences, and mentoring programs. With Lloyd in charge, every African American in the company wanted to get on board, and all of Lloyd's peers wanted to jump in to help. The group really took off, and in time so did promotions for African Americans.

On the other hand, in the mid-1990s I would have dinners twice a year with high-potential women where we would discuss the work-life issues they were facing. In 1997, after a long give-and-take, I challenged the group to create their own version of the African American Forum. They seemed enthusiastic, but much to my surprise, over the next few weeks, I found that some of our top women were balking at the idea. They felt they had made it without any label. They didn't want to be thought of as successful women, they wanted to be thought of as successful executives. After a couple of years, much of that faded, as even the most reluctant grew to enjoy their mentoring and its positive impact on the progress of women in the company.

Back to the quota question about Norway.

The only quota that I ever thought worked was the exposure quota we used at GE—that is, we made sure there was a woman or minority candidate on every slate for the top two thousand jobs. That guaranteed every manager saw the diverse candidates out there and that diverse candidates had a shot.

I spent the first half of my tenure as CEO focused on changing the portfolio and competitiveness. Diversity for me didn't come into play until the '90s.

But today, if you want to field the best team, you simply can't afford a delay.

I've received this question numerous times, from audiences from New York to Sydney:

How did you pick your successor, Jeff Immelt, and how do you think he is doing so far?

I am always thrilled to answer the second part of this question— it's such a layup. Jeff is doing amazingly well, even exceeding my expectations for his leadership. I couldn't be more proud of where he has taken GE and where it is going.

Jeff became chairman and CEO of GE on September 10, 2001, so it was technically his second day on the job when the terrorist attacks changed the game for everyone. Jeff handled the new uncertainty of the business environment with characteristic thoughtfulness and determination. Despite the resulting down- turns in the airline, power, and reinsurance industries, he master- fully navigated the company to modest annual earnings growth from 2001 until 2004.

At the same time, Jeff has made significant changes to the port- folio that positioned GE for future growth. He made major media, medical, financial services, and infrastructure acquisitions, while disposing of slower-growth industrial and insurance assets. He reinvigorated GE's research and development activities with large facility investments in Munich, Shanghai, and Schenectady, New York. And Jeff has put enormous emphasis on diversity at GE, with immediate and positive results.

Several times in this book, I've said that change is good. Jeff sure proves that point.

As for how and why I picked Jeff, I just don't ever talk about that. There were three terrific people to choose from—Jeff, Bob Nardelli, and Jim McNerney. There is no reason to conduct a public autopsy on the process—it's past. Both Bob and Jim have gone on to have spectacular runs in their new roles—Bob as CEO of The Home Depot and Jim at 3M.

What I will say is that at the end of the day, the board and I picked whom we believed to be the best leader for GE, and Jeff is making us all look very good.

This question was posed at a management conference in Reykjavik, Iceland, and during a twelve-person business dinner in London:

What's the future of the European Union?

Long-term, it's very good.

With all the sound and fury about China, some people see the EU as a huge, lumbering bureaucracy that will never get its collective act together fast enough to reach its full potential in the global economy. Maybe that's true in the short run, but in time, the EU will prove naysayers wrong.

Remember, the economic EU is less than fifteen years old. It's already come a long way. Imagine trying to put together the fifty states of the United States today. Now imagine doing that if each state had operated for centuries with a separate government, set of laws, language, currency, and culture, as the members of the EU have. That the EU has done so well in so short a time is actually sort of amazing.

Without question, the EU still has a way to go before it realizes the economic hopes and dreams of its supporters. But its current statistics are enough to give you a sense of the potential to be unleashed. With twenty-five countries, the EU has 450 million people, 50 percent more than the United States, and a GDP of $11 trillion, about the same as the United States, two and a half times Japan, and about seven times China.

These numbers are impressive, but they'll only get better as the EU feels the impact of its newest members, Poland, Hungary, Slovakia, the Czech Republic, and the other nations of "New Europe." In the past decade, from Budapest to Bratislava, from Prague to Warsaw, I've seen the excitement, optimism—and the remarkable achievements—in these countries. A new generation of entrepreneurs and small-business people are thirsting for opportunity and success. Their governments have responded in kind, reducing taxes and providing other probusiness incentives. The result has been significant economic growth, especially in comparison to what's going on in Old Europe.

Yes, Old Europe has problems and a long history. Brussels is filled with bureaucrats, and the individual governments of many countries are fighting tooth and nail to hang on to their hard-earned sovereignty. With their entrenched cultural traditions, France and Germany in particular are lukewarm about the EU, and often act with blatant self-interest.

The paralyzing weight of socialism will gradually give way, and the EU will move steadily forward.

But these problems are not insurmountable. Washington, Tokyo, and Beijing have plenty of bureaucrats too. And as new generations of political leaders emerge across

Europe, and the leadership of the EU itself gains increasing stature with every passing year, the pull of parochial, old-economic-order governments will give way. For example, the French government recently began to ease its rigid support of the thirty-five-hour week and is now proposing that companies be allowed to negotiate directly with employees about work schedules.

In time—and perhaps sooner than many expect—global competitive pressures and the energy of New Europe will have a powerful combined effect. The paralyzing weight of socialism will gradually give way, and the EU will move steadily forward, fueled by an ever-increasing acceptance of capitalism.

This question came at a technology and innovation conference in Las Vegas that spanned three days and featured about twenty speakers. I was one of them.

How do you think corporate boards will change because of the Sarbanes-Oxley Act?

This question, which I heard in various forms and in many locations, including Australia and Europe, reflects a growing attention on governance, a topic for discussion that used to be reserved for shareholder meetings and business school classrooms.

Then, of course, came the postbubble corporate scandals, and people began to ask, "Where the heck were the boards in all these messes? Why didn't they see the funny business?"

Very quickly, laws and regulations were passed to make boards and senior executives more accountable for any corruption that might occur on their watch. In general these rules, such as the Sarbanes-Oxley Act, are a good thing, necessary to restore economic confidence.

But laws will never guarantee good corporate governance.

There is no way that a board's finance committee, comprised of a finance professor, an accountant, and several busy CEOs, all from far-flung locations, can spend a couple of days every month studying a company's books and verify that everything is on the up-and-up. Imagine being a board member of a multinational bank. You have people trading everything, swapping Japanese yen for euros in London, and others betting on U.S. commodity futures down the hall. But even most small companies have too much complexity for a committee to track, with hundreds of transactions every day, near and far.

While boards cannot be police, they must assure themselves that companies have auditors, rigorous internal processes, tight controls, and the right culture for that purpose.

Boards play other roles as well. They pick the CEO and approve the top management. In fact, they should know members of the top team as well as they know their own colleagues. Boards also monitor the mission of the company. Is it real? Do people understand it? Is it being executed? Can it win?

Boards also gauge the integrity of the company. That's huge. They must visit the field operations and conduct meaningful conversations with people at every level, eyeball to eyeball. It is in this subtle, nuanced integrity watchdog role that boards can make a real contribution.

For some boards, Sarbanes-Oxley will require a real change in behavior. They will need to stop thinking about their jobs as eight, ten, or twelve closed-door meetings a year with lovely catered lunches.

For others, it will only reinforce their existing approach.

Now, in the rush to deal with the scandals, perhaps some aspects of Sarbanes-Oxley went too far, for example, the rules that imply the superiority of independent directors over directors who have some sort of stake in the company, either as investors, suppliers, or any other form of business partner.

This new requirement needs a re-look with a big dose of common sense.

There is nothing wrong with directors having skin in the game. For the shareholders' sake, directors should really care about how the

> **Board members cannot get into an us-versus-them dynamic with the very people they are supposed to help.**

company is doing. But the notion that independent directors are better for the company is having the unintended consequence, in some cases, of removing good judgment and experience from where it is needed most.

Take the case of Sam Nunn, the distinguished former U.S. senator from Georgia. Or Roger Penske, the automobile industry entrepreneur. Both were required to leave key GE board committees. Why? After leaving the Senate, Sam joined King & Spalding, a law firm that GE had done business with for decades. In Roger's case, he had a minority interest in a small GE truck-leasing joint venture. Or take the case of Warren Buffett. Activists wanted him off the audit committee at Coca-Cola because of his large ownership stake.

Who would represent the share owners better on key committees than these three people? A professor? An accounting expert? The head of a charitable foundation? Why would share owners ever want company executives answering to people who might need a director's salary to make ends meet? Those kinds of directors are less likely to challenge anything—they're more likely to duck tough issues in the hope they get reappointed.

Let's not forget that boards exist to support and guide, as well as challenge, management. It would be unfortunate indeed if Sarbanes-Oxley ends up making boards primarily adversarial in their approach. Board members can never forget their main job is to make the company work better, not to get into an us-versus-them dynamic with the very people they are supposed to help.

In the final analysis, the best directors share four very simple traits: good character, common sense, sound judgment—particularly about people—and the courage to speak up.

Laws are all well and good. But it is people, culture, processes, controls—and strong directors—that ultimately put compliance in a company's blood.

This question came at a breakfast meeting in Copenhagen with about thirty European managers doing business for their global companies in Scandinavia:

I'm about to be transferred to run our operations in West Africa, and I've been told to expect that 40 percent of my workforce have AIDS or a family member suffering with the disease. Any suggestions for dealing with this problem?

No question ever floored me like this one.

And as if it wasn't disturbing enough on its own, another person at the breakfast, an executive from a consumer goods company, spoke up right afterward. "I'm just back from our operations in Africa," he said. "Try closer to 60 percent."

What can a leader do in such a dire situation? What can a company do?

It is in confronting a societal problem that the results of a winning company and a good culture really come together to make a difference. At the outset of this book, I tried to make the case that winning is great because it inspires people to be happy, creative, and generous.

That was me talking from 20,000 feet. This question brings you right into the trenches.

The manager who asked this question worked for a highly profitable oil company, and I could feel that he really wanted to do something. He'll be able to because his company is winning. He can launch programs to educate the workforce about AIDS. He can provide medical facilities and subsidize the expensive drugs the disease requires. He can really improve the lives of hundreds of people. I'll bet he does.

Winning companies help all the time.

There are more than fifty thousand active volunteers among GE's employees, involved in four thousand projects a year, from mentoring in schools around the world to participating in countless other programs for the disadvantaged. Because of the efforts of GE volunteers, there have been amazing community projects in Hungarian towns, Jakarta slums, and inner-city schools in Cincinnati. Not only were these projects great for the people who were helped, they were equally beneficial for the people doing the helping. Their volunteering in the streets gave their work at the office more meaning and vitality.

In Slovakia, Chris Navetta showed up in 2002 to manage U.S. Steel's newly acquired sixteen-thousand-employee plant in Kosice, a city with 23 percent unemployment in the impoverished eastern region of the country. Chris and his team took a real relic of Communism—a money-losing state-owned enterprise—and with a $600 million investment, turned it into a highly profitable operation. While they were doing that, they poured time and money into Kosice. The list of their contributions is too long to print here, but it includes building an oncology wing at the local children's hospital, remodeling primary school classrooms and providing them with computers, and refurbishing several orphanages and a facility for the blind.

Consider also the outpouring of support from businesses around the world after the tragic Christmas tsunami of 2004. In a matter of days, healthy companies and their people donated billions of dollars in cash and supplies to help people in ravaged communities. It was generosity of the highest order.

I'm not talking here about motherhood and apple pie, or trying to sound like the typical annual report. This is how good business really works. Winning companies give back and everyone wins.

This question came from the reporter who moderated my Q & A session at a management conference for about three thousand people in London:

Do you plan to enter politics?

In a word—never.

It's not that I don't appreciate government. We're all grateful to the public servants who have made national security and the eradication of terrorism their lifework. On top of that, government provides other services that are vital to a thriving society—schools, hospitals, and police, to name just three.

But government, for all the good it does, is filled with all the problems that business has, but nobody seems to have the latitude to fix them.

Basically, government is riddled with bureaucracy, waste, and inefficiency. In a company, you can clean those up, and you have to. In government, they're forever.

Why? For one, because it's difficult to move people up or out based on merit. Most government agencies have no differentiation to speak of. You can work for forty years, never excel or make a dent in results, and still get an annual raise. For another, you just cannot speak or act candidly in government without getting nailed. It is a world filled with compromise, patronage, and quid pro quo.

Yes, all these behaviors exist in business, but managers can rally against them on their own, or join a company that does so as a matter of course.

Finally, governments can afford to be bureaucratic because they don't compete. During the last election season, the governor of Indiana created a big hoopla around the fact that he was going to withdraw the state from an outsourcing project that one of its departments had started in India. There was much cheering him on as a role model of patriotism. It had to make you laugh. It was easy for the governor to withdraw from India—in the public sector you don't have to provide the highest value products or find the lowest cost solutions in order to create revenue. You can just keep raising taxes to pay for everything.

So, as important as government is, it's just not for me. This book makes the point that it is always better to do something you love.

I've taken my own advice on this one.

I've received this question everywhere:

How's your golf game?

Wow, do people love golf! Everywhere I go, perhaps because I stuck a chapter on golf in my last book, people ask about my handicap and whether it's improved since I retired.

The answer is, I don't play anymore.

And, believe it or not, I don't miss it all that much.

My obsession with golf lasted almost sixty years, from my first days playing and caddying at age ten until my first back operation in 2002. I've had two more back operations since then, and thankfully, my back is better now. But I'm sure not inclined to test that proposition with a golf swing. If you've had back problems, you probably understand where I'm coming from.

But in the absence of golf, a whole world of new interests has opened up to me. You can't believe how much time is available when you're not on the golf course all the time! I've loved consulting with several companies and their CEOs. I've also found I'm crazy about modern art, and I'm getting to live out my lifelong devotion to the Red Sox by attending as many home games as I can. I've been able to travel around the world with my wife and four stepchildren and enjoy the sights beyond conference rooms and factories, and been able to meet the many interesting people whose questions grew into this book.

I have always loved new stuff. Looking forward, learning, and growing have always felt good to me. Golf was wonderful. It gave me great friends that I've enjoyed for decades and always will, and all the fun of competing.

But when you can't play, you can't play—and amazingly, the world doesn't even end.

And finally, this question was posed by an audience member at a management conference in Frankfurt attended by about twenty-five hundred people:

Do you think you will go to heaven?

After a few seconds of stunned silence, my first answer to this one was, "Well, I sure hope that's long-range planning!"

But after the audience stopped laughing—they were as surprised by the question as I was—the man who asked this question made it clear that he wanted to understand what I considered my legacy.

First off, I hate the word *legacy*. It just sounds so arrogant. Presidents and prime ministers have legacies. I ran a company and wrote a book or two.

But here we are at the end of this book, and the question did get asked, so I'll attempt an answer.

If there is anything I would like to be remembered for it is that I helped people understand that leadership is helping other people grow and succeed. To repeat myself, leadership is not just about you. It's about them.

I would also like to be remembered as a huge advocate of candor and meritocracy, and believing everyone deserves a chance. And I'd like to be remembered for trying to make the case that you can never let yourself be a victim.

Now, it is no secret that I've made plenty of mistakes in my career. I've made some bad acquisitions, hired some wrong people, and moved too slowly on some opportunities. And that is just a fraction of the list.

As for my personal life, I have four great children and nine terrific grandchildren. My love and admiration for them cannot be expressed with words, and their happy, fulfilling lives today give me no end of pleasure. I had two marriages, however, that did not work out. Life goes on and usually for the better, but no one lives through two divorces and feels proud that they happened.

So, as for heaven, who knows? I'm sure not perfect, but if there are any points given out for caring about people with every fiber of your being and giving life all you've got every day, then I suppose I have a shot.

Given the choice, of course, I'd rather not find out anytime soon!

There's so much more to do.

Acknowledgments

BUSINESS IS ABOUT PEOPLE. In fact, life is only people—family, friends, colleagues, bosses, teachers, coaches, neighbors. At the end of the day, it is only people that matter.

People made this book. First, there were the thousands of men and women around the world who, as my dedication says, cared about business enough to raise their hands and ask the questions that fill these pages. I thank them for candidly sharing their stories, talking openly about the ever-changing challenges of work, and for helping me codify my thinking about how to get it right.

I am also deeply grateful to the people who took an hour or two (and often more) to talk with me about their experiences so that the ideas in this book could be filled with life: Bill Harrison and Jamie Dimon of JPMorgan Chase; Steve Klimkowski of Northwestern Memorial HealthCare; George Tamke, a partner at Clayton, Dubilier & Rice; David Novak, who runs Yum! Brands; Bob Nardelli of The Home Depot; Robert Bagby of A.G. Edwards; Perry Ruddick, the retired vice-chairman of Smith Barney;

Maxine McKew of the Australian Broadcasting Company; Kevin Sharer of Amgen; Jimmy Dunne of Sandler O'Neill & Partners; my old friend Paolo Fresco, former vice-chairman of GE and retired CEO of Fiat; Gerry Roche of Heidrick & Struggles; Joel Klein, chancellor of the New York City public schools; Jim McNerney of 3M; Paolo Monferino of Case New Holland; Dara Khosrowshahi of Expedia; and Chris Navetta of U.S. Steel; and from GE, Bill Conaty, Gary Reiner, Susan Peters, Dennis Dammerman, Mark Little, John Krenicki, and Charlene Begley. Bob Nelson, my financial analyst at GE for many years, was a helpful reader along the way.

Several people don't appear by name in this book, but their ideas were critical in shaping its content. Linda Gosden Robinson, president of Robinson Lerer & Montgomery, shared her considerable experience with us for the chapter on crisis management. For the chapter on work-life balance, I am indebted to Professor Stew Friedman of the Wharton School, and Claudio Fernández-Aráoz, of the executive search firm Egon Zehnder. The chapter on mergers and acquisitions was helped by a long, insightful conversation with M & A expert David Fubini of McKinsey & Company. And my (tiny) newfound knowledge of philosophy is totally thanks to the insights of Nancy Bauer, a professor at Tufts University.

This book started with two pages of scribbled notes about what it could be. The finished product in your hands is thanks to a stellar group of people, most notably the 4Es-and-a-P people at HarperCollins: our wonderful editor, Leah Spiro, whose probing mind and passion for this book never ebbed; Jane Friedman, a fervent believer and unflagging advocate from the get-go; and Marion Maneker, whose deep wisdom guided us all the way. We are also grateful to the terrific team that marketed this book; Joe Tessitore, whose savvy, energy, and decisiveness brought this book home, as well as Brian Murray, Stephen Hanselman, Paul

Olsewski, Keith Pfeffer, and Larry Hughes; the book's designer, Leah Carlson-Stanisic; its copy editor, Anne Greenberg; and Knox Huston, its editorial assistant. Our agent, Helen Rees, was a dear friend and enthusiastic supporter, and Megan LaMothe did tenacious duty as our fact checker.

My assistant, Rosanne Badowski, read every draft of this book, challenged the content, picked apart phrases, and made every chapter better. Her caring and attention were remarkable, and I thank her for the endless hours she gave this project.

Finally, there aren't enough words to thank my wife, Suzy, for the job she did on this book. Her relentless questioning pulled out of me every idea I ever had about business, and her ability to organize and rephrase my (in many cases) random observations made this book so much better than I ever dreamed it could be. I always tell people that Suzy is just about the smartest person I have ever met, and during the last year of writing this book, she has proved it and then some. For every chapter you read in this book, Suzy wrote and rewrote countless drafts, and yet she never took a break from being an amazing mother to her four great kids. Every day, she astonishes me.

For the last year, we have had the greatest time day and night, debating and discussing all the material that went into this book. The conversation never stopped! As I traveled the world, meeting people, answering questions, and asking plenty of my own, Suzy was by my side, listening, analyzing, and opening my mind to what I knew and what more I could know.

It was hard work—and pure joy. Suzy, you made it happen.

Jack Welch
Boston
February 2005

INDEX